Madness Is Civilization

T0385626

Madness in Civilization

Madness Is Civilization:
When the Diagnosis Was Social, 1948–1980

Michael E. Staub

The University of Chicago Press :: Chicago and London

The University of Chicago Press, Chicago 60637
The University of Chicago Press, Ltd., London
© 2011 by The University of Chicago
All rights reserved. Published 2011.
Paperback edition 2015
Printed and bound by CPI Group (UK) Ltd, Croydon, CR0 4YY

21 20 19 18 17 16 15   2 3 4 5 6

ISBN-13: 978-0-226-77147-2 (cloth)
ISBN-13: 978-0-226-21463-4 (paperback)
ISBN-13: 978-0-226-77149-6 (ebook)
DOI: 10.7208/chicago/9780226771496.001.0001

Epigraph (p. vii): From "Twisted" by Annie Ross. Used by permission.

Library of Congress Cataloging-in-Publication Data

Staub, Michael E.
    Madness is civilization : when the diagnosis was social, 1948–1980 /
Michael E. Staub.
        p. cm.
    Includes bibliographical references and index.
    ISBN-13: 978-0-226-77147-2 (cloth : alk. paper)
    ISBN-10: 0-226-77147-4 (cloth : alk. paper)   1. Mental illness—United
States—Sociological aspects. 2. United States—Social conditions—1945–
I. Title.
    RC455.S79 2011
    362.196'89—dc22

                                                        2010045772

♾ This paper meets the requirements of ANSI/NISO Z39.48-1992
(Permanence of Paper).

For my family

My analyst told me
That I was right out of my head
He said I'd need treatment
But I'm not that easily led
He said I was the type
That was most inclined
When out of his sight
To be out of my mind
And he thought I was nuts
No more ifs or ands or buts

ANNIE ROSS, "Twisted" (1952)

Contents

Contents

Figures

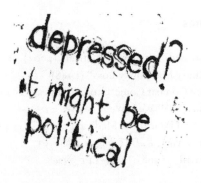

FIGURE 1 "depressed? it might be political." Feel Tank Chicago, from the First International Parade of the Politically Depressed. Chicago, May 1, 2003. Reprinted by permission.

Introduction

"Depressed? It might be political."

So stated a slogan (available as both T-shirt and refrigerator magnet) for an academic conference at the University of Chicago in 2003 on the role of feelings in political life. The bitter joke of the slogan played on the phenomenal success of an ever-growing variety of psychopharmaceutical drugs for panic, social phobias, anxiety, and depression—such as Zoloft, Prozac, Celexa, or Paxil—any one of which could be promoted with the tagline "Depressed? It might be chemical." At the same time, the conference slogan also served as anguished commentary on the George W. Bush administration's egregious disregard both at home and abroad for the rules of law.

The slogan proved particularly prescient. Within only a few years, Americans saw shocking images and heard sordid tales of torture and abuse—at the prison at Abu Ghraib in Iraq, the US military installation at Guantánamo Bay in Cuba, and at secret prisons (or "black sites") operated by the Central Intelligence Agency—as they also learned the news of devastation and death in the predominantly African American Lower Ninth Ward of New Orleans after Hurricane Katrina. Americans experienced as well the first years of Chief Justice John G. Roberts's Supreme Court (the most conservative in modern memory) and witnessed the electoral successes of a far-right Tea

Party movement. These developments would make it especially difficult for many on the American left to imagine how a better, more humane world might still be possible.

Yet the slogan had further served as a subtle (if ironically and self-critically nostalgic) gesture toward the 1960s and early 1970s when psychological disorders were understood more in social and political (and less in strictly individualized) terms. Depressed? In those bygone days many believed that the principal causes of mental illness could be unhealthful familial dynamics or socioeconomic stresses. Mental illness might also be traceable to the emotional debilitations of racism, militarism, or patriarchy. In that former era, moreover, a great many influential critics both inside and outside the psychiatric profession argued that persons who suffered from mental disorders would never be cured through biomedical treatments alone. Pills could not solve emotional problems that sprang up amid the squalor of the urban ghetto or within the soullessness of the military industrial complex or, for that matter, many heterosexual marriages. These critics argued fervently how crucial it was to understand that environment played a decisive role in the etiologies of mental disturbances, and that it was the environment that needed to be transformed.

The 1960s and 1970s remain well remembered as a moment when the hippie denizens of the First World romanticized the rebels of the Third, and Che Guevara, Frantz Fanon, and Ho Chi Minh were heroes in the West. We acknowledge that epoch as a time when white styles mimicked black ones and an essay called "The Student as Nigger" (written by a white activist) resonated powerfully with an entire generation of white, middle-class progressive youth.[1] However, the 1960s and 1970s have not been adequately analyzed as a moment when a significant portion of the populace also believed madness to be a plausible and sane reaction to insane social conditions, and that psychiatrists served principally as agents of repression.

A paradigmatic example came from the anti–Vietnam War movement. It was the fable, possibly true, of a troubled young man who sought out counseling after he learned he had been drafted for military service in Vietnam. He informed his psychiatrist that he felt shame and guilt because he was not eager to fight for his country. Should he hate himself for his cowardice? The psychiatrist asked the young man to describe his feelings about his parents and his childhood; he asked him to recount his dreams. The psychiatrist deliberated, and then told the young man he suffered from passive aggression. He insisted the young man "pull himself together." And so the young man stiffened his spine and went off to war—and returned in a pine box. From the perspective of the antiwar movement, the moral of the story was unambiguous: The psychiatrist had "acted as a recruiting officer for the army, all the more effective for his disarming smile."[2] The shrink had the young man's blood on his hands.

No period in American history witnessed as much critical attention and cultural energy lavished on issues relating to madness as the 1960s and 1970s. Not only medical literature but also popular films and music, plays and novels, performance art, and mainstream news media and popular magazines discussed and represented mental illness and the asylum almost incessantly. Insanity also served as subject and the insane asylum as setting for dozens of books and articles that ranged across the social sciences.

It is a main premise of *Madness Is Civilization* that in many of these accounts mental illness both operated as a subject in its own right *and* as an occasion for addressing a host of other political, emotional, and social concerns. This book thus reads the profusion of texts produced on mental illness and the mental hospital in the disciplines of psychology, anthropology, sociology, and the law with and against the medical literature. But it also reads medical texts as themselves political documents.

This book further argues that the origins of the ideas conventionally attributed to the diffuse movement that came in the later 1960s to be known as *antipsychiatry* must be located in the very different political climate of the early postwar era. Classic antipsychiatric notions—that madness was a kind of protest against unjust social conditions, that psychiatry was social control in the guise of "treatment" and that the regimens of antipsychotic medications and procedures like electroshock therapy punished deviance and enforced conformism, that asylums were gulags or concentration camps for society's undesirables, or that "mental illness" was a hallucinatory construct with no basis in serious science—are now, in the early twenty-first century, frequently dismissed and denounced as sure signs of the counterculture's loopy excesses. The three leading figures associated with antipsychiatry—R. D. Laing, Erving Goffman, Thomas Szasz—are now often linked derisively with the quite dissimilar historical project of French philosopher Michel Foucault and his *Madness and Civilization* (1965). All are summarily identified as products of the 1960s, with the popular success of their ideas typically attributed to the "feverish atmosphere" of that decade.[3] Foucault's questioning of reason's superiority to madness and his skepticism that enlightened treatments were more humane than early modern ones certainly lent additional cachet to antipsychiatric impulses. Yet the shorthand merger of Laing, Goffman, and Szasz with Foucault misses the point that the efforts of the first three were based on direct ethnographic and clinical encounters. Even more importantly the collapse and dismissal of these thinkers' diverse projects misses the intimate inseparability of the histories of antipsychiatry and psychiatry.

A major contention of this book is that precursors to antipsychiatric ideas were inextricable from a broader turn to social diagnoses within *mainstream* psychiatry and were, furthermore, absolutely essential to psychiatry's dramatic rise to broad cultural influence and legitimacy in the first decade of the Cold War. The research into the psychodynamics of mental illness mandated by the National Mental Health Act (signed into law in 1946) and by the National Institute of Mental Health (formally established in 1949) as well as the publication of the first edition of the *Diagnostic and Statistical Manual of Mental Disorders* (DSM-I) in 1952, all signaled a commitment to situate the origins of mental illness in the interplay between the self and societal forces and to broaden the mission of the psychiatrist beyond the treatment solely of the most intractable cases of mental disease. Psychiatry now intentionally addressed itself also to the daily tribulations of "the worried well." These moves meant a vast widening of the net of those believed to be at risk of mental problems, which gave psychiatry a far more secure footing in the postwar era (and ultimately far more government-sponsored funding). The turn toward social analyses of individual problems also reflected sincerely held (and essentially progressive) beliefs that analyzing interpersonal relations and environmental conditions offered an exciting key for the curing of individual psychological difficulties.

The turn toward social diagnoses for madness had a double aspect all along. On the one hand there was unquestionably an impetus to foster more humane and sympathetic treatment of the mentally ill. Yet on the other hand, and often simultaneously, all through the postwar period representations repeatedly released "mental illness" from any reference to actual psychic disorder, which permitted attention to madness to serve usefully as political critique. Mental illness became (to paraphrase Claude Lévi-Strauss) good to think with. From the 1940s to the 1960s, prominent American psychiatrists and social scientists conducting open-ended and often unsettling quests for the sources of mental illnesses invariably struggled with far larger conundrums concerning the relationships between the individual and his or her social environment. It was only against this background that, by the late 1960s and early 1970s, a growing perception that the entire society was becoming a lunatic asylum could spark such an extraordinary range of oppositional projects. The critical reflections on mental illness and social conditions put forward in the postwar decades eventually came to offer the counterculture an invaluable vantage point for articulating profound disgust at society-wide hypocrisies and cruelties. In short, the countercultural activists in the 1960s and 1970s who conjoined analyses of mental illness with political reflections were hardly the first to do so.

At the same time, however, this book also demonstrates that antipsychiatry was not solely a left-leaning development. On the contrary, throughout the postwar decades there were passionate and powerful right-wing and conservative critiques of the rise of psychiatric expertise. Appeals to small-town values of hard work, responsibility, and stoicism in the face of life's turbulence alternated with paranoid reports that state psychiatric facilities might serve as detention centers for political dissidents. The roots of the conservative backlash against antipsychiatry that set in from the mid-1970s on, then, can already be found in a hostility to psychiatry's ascendance in the 1950s, even as, and however paradoxically, that same populist 1950s suspicion of the rise of psychiatry fueled the antipsychiatric movement in its 1960s and early 1970s heyday.

As it turns out, both psychiatry and antipsychiatry were ideologically all over the map. This became even clearer in the late 1960s and 1970s as feminist, gay liberation, and Black Power activists and members of the radical therapy and psychiatric survivors movements all took potshots at mainstream psychiatry. To make the story even more intricate, these protesters found the social theories of mental illness that had been so central to mainstream psychiatry's ascent and growing legitimacy from the 1940s to the 1960s now extremely useful for *attacking* psychiatry. As the New Left and the counterculture turned against psychiatry in the 1970s—accusing it of complicity in "adjusting" young men to serve in Vietnam and in policing student activism and Black Power, as well as of endemic homophobia and misogyny—they were relying on social theories developed by psychiatrists in prior decades.

Finally, in another odd twist, the antipsychiatric radicals and feminists of the 1970s ran squarely into many of the same conceptual impasses in thinking about the relationships between individuals and society that had stymied psychiatric professionals for decades. What were the mechanisms of interaction between the individual and the social environment? What could or should the direction of social change be? Was it best to start with the individual or with the conditions? Were therapeutic interventions politicizing or depoliticizing?

And yet none of the shortcomings of or difficulties encountered by antipsychiatry justify how it has been either derided, summarily ignored, or removed from its historical context. The backlash that subsequently ensued against the obvious grandiosity and falsity of the most extreme versions of antipsychiatric sentiments also brought with it a near-total erasure of the best insights put forward during the era when the diagnosis was social. That erasure remains surprising not only because of the power and breadth of antipsychiatric thought throughout the postwar period, but also because of antipsychiatry's many overlaps with mainstream psychiatry. It is no less surprising in view of the international scope of the antipsychiatric movement. Mental illness—and schizophrenia in particular—was, after all, a focus for major fascination, sustained reflection, and investigation not only in the United States but in the United Kingdom, Italy, the Netherlands, France, and West Germany as well.[4]

Histories of the political upheavals and cultural (and countercultural) movements of the 1960s all too routinely do not discuss antipsychiatry at all and certainly do not integrate the ambiguous history of antipsychiatric thought into their accounts in any sustained or meaningful way.[5] Histories of psychiatry, meanwhile, have inadequately attended to the mutual entanglements of psychiatry and antipsychiatry and, more generally, have neglected to analyze the extraordinary outpouring of social theorizing engaged in by psychiatrists and professionals in related disciplines in the postwar decades.[6] Those authors who do bother to make passing mention to antipsychiatry routinely do so with confident condescension. Thus Edward Shorter sarcastically remarks on how antipsychiatry came to occupy "the catbird seat among intellectuals both in the United States and Europe" by the late 1960s, and Jonathan Engel states that Thomas Szasz was "a paranoid kook who was sloppy with his facts."[7] Allan Hobson and Jonathan Leonard declare Laing and Szasz to be members of the "lunatic fringe" and blame them as well as Goffman for "increasing public doubts about the existence of mental ills and worsening the [mental] hospitals' already battered image."[8] Derogatory declarations like these from respected scholars have largely gone unchallenged and unmodified for more than a quarter century.

Revising this routine erasure and reflexive dismissal of antipsychiatry as a potent and complex intellectual and cultural force in postwar American life and contextualizing it within broader postwar trends has been a primary task of this book. The stories of psychiatry and of the upheavals of the 1960s have all too typically been told separately. And yet these only seemingly disconnected histories were all along, as this book demonstrates, integrally intertwined.

This book provides an intellectual and cultural chronicle of that time (running from the late 1940s to the early 1980s) when many leading psychiatrists and social scientists enjoined one another as well as the general public to seek the causes of mental illness in societal sicknesses. It also aims to disentangle the all-too-often jumbled-together contributions of the antipsychiatric triumvirate of Laing, Goffman, and Szasz and situates their respective projects in preexisting and contemporaneous debates. For Laing, for example, as for anthropologists Gregory Bateson and Jules Henry and psychiatrists Lyman Wynne and Theodore Lidz, among others, the turn toward the social meant above all a focus on *interpersonal dynamics*. Parents in nuclear families with mentally ill children were held responsible for "double-binding" them, and thus for driving those kids insane. For Goffman, by contrast, thinking about madness as a socially produced problem above all meant focusing on the damages done by the *institutional setting* and the coercive means employed there. And quite unlike Laing, Goffman's fascination with mental institutions and what they could do to vulnerable inmates grew out of his interest in "thought reform"—commonly known as "brainwashing." It was Goffman's innovation to turn what had been a Cold War (and preeminently right-wing) ideological preoccupation into a theory whose applications came quickly to mean so much to radical activists in the 1960s. As for Szasz and his many admirers (especially in the legal profession), in yet a third variant, theorizing madness in social terms meant that the very category of mental illness was a *social construct*. And again, though also in a manner quite distinct from either Laing or Goffman, Szasz's relentless assault on psychiatry was rooted in 1950s popular discussions concerning a new therapeutic culture, and especially the potentially insidious impact of psychiatric expert testimony on American jurisprudence. Yet while Laing and Goffman believed that madness, while socially produced, was quite real, Szasz was skeptical on exactly this point—a position that could, as it turned out, be used to advance both right- and left-wing agendas.

The anti–Vietnam War movement, in turn, as well as the radical therapy and psychiatric survivors movements, took yet a fourth position, one that built on all three prior conceptualizations. The argument was not just that mental illness was socially produced and/or constructed, but that it was above all also a *political phenomenon*, both in the sense that critics of the status quo were deemed crazy and in the sense that going crazy could be a morally healthful response to grotesque social injustices.

There was, moreover, a fifth form of social diagnosis that will be discussed in these pages: *feminism*. The feminist movement advanced an extraordinarily important strand of antipsychiatric thought and numerous experiments in radical therapy. This book will additionally argue, however, that there were peculiar but remarkable overlaps between feminist therapy and the juggernaut of popular psychological self-help and efforts at self-actualization that came to dominate so much of American culture from the 1970s onward. The many shared emphases that evolved between the counterculture and pop psych would also find expression in the "human potential" movement—a broad-based cultural trend headlined by *Time* magazine in 1970 as "the revolution in feeling."[9]

And here the story gets trickier still. Pop psych represented yet another new form of antipsychiatry—indeed a massively successful one. It banked expressly on widespread popular suspicion of professional experts. Yet it also marked the beginning of the backlash *against* the social diagnosis. Pop psych emphasized individual responsibility and possibility—without the social criticism, and in explicit rejection of social theories of mental illness. All the more ironic, then, is that the increasingly permeable boundaries between pop psych and radical therapy would come to be used, in the antileft backlash gathering force from the later 1970s on, as sufficient grounds to dismiss all the radical forces of the 1960s–1970s, including antipsychiatry and feminism, as self-indulgent exercises symptomatic of a "culture of narcissism."[10]

The official death announcement for the social diagnosis would come from within psychiatry. From the mid-1970s onward, in an imaginative rescue operation, the weaknesses in psychiatric practice and concepts exposed by antipsychiatry ended up being used by mainstream psychiatrists to lay the groundwork for a thoroughly reconceived biochemical paradigm. The results of these labors, published in 1980 as DSM-III, inaugurated a crucial shift from speculation about etiology to an emphasis on measurable observation of symptoms and their remediability and facilitated a new era of research into individual biochemical anomalies.

Yet the social diagnosis would not disappear. In the first decades of the twenty-first century, revised and refined social diagnostic thinking and socially attuned treatments have been experiencing a renaissance. To reconstruct this story, with its many unexpected shifts and reversals, thus not only corrects the historical record. The issues raised also have powerful ongoing resonance not least because they remain unsettled.

Early postwar efforts by psychiatrists to fortify their position by expanding their reach into the wider populace made inescapably apparent just how blurry was the line between mental illness and mental wellness. So too the move made by mainstream psychiatrists to investigate and theorize individual psychological issues in socially contextualized terms pushed to the fore of both professional and popular reflection enduring enigmas of the mechanisms of interaction between individual selves and social contexts. This in turn explains much about the ferocity of the conflicts that ensued within psychiatry and related social sciences as well as the wider culture. To put it another way: It is the ultimate unresolvability of the riddles of the relationships between an individual's biochemistry and his or her social context, as well as of the boundaries between normalcy and abnormality, that explains the extraordinary outpouring of intensity in the decades of debates about madness, and the (at once ardent and mutually contradictory) political conclusions that were drawn in those debates. In grappling with the intersections of psychiatry and politics, after all, what is at stake is nothing less than how to feel and think about such matters as the institution of the family, the nature of the human self, and the prospects for (and limits of) social change.

Part One: When the Diagnosis Was Social

1   Society as the Patient

There is a growing realization among thoughtful persons that our culture is sick, mentally disordered, and in need of treatment.   **Lawrence K. Frank, 1948¹**

I

The postwar era in the United States witnessed an extraordinary spike in attention given to the status of Americans' mental well-being. Debating what it meant to be mentally well and mentally ill became a national pastime as all things psychological became the focus for unprecedented fascination. This fascination took a myriad of popular forms. Magazines ran self-administered "diagnostic tests" to "determine how normal you really are."² Articles advised anxious parents on how they might most effectively engage in "building" the "best possible mental foundation for mental health" of their children.³ There were nationally broadcast television programs on the subject of mental health, and there was the introduction of a Mental Health Week to publicize the message (and the dilemmas) of mental illness. *The Basic Writings of Sigmund Freud* appeared in a new edition in 1947 and, notwithstanding its unwieldy length of a thousand pages, sold over a quarter of a million copies. And syndicated columns with titles like "The Worry Clinic" or "Let's Explore Your Mind" drew readerships in the tens of millions. At the same time, and all through, there was a recurrent effort to theorize the deeper psychic illnesses that were said to course through American culture—efforts (as the title of a book published in 1948 put it) that conceived of "society as the patient."[4]

This chapter explores how the postwar explosion of interest in all things psychological can be understood as rooted in lessons taken from World War II. In particular, the concern over traumatic experiences of soldiers in combat along with the attempts better to understand the "personality structure" of the Nazi opponents was to have tremendous consequences for the practice of psychiatry and for a social psychological analysis of US domestic politics. During the war military psychiatrists witnessed the degree to which the onset of mental disorder represented a reaction to environmental stress; after 1945 these psychiatrists broadly applied their wartime observations of the impact that a conflict-ridden environment had on psyches to an exegesis of how the daily lives of average Americans probably also contained submerged pathogenic qualities. Moreover, psychiatric diagnoses of American society began increasingly in the postwar era to articulate moral and political values; for instance, "undemocratic" attitudes (such as antiblack racism or anti-Semitism) came widely to be interpreted by social psychologists and psychoanalysts as quite likely reflective of individual psychopathology or reactions to environmental influences—and the challenge was properly to identify this dynamic. If psychiatry was to be understood as a branch of medical science, it was additionally believed by many of its leading postwar practitioners to be a science with a social mission.

There was also increasing attention among researchers in the social sciences to the relationship between early experiences within the family and the later capacities of average Americans to develop properly beneficent and appropriately democratic personalities. "If men be good, government cannot be bad," William Penn had observed in 1693. This maxim rather remarkably came to be understood as so apt an expression of "the interlocking bonds of affection that give strength to social structure," as Harold D. Lasswell, a leading figure in the field of political psychology, wrote in 1948, that investigations into the possible connections between psychology and politics absorbed scholars across many disciplines.[5] Americans, or so one line of argument went, had too often been inadequately nurtured as children, and thus grew to adulthood insufficiently affectionate and unable to maintain genuine and intimate personal relations. The grim news from psychiatrists and social psychologists by the early 1950s was that many Americans ran a high risk of developing mental illnesses because they had been raised in families that had not provided them enough warmth; and an interwoven argument was that many of these same persons were also at risk of being lured by right-wing ideologies. Indeed, as one theory had it—and as the authors of the massive social psychological tome on the origins of prejudice, *The Authoritarian Personality*, argued forcefully in 1950—the aggressions a person directed toward members of ethnic or racial minorities could be interpreted as the result of a frustrated search for affirmation. Drawing on wartime analyses of Nazi Germany, as well as on studies of race relations and the strong appeal of right-wing politics also in the United States, the authors dramatically concluded that a "failure in superego integration, inability to establish emotional relationships with others, and overcompensatory reactions to weakness and passivity are among the important sources of potentially fascist trends within the personality."[6] While many scholars would soon reject the specific theses put forward in *The Authoritarian Personality*, the questions the book had raised about the psychic fragility of American democracy and the mechanisms of interaction between individual psychological development, familial dynamics, wider social environment, and ideological convictions would preoccupy the social sciences for many years to come. Most importantly, as with postwar psychiatrists' efforts to address not only psychosis but also a broader range of disturbances and maladjustments in daily American life, so also with the investigation into the connections between psychology and politics: the effect was to foreground just how indeterminate was the line between illness and health. This indeterminacy, far from inhibiting the growth of psychiatry's influence and prestige, instead facilitated it.

The dominant assumption in postwar American psychiatry was that society played a grievous role in the etiology—or "triggering off"—of mental disorders.[7] This in itself was not a postwar innovation. As long ago as the late nineteenth century, French sociologist Émile Durkheim had analyzed statistical records and other data to explore how societal stresses (like the loss of social position) resulted in an elevated incidence of suicide; epidemiological research throughout the first half of the twentieth century continued to provide compelling evidence that environmental factors posed a risk in the etiology of mental illness.[8] Social participation and social detachment were seen as especially important in this regard, with isolated individuals shown to be "much more likely to commit suicide than are persons who are closely integrated in group life."[9] For related reasons persons who lived in the heightened anonymity of cities were found to run a higher risk of mental illness than persons who lived in rural areas.[10] Nor were city dwellers all equally liable to go insane. In *Mental Disorders in Urban Areas: An Ecological Study of Schizophrenia and Other Psychoses* (1939), medical sociologists Robert E. L. Faris and H. Warren Dunham had determined that the incidence of psychosis in Chicago was unevenly distributed across the strata of socio-economic classes; the slum dweller ran a far greater chance of developing schizophrenia than persons who lived elsewhere in the city. Faris and Dunham could not settle the puzzle of whether individuals predisposed to mental illness were the most likely to "drift" to the poorer neighborhoods in urban centers or whether the slums produced psychosis.[11] But their work nonetheless prompted research into causal links between the "social disorganization" of urban existence and heightened rates of mental illness; postwar epidemiological studies further confirmed at least partial aspects of what came to be called the "urban hypothesis" of mental disorders.[12]

At the same moment a corollary hypothesis began to gain traction. It postulated that psychosis did not exist in "traditional" societies due to those cultures' social cohesiveness. Various anthropological researchers found that members of "primitive" cultures simply did not evince psychotic symptoms.[13] If schizophrenia resulted from an inability to integrate oneself socially, scholars speculated that individuals in close-knit cultures were going to be far less susceptible to the emotional disorders of civilization; indeed, anthropologists also found that psychosis became a problem in traditional cultures only *after* members of those groups began to have extensive contact with Western peoples.[14] As the writer of an article from 1942 in the *American Journal of Psychiatry* observed, there was no "schizophrenia among primitives" because mental illness represented "the peculiar curse of civilized man."[15] Or as a medical sociologist summarized this view again with more measured phrasing a decade later in 1952: "It appears that schizophrenia is less frequent in cultures which are homogenous and have intimate contacts than in cultures which are heterogeneous and have impersonal and hostile contacts."[16] Thus it was argued that the very fact of living in modern society effectively produced psychosis, though in truth much available evidence contradicted this conclusion. For instance, a historical review of mental hospital admission rates conducted in the late 1940s disclosed no increase in rates of mental illness since the nineteenth century despite industrialization and urbanization.[17] Other researchers in the late 1940s concluded that schizophrenia was most likely ubiquitous in all human cultures.[18] None-theless, the position that civilization promoted mental difficulties came to dominate postwar discussions. As one of the nation's foremost psychi-atrists, Francis J. Braceland, declared in 1947, "it would not be surpris-ing to see the incidence rates of psychoneurosis take an upward turn" in the years and decades ahead. In this fashion Braceland worked to posi-tion strategic arguments as though they were self-evident facts, noting how "civilization in its advance brings with it the seeds of neurosis."[19]

The rising cross-disciplinary fascination with diagnoses of society's illnesses was not the only reason for the post–World War II decline in a biological disease model of mental illness that had been initially ad-vanced in the early twentieth century by prominent German psychia-trist Emil Kraepelin. The biological model was also running into trouble because it had been unable to solve the problem of etiology. Indicative of the new hostility to biologism were the pronouncements of popu-lar journalist Albert Deutsch, who wrote in his influential account, *The Mentally Ill in America* (1949), how Kraepelin had fallen "far short of his aim to create order out of the existing chaos in psychiatry" specifi-cally due to the limitations of his neurobiological approach. According to Deutsch, while Kraepelin had "provided a valuable key to the un-derstanding of the *what* and the *how* in mental disorder," the "greatest question—the *why*—still remained wrapped in deep mystery." This was, Deutsch asserted, because the disease model had resulted in "static con-ceptions of mental disorders," a problem only the investigation of social factors could begin finally to solve.[20]

While some experts in American psychiatry remained committed to a Kraepelinean approach, increasing numbers of leading psychiatrists argued that a biological disease conception of mental illness was both unsatisfactory and inadequate. In 1948 psychiatrist Robert H. Felix—who would become the first director of the National Institute of Men-tal Health (NIMH) in 1949—summarized the postwar consensus of mainstream psychiatry when he proposed how "the impact of the so-cial environment on the life history, and the relevance of the life history to mental illness are no longer in serious question as clinical and re-search findings."[21] Also in 1948 Karl A. Menninger, one of the nation's most renowned psychiatrists, expressed comparable views, writing that there was "no proof" that "a special tendency to schizophrenia" was "transmitted by heredity." However, Menninger went on to remark that there existed "much proof" that "those individuals who later become schizophrenic" had suffered emotional "injuries" early in life. As Men-ninger outlined:

It may be the death of a mother, or neglect or harshness by the mother, incessant quarreling between the parents, hopeless rivalry with a much more popular or much more beautiful sister. Perhaps any, perhaps all of these things can do it. Some of them may occur even in the most gentle and kindly and affectionate of families. . . . The girl who is jilted by a lover at 21 and then develops schizophrenia may well have had a much more serious disappointment 18 years before that, and perhaps many others, but the final disappointment acts like the straw that broke the camel's back.[22]

Likewise, psychologist Bruno Bettelheim, then director of the Sonia Shankman Orthogenic School in Chicago, a leading residential institution for the treatment of emotionally disturbed youth, underscored the social, not biological, sources of mental disturbance. Arguing that "certain factors originating in society interfere with our work and create specific emotional difficulties," Bettelheim further demanded that children at his school be kept as far removed from parents as possible because parents, in their confused desire to meet (often conflicting) social expectations, incoherently mixed intermittent indulgence with imposition of strict values and thus "may actually impede mental health" of children. As Bettelheim intoned: "The very fact that we had to try to create a total therapeutic environment is itself some reflection of recent changes in thinking on mental health within our society."[23]

It was a widely promoted position, moreover, that psychiatry could play an essential role in healing the psychic wounds of postwar America. As William C. Menninger, brother of Karl and the first psychiatrist ever to serve as brigadier general in the United States Army, as well as president in 1946 of the influential Group for the Advancement of Psychiatry and president of the American Psychiatric Association in 1948, predicted in 1951, his profession "can and will make an important contribution towards the solution of some of our social problems."[24] Such an expanded public role for psychiatry was especially vital at a historical moment when, as Menninger wrote to mark the first nationwide observance of Mental Health Week in May of that year, "the world could never before have had more grief and unhappiness and human turmoil than currently exists."[25] As priorities Menninger named the desperate need "to find ways and means of more satisfactorily sublimating man's aggressive instinct," to diminish fear, superstition, and anxiety, to counteract impulses toward materialism and instead help people "gain greater satisfaction in life," and to teach young people "not only the *facts about* life,

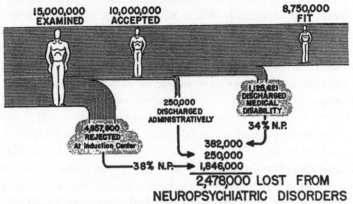

FIGURE 2 "Military Manpower Loss (Due to Mental & Physical Conditions)." *Bulletin of the Menninger Clinic* 12, no. 1 (1948). Courtesy of the *Bulletin of the Menninger Clinic.*

FIGURE 3 "From Combat Come Two Casualties." *Bulletin of the Menninger Clinic* 12, no. 1 (1948). Courtesy of the *Bulletin of the Menninger Clinic.*

but a worth-while *way of* life."[26] Thus, as Robert Felix wrote in 1947, having identified the roots of mental disorders in societal terms meant as well to interpret mental illness as preeminently constituting "a public health problem" for which preventive mental health treatment programs needed desperately to be made far more extensively available.[27]

The conception of mental illness as a matter of considerable urgency developed further in direct relationship to lessons gleaned from the extensive firsthand experiences of American military psychiatrists during World War II. Already World War I had focused psychiatric concern on the problems of "shell shock" and "war neurosis." World War II presented exponentially larger problems. As an article in *Mental Hygiene* stated in 1947: "Never before were psychiatrists, psychologists, and psychiatric social workers employed on such a vast scale as members of neuropsychiatric teams as in the war recently won."[28] World War II transformed the place of psychiatry within medicine as well as within American society. In early 1944 psychiatry became a division within the Office of the Surgeon General of the United States Army, and William Menninger was appointed its first director; the war also drew hundreds of physicians into psychiatry and greatly expanded the membership of the American Psychiatric Association.[29] And as physicians who had examined soldiers with psychological disorders concluded, environmental stresses were the key to understanding the etiologies of mental maladjustment. Or as Albert Deutsch wrote, "the observations of military psychiatrists provided the basis for a remarkable stimulus to postwar study of the social aspects of mental disorders."[30]

Almost as soon as the war ended, psychiatrists began openly to discuss the often-startling data that revealed that the incidence of mental disorders among American soldiers was far greater than anyone might have imagined. As William Menninger disclosed at the annual meeting of the American Psychiatric Association in 1946, close to two million men were rejected for military service during the war as a result of "neuropsychiatric disorders," and an additional one million men had become "neuropsychiatric admissions" to army hospitals in the years from 1942 to 1945. Menninger reported as well that more than a half million men had been discharged from military service on account of "personality disturbances."[31]

No less troubling were the implications for social relations implicit in the findings of military psychiatrists Roy R. Grinker and John P. Spiegel. Based on their study of the psychological impact of combat stress on Air Force bomber pilots, Grinker and Spiegel found that there was a tendency of bombardiers to collapse psychologically after a certain unspecified (and widely varying) number of missions. Everyone appeared in the end, according to them, to have "a fixed limit of tolerance to the physical and emotional stress of combat." (To be clear, the men's stress was not due to the killing of others—which Grinker and Spiegel barely if ever dis-

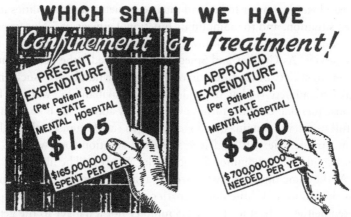

FIGURE 4 "Which Shall We Have, Confinement or Treatment!" *Bulletin of the Menninger Clinic* 12, no. 1 (1948). Courtesy of the *Bulletin of the Menninger Clinic.*

MEDICAL EDUCATION

 4% (OF 5000 HRS.)
PSYCHIATRIC
TRAINING

MEDICAL PRACTICE

30 TO 50% OF ALL PATIENTS

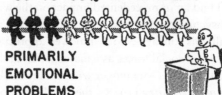

PRIMARILY
EMOTIONAL
PROBLEMS

FIGURE 5 "Medical Education, Medical Practice." *Bulletin of the Menninger Clinic* 12, no. 1 (1948). Courtesy of the *Bulletin of the Menninger Clinic.*

cussed—but rather terror at their own helplessness as well as guilt over the loss of comrades.) Once a man passed his limit, he experienced what the psychiatrists rather euphemistically labeled "operational fatigue," which meant that all his accumulated fear simply overwhelmed him and he became unfit to fly. Grinker and Spiegel further speculated that the vulnerability felt during combat resulted in "a reactive state in which the ego loses its power to control intense anxieties and hostilities in the given situation, and to maintain its functional efficiency." Nor were the consequences of these breakdowns solely confined to time spent in military service. As Grinker and Spiegel also observed, "the possible implications to society of the future in returning large numbers of such angry, regressed, anxiety-ridden, dependent men to civilian life" were far from inconsequential. Of the returning veteran they added, "he is so unhappy, so full of intense longings, so inadequate to satisfy himself through his own activities, he will be driven to seek a solution somewhere." And Grinker and Spiegel ominously inquired: "Where will he find it?"[32]

At the same time there were strong assurances in the popular media that the emotional difficulties experienced by so many veterans represented neither a disgrace to the US military nor a danger to the general public. The vast majority of these men were, or so it was reported, responding remarkably well to new therapies and treatments. As war correspondent John Hersey observed late in 1945 in a lengthy report for *Life* magazine about a mental hospital's efforts to rehabilitate "nervously wounded" men (accompanied by still photographs from director John Huston's still-unreleased documentary film about the hospital), the innovative psychiatric care received by these veterans meant that most of them were "no worse off, in fact sometimes better off, than millions of their fellow citizens with minor neuropsychiatric disorders who have not had the benefit of a psychiatric service like that of the U.S. Army."[33] Strikingly, the depiction of psychiatry was as a sort of salvation.

Without a doubt the traumatic experiences of soldiers in combat during World War II had an unprecedented impact on the wider practice of psychiatry and psychology. For instance, William Menninger worked strenuously to rally his colleagues to a "renewed appreciation of the importance of stress from social forces as a major factor in the causation of psychiatric casualties."[34] As Menninger wrote in his book for a popular audience, *You and Psychiatry* (1948), the psychiatric observations of soldiers who collapsed after combat had general implications for understanding the reactions of all persons to all sorts of only seemingly banal social pressures:

> More than half a million men, 49% of all discharges from the army for mental or physical defects, were discharged because of their inability to make the adjustments demanded of them. . . . None of those men were any "crazier" or more "insane" than you or I. . . . The pounding of German 88 guns and the diving

Japanese Kamikazi planes are totally different stresses from living with a wife and three kids in the attic of an in-law's house or
not being able to find a job. But the effect on the personality is
very much the same.

Ego does the best it can, but sooner or later, in this complex
civilization it may be overcome by troubles that result in hurt
and worry. These hurts and these worries are symptoms . . . of
emotional conflict [that] can become so severe that they incapac-
itate a personality for living normally.[35]

By the early 1950s, Menninger had come to believe that *love* was
the key to immunizing individuals against the ravages of emotional ill
health. "I feel strongly," he wrote in 1953, "that unless we teach our
children how to love and we ourselves learn how to love, we never become a contributing social being." In an astonishing precursor to an
argument that would be made even more forcefully more than a dozen
years later by renegade psychiatrist R. D. Laing as well as other celebrity
gurus of the 1960s counterculture, Menninger added dramatically that
without adequate love, "we remain a hermit, or in our technical jargon,
a 'schizophrenic.'" And he concluded: "Our mental health depends on
our capacity to love."[36]

II

Meanwhile, the political lessons drawn from psychiatry and psychoanalysis in the wake of the war were uneven and contradictory. Democracy
itself—so scholars in a variety of disciplines had begun to argue—depended on Americans' capacity to love. But the problem lay in the American family. As with the more general expansion of psychiatry's mission,
and with the turn to a focus on social sources for mental disorders, so
too with the growing effort to theorize the relationships between psychology and politics, the experiences of World War II were extremely
significant, albeit for completely different reasons. Rather than analogizing between the reactions of American soldiers to combat and the
stresses of daily existence in America, social scientists who were interested in politics sought to draw lessons from an examination of the Nazi
enemy. Attention focused on the possible relationships between individual psychological development and adherence to political ideologies. If
the psyche of the individual was vulnerable especially while young, and
if there existed a decisive link between the development of personality

and the evolution of ideological values, then environment (particularly within families) required close scrutiny.

Especially influential in this regard were the writings of the psychoanalytically inclined political scientist Harold D. Lasswell, who was confident that his theories about Nazism and about nurturance and American family life were mutually applicable. Nazism was clearly on Lasswell's mind when he noted in *Power and Personality* (1948) that "the ascendency (the 'charisma') of many so-called natural leaders turns out to be that of the successful delinquent," sharply adding: "No one can look at the psychological structure of the tyrannies of recent world politics without recognizing that such political leadership is juvenile delinquency on a colossal scale."[37] But Lasswell was particularly fascinated with thinking through the appeals of right-wing politics for its many followers.

Lasswell posited that the pathologies of personality and the pathologies of politics had to be recognized as inseparable entities, and that the maintenance of democratic societies depended on the maintenance of the populace's mental health. Right-wingers, in his view, were emotionally unstable. As Lasswell wrote, the same person who struggled unhappily within himself tended overwhelmingly to pursue power "as a means of compensation against deprivation." Thus when persons in a society routinely experienced feelings of anxiety and low self-esteem, they were more likely to take on antidemocratic political attitudes. Drawing directly on psychodynamic theories on social anxiety advanced by psychiatrist Harry Stack Sullivan, supervisor at the prestigious Chestnut Lodge Sanitarium in Maryland (whom Lasswell knew well and with whom he had often collaborated), Lasswell argued:

> The newborn member of society must receive enough positive indulgence from the human environment to enable him to be indulgent toward himself and others. Such a basic character formation operates selectively as an enduring predisposition in subsequent life situations. It makes it possible for the person to supply himself with indulgence in circumstances in which a favorable ration of indulgence is not accorded to prodemocratic conduct by the environment. This is the basis for the extraordinary capacity of some human beings to remain generous, warm, enduring, hopeful and spontaneous when others project blame, dash themselves to pieces or retire, trailing clouds of regressive fantasy. Democratic characters have a durable positive image of the potentialities of human nature.[38]

But Lasswell's ambition went beyond diagnosis and identification of the lasting damages done by early emotional deprivation. What was required, according to Lasswell, was the full-scale development of a "social psychiatry" (not his coinage, but a term that was coming increasingly into use and reflected Lasswell's interdisciplinary inclinations).[39] In Lasswell's opinion the aim of social psychiatry would be to function unabashedly as a "value-oriented" branch of medicine, one committed to an exploration of "the entire social process for the purpose of discerning and abolishing whatever impairs the self-respect of human beings." This branch of medicine, Lasswell proposed, would ideally become "coterminous with" American democracy, not least because it would operate to safeguard US society against authoritarian impulses—and Lasswell did believe that these lurked not just overseas but also at home. In this respect, what became so very important was that individuals know warmth and affection, and that they know how to love. "Personalities fit to participate in the democratization of society must love themselves enough to love all," Lasswell wrote. The problem thus was how to raise loved and loving children since, as Lasswell added, "Progressive democratization depends upon finding the ways of dealing with children which do, in fact, aid in the formation of democratic character, transmit democratic perspectives and foster the acquisition of democratic skills."[40] The inadequate affirmation and nurture that William Menninger would a few years later identify as the source of schizophrenia, Lasswell saw as the source of antidemocratic politics.

By the time sociologist Theodor W. Adorno and social psychologists Else Frenkel-Brunswik, Daniel J. Levinson, and R. Nevitt Sanford, a research team based in Berkeley, California, published *The Authoritarian Personality* (1950), a project dedicated to the unraveling of the relationship between personality and political values, the idea that personal psychological development and political values and identities were deeply intertwined had already been for several years in wide circulation within psychiatric and psychoanalytic circles—and by no means only because of Lasswell. A main trend in psychoanalytic and social psychological studies of both antiblack racism and anti-Semitism was to argue that racism functioned as a compensatory or defense mechanism, an unconscious means to manage deep feelings of humiliation that were too awful and difficult consciously to contemplate. For instance, it had been theorized since the 1930s that when routinely frustrated, human beings responded with acts of aggression, and that this aggression was often directed against individuals or groups deemed lesser or worthless.[41] Additionally,

social psychologist Erich Fromm had proposed in 1941 that when social conditions squelched individual self-expression, this offered rich soil
for the flourishing of an "authoritarian character" that displayed "the
simultaneous presence of sadistic and masochistic drives."[42] Such persons sought to surrender themselves to a master (not least so as to avoid
responsibility for their own aggressive actions) even as they sought also
to dominate others and to inflict pain upon them. And psychoanalyst
Ernst Simmel had contributed the insight that also the "relatively normal, well-adapted person" "regressed" at moments of social panic or
crisis. Under such circumstances it became possible for a society to experience "mass psychosis" and for there consequently to be outpourings of
venomous hatred (like the virulent anti-Semitism witnessed across Nazi-
occupied Europe).[43] In addition to citing this scholarship, the authors of
The Authoritarian Personality also understandably thought to reference
Harold Lasswell, since he had, after all, offered further support for "the
psychoanalytic axiom that the first social relationships to be observed
within the family are, to a large extent, formative of [political] attitudes
in later life."[44] The Berkeley research team intended to defend and refine
this axiom, seeking more precisely to determine correlations between
pathological personality factors and destructive ideological opinions, including the hatred of ethnic and racial minorities.

Did persons who harbored resentments and hostilities toward minorities share a specific character structure that might be labeled "authoritarian"? Was it possible to extrapolate from an individual case study to
the population as a whole? What was the link between the individual
who possessed an "authoritarian" personality and the ability of states to
carry out policies whose aim was to "scapegoat" so-called undesirable
groups? And did the presence of authoritarian personalities within a society not only make fascism possible but also ensure that fascistic policies
could be carried by popular consent? Integrating an innovative array of
social psychological methods, the Berkeley researchers sought to make
sense of these questions through the collection of a mass of empirical and
statistical evidence. They interviewed more than two thousand subjects
and took their life histories. They devised elaborate questionnaires. They
showed their subjects dramatic images and asked them to invent stories about them. (This technique first introduced in the mid-1930s was
known as the Thematic Apperception Test.[45]) And they developed several
scales to quantify their findings. There was the "A-S scale" (for "anti-
Semitism") and the "E scale" (for "ethnocentrism"); there was the "PEC
scale" (for "politico-economic conservatism") and—most famously—
the "F scale" ("f" for "fascist"), each of which was intended to measure

an individual's tendency toward prejudiced and undemocratic values as a corollary of personality factors. The result was the most comprehensive study ever undertaken on how political attitudes related to personality traits. And what the Berkeley researchers finally argued was that there did in fact exist "the *potentially fascist* individual, one whose structure is such as to render him particularly susceptible to anti-democratic propaganda."[46]

Several points bear emphasis. For one thing—and although it left unclear whether pathological personality traits were innate or produced by early parent-child interaction, while at the same time it certainly did also attend to the impact of the wider social environment—*The Authoritarian Personality* definitely took the view that there were strong correlations between character structure and ideological attitudes. Additionally, while the book was framed principally as a study into the nature of prejudice, and the subjects were tested to measure the extent of their ethnocentrism, racism, and anti-Semitism, it also had much to say about the combination of ambivalent submission to authority figures and cruelty and aggression toward those more vulnerable that the authors identified as characteristic of antidemocratic and even incipiently fascistic impulses. In other words, racist attitudes, authoritarian submission, and tendency toward aggression were understood to be all part of the same package—complementary components of a unified psychological profile.

Finally, and despite the reams of seemingly objective scientific data marshaled, the book was without a doubt intended as a political intervention into discussions about what Americans *should* value. It sought to position prejudice as antithetical to democracy. In pursuit of this cause the authors unfortunately—although tellingly—did not hesitate to strategically portray the prejudiced person as both latently homosexual and mentally disturbed (even while the study had also tested for homophobia as an indicator of potentially fascist traits). Indeed, the authors of *The Authoritarian Personality* did not—or perhaps could not—resist casting the bigot in the most unflattering terms. The bigot was a sexually frustrated and pathetic wimp. Unloved as a child, his authoritarian parents had doled out their affections in tiny spoonfuls. This led him to grow to adulthood in pitiful search of tenderness, while masking his erotic attraction to other men by acting macho. He hated himself for being weak, and he turned that hatred against scapegoats. For the authors of *The Authoritarian Personality*—and in this way again strongly echoing the arguments advanced by Fromm, Simmel, and Lasswell, among others—the person who hated was psychologically deficient and emotionally damaged.

At the same time, and by contrast, the Berkeley researchers gave the un-biased individual a clean bill of mental health.

The Authoritarian Personality quickly emerged as one of the most significant and widely critiqued texts published in the postwar era.[47] It was a landmark text in the field of social psychology and also a ma-jor contribution to an emerging postwar discussion about the fortitude and resilience of American democracy. Yet far from finding it gratifying and useful that so many unpleasant aspects of human nature were being made explicable, *The Authoritarian Personality* would rapidly be sav-aged both on conceptual and substantive grounds. (In 1958 two retro-spective observers noted that *The Authoritarian Personality* was "one of the few books known to have been criticized before it was published!"[48]) The reasons for the almost instant umbrage taken were several.

First, *The Authoritarian Personality* pointed an accusatory finger at American society as a whole, deeming the phenomenon of vulnerabil-ity to antidemocratic attitudes to be far more pervasive than had been previously assumed. A 1946 study by psychologists Gordon W. Allport and Bernard M. Kramer already had ventured the view that "it would seem a safe estimate that at least four-fifths of the American population lead mental lives in which feelings of group hostility play an appreciable role."[49] Here now was a blockbuster book that, while reducing the es-timate of the proportion of Americans afflicted, raised the stakes by re-directing the conversation away from the rather mundane phenomenon of "feelings of group hostility" to the far more dramatic tendency to "authoritarianism." A feature piece in the *New York Times Magazine* in 1950 promoting the conclusions of *The Authoritarian Personality* flatly asserted "it can be said that about 10 per cent of the population of the United States probably consists of 'authoritarian men and women' while as many as another 20 per cent have within them the seeds that can grow into authoritarianism."[50] Having just defeated German and Italian fas-cism, Americans were not eager to learn that it *could* happen here, that the United States also possessed the potential for fascism.

Second, *The Authoritarian Personality* insulted those with tradition-ally conservative values, expressly tarring conservatism as *both* an incip-ient form of authoritarianism and fascism *and* a sign of mental disorder. The book also suggested that many conservatives were "phony" in their patriotism, waving the flag while hating the democratic institutions they claimed to honor. Authoritarian individuals often appeared well ad-justed, but that was only because they externalized their seething resent-ments onto others (rather than being able to reflect self-critically). Notably, then, while prior studies (not incidentally produced in the wake of the Great Depression) had emphasized the tendencies toward prejudice especially among members of the lower class and the economically vulnerable, *The Authoritarian Personality* cast aspersions on mainstream, also prosperous, Americans.

In addition a number of scholars found serious flaws with personality studies as a methodological enterprise. In 1950 sociologist Nathan Glazer expressed irritation at what he took to be the tautological quality of the Berkeley team's approach and at its political implications. "When the researcher, on the basis of a subject's agreement or disagreement with a series of statements composed by the researcher himself, proceeds to determine the nature of the subject's thought-processes," Glazer rhetorically inquired, "is he not moving in a circle?" (Glazer was especially huffy about Adorno and his colleagues' "rather simple and simpleminded assumptions about what is progressive or liberal," and "their assumption that opposition to intermarriage can only be a sign of prejudice."[51]) In 1954, in an anthology dedicated to assessing the strengths and (above all) weaknesses of *The Authoritarian Personality*, one contributor also made the telling critique that Adorno and his associates had completely neglected to explore "Leftist authoritarianism."[52] Other contributors decried the Berkeley team's disregard for social conditions and overemphasis on individual character, contending that *The Authoritarian Personality*'s methodology was "unsound" because "from a practical standpoint, it tends to perpetuate the implication that the level of organization of sentiments is a kind of universal, an intra-psychic process which bears little relation to environmental conditions."[53] And in 1958 a leading sociologist chose to present his discussion of authoritarian personality research in the past tense, while also articulating disdain for the presumption that racism was a sign of mental disturbance; he sarcastically noted that the very notion of an authoritarian personality "lent itself nicely to precisely the kinds of study which psychologists and social psychologists were prepared to undertake," just as it also "fitted in nicely with the general view that racial prejudice is basically wrong and unhealthy."[54] By the later 1950s a perspective that prejudiced attitudes could be linked to mental illness was in the process of being actively repudiated.[55]

Finally, and related, was how pessimistic and despairing about human nature the entire social psychological field of personality studies in the immediate postwar years had been. It was not that prejudiced persons could never change, but that such persons were highly resistant to attempts to alter their racist character. For instance, while well-publicized and coordinated efforts to combat bigotry with accurate information about minority groups had initially been presented by leading social psychologists as the best weapon against intolerance, after 1945 the conviction that such efforts really worked began to dim considerably.[56]

By the early 1950s new Cold War ideological factors required a revised (and less gloomy) theory of white racism. As America claimed its postwar place as a beacon for democracy in the world, the dirty linen that had been slavery and remained as racial segregation required political and intellectual redress.[57] It was no longer palatable by the mid-1950s to argue within social psychological circles that a good number of American citizens could easily succumb to political values that were potentially fascistic.

Social progress and individual reform were presented by the early 1950s as eminently achievable. For instance, a significant contribution to the emphatically upbeat direction in child clinical studies was sociologist Mary Ellen Goodman's *Race Awareness in Young Children* (1952). Drawing her analysis from data collected in three nursery schools, Goodman rejected the disquieting argument that people could not change their natures. She wrote that "the thoughts and feelings of our four-year-olds, white or brown, do not come out of the blue. Neither do they come simply and directly from parent to child." And she also ended her study with these lofty sentiments:

> There are no inevitabilities here. What is more, there are no monolithic attitudes springing from monolithic sources. Monoliths are massive and resistant. But the very complexity of the process of attitude-generation, as we have seen its early stages in our four-year-olds, is promising. It means that there are a great many possible points of attack, no one of which is necessarily highly resistant. . . . It is heartening to remember that there is an antithesis to the principle of the vicious circle in human affairs. *The benign circle operates too, and we who have young children in our charge can touch the springs to help set it in motion.*[58]

In this way clinical studies of children's racial attitudes conducted in the early 1950s began overwhelmingly to reject a theory that children were predisposed from early on to particular political attitudes, favoring instead a far more open-ended and hopeful interpretation that democratic (and nonauthoritarian) values could be schooled effectively into the ignorant and the very young.

Also notable was the work of prominent social psychologist Marian Radke-Yarrow and her team at the Philadelphia Early Childhood Project. Radke-Yarrow's project tested over two hundred children in six Philadelphia public schools, concluding that any child might be educated to racism, but also that any child could be educated to tolerance. In 1951, when *Commentary* magazine reported on the Philadelphia Early Childhood Project, it observed how the project's findings appeared to undermine the dark conclusions in *The Authoritarian Personality* "that the educator is powerless to alter the consequences of unsound parent-child relationships."[59] Or as Radke-Yarrow herself noted in 1953, researchers "must not now" continue to treat the "importance of personality systems" as "the key to the problem" of racial prejudice, but rather take more fully into consideration "the social field" in which the prejudicial behavior occurred.[60] The larger preoccupation of the Philadelphia Early Childhood Project was in understanding how this research might be "an aid in controlling anti-Democratic propaganda and demagogues within our society and in educating for democratic group living."[61] As Radke-Yarrow and her coauthor Helen G. Trager announced in the indicatively titled *They Learn What They Live: Prejudice in Young Children* (1952), their ambitious aim was nothing less than to offer parents a guidebook for how to raise children who could "learn to live democratically."[62]

There was hope for adults as well. In this regard psychologist Kurt Lewin's "change experiments" proved pioneering. Lewin's research into group dynamics proposed that individuals in small, participatory, and process-oriented groups could effectively work to eliminate their own and each other's antidemocratic and authoritarian feelings and learn to help resolve social conflicts. Lewin argued that racial prejudices "should not be viewed as individual character traits" but rather as "anchored in cultural standards," and that the "stability" and "change" of such prejudices "depend largely on happenings in groups as groups." And Lewin believed that small groups might transform "a multitude of unrelated individuals, frequently opposed in their outlook and their interests," into "co-operative teams not on the basis of sweetness but on the basis of readiness to face difficulties realistically, to apply honest fact-finding, and to work together to overcome them."[63] As Lewin noted in 1945, "democracy" represented a meaningless abstraction to people until they actively experienced it. The principles of democracy, Lewin wrote, "might be *clarified* by lectures but they can be *learned*, finally, only by democratic living." He added: "The 'training on the job' of democratic leaders is but one example of the fact that teaching democracy presupposes establishment of a democratic atmosphere."[64] Lewin's ideas led directly to the first "T-group" (or training group), established in 1947 at the National Training Laboratory in Group Dynamics in Bethel, Maine; these experiments with using small groups to effect social and political change were the forerunners for approaches that would be elaborated further in the New Left and counterculture and for what came still later to be known as sensitivity training.

By the early 1950s there were social psychological trends toward a new model of politics and personality, a model that offered a more optimistic reading of human nature. This manifested in a variety of ways. For instance, it was reiterated that a reduction in the social distance between groups that feared or hated each other could likely diminish the perpetuation of stereotypes held by members of both groups.[65] It was also argued that the degree of social alienation or anomie tended to define a person's political values, but that the anomie could be alleviated.[66] And it was argued that prejudiced feelings were the result of weak egos, but that weak egos could be effectively bolstered. The selves of citizens could be repaired through early childhood intervention or even later. The argument that persons raised racist were immune to later social forces went quickly out of fashion in the course of the 1950s and was rapidly replaced with an argument that racists were really quite capable of attitude improvements—given adjustments in their social circumstances.

Leading social psychologists actively used their research and academic expertise to combat racial inequality, most memorably on behalf of the plaintiffs in the Supreme Court desegregation case, *Brown v. Board of Education of Topeka*. Fittingly, for instance, findings from Radke-Yarrow's Philadelphia Early Childhood Project were entered as evidence for the plaintiffs to dramatize how children might unlearn prejudiced attitudes in integrated social environments.[67] Most famous, however, was "The Effects of Segregation and the Consequences of Desegregation," an appendix to the briefs submitted to the Supreme Court (signed by thirty-two social scientists, including many social psychologists) on behalf of the plaintiffs that emphasized the psychological illeffects of segregated life on minority children. As a coauthor of the report, psychologist Kenneth B. Clark had long argued that segregation inflicted tremendous potential psychic wounds upon members of an oppressed minority.[68] And as the report from the social scientists on behalf of the plaintiffs in *Brown* noted, "minority group children learn the inferior status to which they are assigned—as they observe the fact that they are almost always segregated and kept apart from others who are treated with more respect by the society as a whole."[69]

Moreover, and however problematic a line of argument this proved in hindsight to be, it was at this moment almost a standard reflex among social scientists to say that the mental disorders witnessed in African American children were responses to stresses inherent in living in a segregated society. For instance, as Clark wrote in 1955, a member of a disrespected minority often defied the dominant values of his society by engaging in criminal or delinquent activity largely as "a reaction, fundamentally unconscious and inarticulate, against society for its isolation, rejection, and chronic humiliation of himself."[70] In effect, if African Americans tended to exhibit signs of mental illness, it was an ill society that made this so. As a psychologist in 1953 had dramatically described the process, although an African American might often appear to possess a personality "which clinicians would ordinarily consider to be schizoid and hence 'abnormal,'" the truth of the matter was that this merely reflected "an 'adjusted' personality organization for Negroes in American society, since it is reality-adaptive and adaptable, and since it serves to protect the core or ego aspects of personality and to maintain them at levels sufficient for psychologically adequate functioning."[71] It was on the basis of ideas such as these that Clark and his colleagues concluded that only full desegregation could be the means to reverse deeply ingrained and problematic psychological patterns of personality.

That a segregated society compromised the African American family's ability to foster healthful and sustaining emotional relationships also emerged in the postwar years as almost entirely uncontested social scientific and psychiatric common sense. Time and again medical experts located in the black family an environment festering with the rich potential for mental pathology. Psychiatrists Abram Kardiner and Lionel Ovesey advanced just such a perspective in their influential study, *The Mark of Oppression: Explorations in the Personality of the American Negro* (1951), which took as fully representative the unfortunate situation of the black father who—unable to find employment—acted like a humiliated child within his own family. Meanwhile, Kardiner and Ovesey saw the black woman who now supported not only her children but also her husband as having assumed "the psychological position of the father, in which case she automatically elevates the female role as provider and derogates the established role of the male."[72] For mental health experts, the psychological consequences of this inversion of appropriate Cold War era gender roles was often interpreted as profound. As a contributor to the *American Journal of Psychiatry* summarized in 1956:

The Negro male child in a lower-class environment has difficulty in identifying with either parent. Whatever the affective
ties with his mother, he finds that she has a constant fear that he
will follow in the father's footsteps as an insecure breadwinner.
If he submits to the mother's demands, he may be regarded as
a sissy by his father and his age mates; for this he despises himself. Should he identify with his father? Yet the father image has
already been damaged by the constant stream of rebukes and
slurs thrown at him by the mother. A father identification may
mean freedom from the mother's control, but it also separates
him from the only safety and security he knows. Ambivalence toward both figures results; part of him is frustrated and repressed,
whatever his choice. Actually, the inconsistency of his discipline
may lead him to a rejection of both parents and to a certain hard
shrewdness with an atrophied superego.[73]

This was not all. A study of "psychoneurotic" breakdowns among African American soldiers in combat concluded that these breakdowns no
doubt arose "out of the relatively harsh childhood experiences of the Negroes."[74] Blacks were seen to suffer from higher levels of "self-abasement"
than whites.[75] Blacks had a special problem with anger, choosing to deny
or conceal such feelings for fear of losing control in the face of persecution.[76] Or conversely, blacks had delusions of persecution and saw discrimination everywhere—even "where none exists"—so that they might
claim such delusions "as an alibi for their own inadequacies."[77]

White psychologists and psychiatrists remained no doubt solidly
convinced that they pursued a greater good when they advanced these
devastating critiques of the postwar black psyche. Psychiatrist Viola M.
Bernard likely spoke for many in her profession when (in 1956) she emphasized how "as the choice of the lesser evil it seems preferable, from
the mental health standpoint, for some Negro children to suffer the tran-
sitional and current psychological hardships of desegregation which
are relatively more recognizable and correctable, than to experience the
more insidious and less treatable lifelong psychic damage from segregation."[78] Yet statements such as these cannot erase the fact that there
emerged a remarkably long list of (however unintentional nonetheless
disturbing) Cold War liberal perspectives promulgated by leading social
scientists and psychiatrists that cast the black psyche as damaged and
pathological and thus in seeming need of emotional uplift through en-
hanced contact with white culture.[79]

While scholarship has noted the condescension toward African Americans also in progressive analyses of race relations, it has less often observed how the report on behalf of the plaintiffs in *Brown* also rendered white personalities as potentially no less wounded by segregation due to the subterfuges and con games of a society that validated the standards of white supremacy. White children came of age having to learn "the moral, religious and democratic principles of the brotherhood of man and the importance of justice and fair play" from individuals and institutions that "in their support of racial segregation and related practices, seem to be acting in a prejudiced and discriminatory manner." Such sharp discrepancies between democratic ideals and racist practices bred in white children "confusion, conflict, moral cynicism, and disrespect for authority," which, in turn, and "as described in *The Authoritarian Personality*," led these same white children "to despise the weak, while they obsequiously and unquestioningly conform to the demands of the strong whom they also, paradoxically, subconsciously hate."[80] In short, and however surprising in view of its general pessimism, *The Authoritarian Personality* did eventually come to make an essential contribution to 1950s efforts by leading social psychologists to argue against legal segregation. (Notably, the report to the Supreme Court coauthored by Clark included as signatories both Else Frenkel-Brunswik and R. Nevitt Sanford, the social psychologists who had coauthored *The Authoritarian Personality*, as well as psychologist Gordon W. Allport, one of the book's chief defenders.) *The Authoritarian Personality*, although trounced by social scientists throughout the 1950s, nonetheless became a lasting potent cultural force. It continued to be drawn upon for diverse political purposes in subsequent years, even as what lessons might be taken from the text would remain unresolved.

III

In the 1950s opportunities in the field of mental health grew at an extraordinary rate as funding for both psychological and psychiatric research expanded exponentially. In 1950 the budget for the NIMH had been $8.7 million; by 1960 its budget jumped to over $100 million.[81] And in the six years between 1950 and 1956 alone, the number of psychiatrists in the United States climbed 57 percent as the membership in the American Psychiatric Association increased from 5,500 to over 8,700.[82] Nonetheless, there were repeated complaints from mental health professionals that supply still severely lagged behind demand. As of 1955 fewer than 5 percent of all doctors in the United States were psychiatrists, and of this number more than half were affiliated with public mental institutions. In these institutions every doctor was assigned to supervise between two hundred and three hundred patients, despite the fact that the American Psychiatric Association recommended that there should be one psychiatrist for every thirty acute or 150 chronic cases.[83] Or as a widely discussed survey of manpower trends in the field of mental health observed in 1957, the very fact that the United States currently had "one psychiatrist for every sixteen thousand people" represented nothing if not "an alarming ratio."[84] The reason why so relatively few medical students chose psychiatry as their specialty was entirely monetary; psychiatrists remained among the lowest paid among medical professionals. As *Newsweek* drily observed, even in private practice, the psychiatrist could "see only one patient an hour [while] other doctors see from four to ten."[85]

Meanwhile, psychiatrists and their allies kept hammering on the argument that America was in the grip of an unprecedented mental health crisis. In 1953 NIMH director Robert Felix warned a congressional committee that "mental illness has reached epidemic proportions."[86] That same year Kenneth Appel, president of the American Psychiatric Association, described "the rising burden of mental illness" as "a bigger problem than cancer, tuberculosis, and infantile paralysis combined."[87] The reported numbers on mental illness in America were presented as staggering—even if the statistics marshaled varied considerably. It was widely announced in 1955, for instance, that "people were cracking up at a rate which promises that, out of every twelve American children born each year, one will end up a serious mental case before he dies." It was additionally reported that approximately ten million Americans suffered from some form of mental illness, and that "some 25 per cent of the nation's labor force have been estimated to be emotionally disturbed."[88]

The possible consequences of widespread mental illness on the US economy also emerged as a key argument for the further expansion of psychiatry and of public psychiatric facilities. As journalist Mike Gorman wrote in *Every Other Bed* (1956), his powerful exposé of the routine mistreatment of the nation's mentally ill: "In terms of industrial productivity, at least one million man-years are lost each year because of mental illness." Gorman added: "This is an economic loss of several billion dollars a year in wages, and several hundred million dollars a year in lost federal income taxes."[89] A full-length study conducted in 1958 by the Joint Commission on Mental Illness and Health confirmed these troubling numbers.[90] There were additional suggestions that the future fate of the country in its Cold War with the Soviet Union could hang in the balance if the United States did not begin to address its mental illness epidemic far more aggressively.[91] Psychologist George W. Albee argued for the urgent need to double the number of practicing psychiatrists in the nation, and to do this as soon as possible, not least since "as our population continues to grow too, and as the rate of mental disorder in the population continues to increase, the need rises along with the supply of psychiatrists."[92] By 1961 it would once again be observed—this time in Senate hearings—that one in twelve Americans would be placed in a mental hospital during their lives.[93]

Through the 1950s William Menninger kept pushing the point that severe psychosis was not the only reason more psychiatrists and more funding for psychiatric research were desperately needed. The endless numbers game—one in four workers, one in twelve children, one in sixteen or possibly even one in ten Americans would suffer a breakdown and be institutionalized during their lifetimes—missed the point entirely. As Menninger explained in 1956 before the National Association for Mental Health:

> Even the most startling of these figures . . . refer only to extreme cases of mental disorder. [They] overlook the common, everyday emotional disturbances which can be as upsetting and incapacitating as many of the physical illnesses. When we take these into account, the toll of mental ill health must be reckoned as one in one, for there isn't a person who does not experience frequently a mental or emotional disturbance severe enough to disrupt his functioning as a well-adjusted, happy and efficiently performing individual.[94]

Americans appeared increasingly willing to take Menninger's message to heart. As *Life* magazine summarized the mood in the country in 1957, the 1950s had become "the age of psychology in the U.S.," a moment in which "the science of human behavior permeates our whole way of life—at work, in love, in sickness, and in health."[95]

By the mid-1950s Americans routinely heard that psychological thinking was everywhere around them—informing the minutiae of existence. "Psychology has burst out of the consulting room and clinic, spreading all through life and leaving nothing untouched," declared *Time* magazine in a cover story on psychiatrist Carl Jung in 1955.[96] As historian Roy Porter has written, the 1950s in the United States witnessed "the psychiatrization of everything," a mood contemporaneously

captured by the psychologically self-aware and sweetly satiric lyrics sung
by gang members to their neighborhood cop in Leonard Bernstein and
Stephen Sondheim's *West Side Story* (1956):

> Officer Krupke, you're really a square;
> This boy don't need a judge, he needs an analyst's care!
> It's just his neurosis that oughta be curbed.
> He's psychologic'ly disturbed!
> We're disturbed, we're disturbed,
> We're the most disturbed, like we're psychologic'ly disturbed.[97]

Likewise, a *New Yorker* cartoon from the early 1950s also humorously
illustrated how Americans had become aware of the flimsy line divid-
ing mental well-being from mental illness, as a middle-aged woman per-
plexedly asked her psychiatrist: "You mean all these years I just *thought*
I had a happy childhood?"[98]

The intertwined postwar success stories of psychiatry and social
psychology had initially been conjoined with a grim assessment of the
American family's dark underside. Americans remained susceptible to
the lures of authoritarianism not least of all due to the limitations on
love that parents were providing their children. Or so Adorno and his
research team had speculated. Yet even as this downbeat theory on family life became less and less acceptable as the 1950s proceeded, a new
psychiatric challenge began to be posed to the nuclear family. This time
it was not that the family served as a potential seedbed for fascist convictions, however. The subtly poisoned atmosphere in dysfunctional families was instead increasingly identified as a key factor in the onset of
childhood and adolescent schizophrenia.

2

Enough to Drive Anybody Crazy

Long before a thermonuclear war can come about, we have had to lay waste our own sanity. We begin with the children. It is imperative to catch them in time. Without the most thorough and rapid brainwashing their dirty minds would see through our dirty tricks. Children are not yet fools, but we shall turn them into imbeciles like ourselves, with high IQs if possible. . . . Specifically this devastation is largely the work of *violence* that has been perpetrated on each of us, and by each of us on ourselves. The usual name that much of this violence goes under is *love*.   **R. D. Laing, 1967**[1]

I

In 1960 Scottish psychoanalyst Ronald D. Laing concluded his first book, *The Divided Self: A Study in Sanity and Madness*, with a case study of a psychotic—one of the more chilling and consequential psychiatric case studies of the post-Freudian era. "The Ghost of the Weed Garden" recounted the life story of Julie who was in her mid-twenties when Laing met her; she had been institutionalized at the age of seventeen when she was diagnosed with hebephrenia, a form of schizophrenia whose onset coincided with adolescence and whose symptoms typically included fragmented speech and flat affect. Julie heard voices and suffered from delusions of persecution. She believed the world was coming to an end. She believed she was not a real person and that she was worthless. She also spoke an incomprehensible gibberish, or "schizophrenese," as psychiatrists labeled it. Yet a statement she repeated appeared to Laing to have a special significance; Julie said that "a child has been murdered."[2]

What child had been murdered? Julie said only that the child had been wearing her clothing when it died. Was she the child? Julie could not be sure. How did she know a child had been murdered? A voice had told her; very possibly it was the voice of her brother (though she had no brother). Who had murdered the child? Again, Julie could not give a clear answer; perhaps she was the murderer—or perhaps it was her mother.

Julie had a great deal to say about her mother. Her mother had never loved her; her mother had wished Julie had never been born. But these statements seemed further indications of the young woman's madness, especially in light of how devoted her mother had been during Julie's many years of institutionalization. Yet Julie remained adamant in her accusations: Her mother had never permitted Julie to have a life of her own. As for Julie's mother, she remembered her daughter above all as a happy child. She recalled how healthy and good Julie had been—undemanding to a fault. "I've always tried my best to be a good mother to her," she told Laing (to which Laing added this portentous comment: "We shall have occasion to remember this last sentence") (200).

Over time Laing began to piece together an interpretation of Julie's utterances, concluding that Julie would never have become insane if not for her family. That had certainly never been their intention; they had always wanted what was best for her. Nevertheless, they had unwittingly—if systematically—colluded to kill Julie's sense of selfhood, squeezing any sense she possessed of herself as real or alive out of her at a tender age.

There is a good deal more to the case study of Julie, but what becomes immediately manifest even in a brief limning of the story is the contradictoriness of the searing emotional impact it would have. Laing's theories of parental and familial dysfunction were shortly to emerge as monumentally influential. During the high-water mark of his career in the later 1960s, Laing would ever more vigorously express views that both justified and validated moral outrage at one's own family and the very concept of family values. In *The Politics of the Family* (1969), for example, Laing spoke derogatorily of the family as a shared fantasy whereby individuals essentially conspired to accept that what they constituted together represented something meaningful. Self-destructive patterns established early in life continued to deform later social interactions.[3]

Yet it is also noteworthy how slender were the reeds of clinical evidence upon which Laing rested his diagnosis of intrafamilial devastation. This was already apparent in the story of Julie. To be sure, Julie's childhood had been less than perfect; for instance, while in her early teens she was understandably crushed to learn of her father's secret extramarital affair. But Laing believed the hurt done to Julie's sense of self had commenced far earlier—when she was still in her infancy. For example, Julie's mother told Laing how much she had disdained the familiar game in which a parent picks up an object thrown by her infant, retrieving it so the child might repeat the action of throwing the object once again. Instead, Julie's mother practiced her own preferred game. *She* threw an object and required *Julie* to return it to her, so that *she* (the mother) might throw it away again. To which Laing acidly observed: "It is hardly necessary to comment on the implications of this inversion of roles for Julie's failure to develop any real ways of her own" (203). For Laing the consequences of incidents like these were almost too obvious to spell out. Julie grew to experience herself as "a dead thing" because she had been taught subservience and obedience (224). In Laing's view, the awful calculus of Julie's early family life was clear: She was "an existentially dead child" who received "the highest commendation" from her mother precisely because Julie became so expert at expressing nothing but what was requested of her (201). And this violence against Julie had all been accomplished in the name of love.

There are three interwoven assumptions buried to various degrees in Julie's story that require emphasis. First, there was the concept that the etiology of mental illness must be sought within interpersonal relations within the family, *not* in biochemical anomalies. A second important idea was that a human mind could—through repetitive emotional injuries—be conditioned to insanity. Third, there was the crucial point that the problem that caused mental illness was inauthenticity and (what the anthropologist Jules Henry would soon call) "shamming," for instance, that Julie's mother declared herself to be loving when in truth she had been withholding love. Subsequently, there would be a fourth theme in Laing's work: His analyses would begin to point beyond the family to something fundamentally sick in social relations writ large. These four central ideas—the social rather than biological etiology of madness, the malleability of the human mind, the idea of shamming and inauthenticity as poisoning human relations, and the idea of a sick society—would be developed into a complex interlocking conceptual frame in which each factor had different weights at different points and yet in which thinking about each of the factors evolved interdependently with thinking about the others. Ultimately these theories of madness produced a convincing schema for understanding both individual human nature and social problems.

Significantly, the ascent of family-focused explanations for the onset of schizophrenia coincided with unsuccessful efforts to locate a biological etiology for mental illness. This failure to advance biochemical explanations was not for lack of trying. There were laboratories across the United States engaged in clinical research that explored any number of possibilities—from disturbances in oxygen consumption in the brain to abnormal differences in amino acid patterns to possibly genetic endocrine and enzyme defects to cerebral serotonin deficiencies or immunological problems. Still, by the end of the 1950s, a scientist at the National Institute of Mental Health (NIMH) could only conclude his comprehensive review of the current state of biochemical research into the etiology of schizophrenia by stating that while there was "no cause for discouragement," it was also accurate to acknowledge "how large is the haystack in which we are searching for the needle."[4] In other words, and although the medical model for schizophrenia remained a persuasive paradigm for many psychiatrists, this model was not yielding results, thus leaving the door wide open for continued investigations into approaches that emphasized a new familial and social model of mental illness.

Eventually the profusion of theories about the possible roots of madness in interpersonal interactions within families would provide an unlikely vehicle for a fundamental rethinking of everything that was wrong with so-called normalcy. Medical and social scientific research across the United States and the United Kingdom during the 1950s advanced the premise that familial problems were often the cause of a child's schizophrenia. This new model of mental illness would subsequently transform into one of the most powerful moral cudgels young people in the 1960s could use to explain their ever-more-fervent opposition to the perceived tyrannies of the nuclear family.

Yet while it may seem incongruous in view of subsequent developments, it remains important to understand that Laing and all the other medical and ethnographic researchers who pursued theories of the familial etiology of mental illness were initially not at all seeking through their research to disrupt a Cold War consensus about the desirability of nuclear families. They did not intend their investigation into the family origins of mental illness as a critique of the family as an institution. On the contrary, it is apparent that they did not question the prevailing ideal of strong and at once authoritative and caring fathers and of nurturing, self-sacrificial mothers. Their analyses of what had gone wrong in families that produced schizophrenic offspring contributed above all to a policing reinforcement, not interrogation, of conservative gender ideals. If there was a problem with the child's mental health, this was due to a considerable degree to pathogenic parents, which most frequently could be translated to mean "schizophrenogenic mothers."

II

A crucial contribution to the familial etiology school had come in 1948 from Frieda Fromm-Reichmann, director of psychotherapy at the Chestnut Lodge Sanitarium in Rockville, Maryland, at that time probably the most liberal private psychiatric hospital in the United States. In advancing her new concept for the diagnosis and treatment of schizophrenia by psychoanalysis, Fromm-Reichmann drew especially on the interpersonal theory of psychiatry and mental illness articulated most prominently by Harry Stack Sullivan, with whom she worked closely at Chestnut Lodge.[5] Sullivan had argued that schizophrenics were invariably socialized to feelings of anxiety and insecurity due to the disapproval they repeatedly experienced during childhood from persons closest to them.[6] Seeking further to specify the source of these early pathogenic encounters, Fromm-Reichmann wrote:

> The schizophrenic is painfully distrustful and resentful of other people, due to the severe early warp and rejection he encountered in important people of his infancy and childhood, as a rule, mainly in a schizophrenogenic mother. During his early fight for emotional survival, he begins to develop the great interpersonal sensitivity which remains his for the rest of his life. His initial pathogenic experiences are actually, or by virtue of his interpretation, the pattern for a never-ending succession of subsequent similar ones. Finally he transgresses the threshold of endurance. Because of his sensitivity and his never-satisfied lonely need for benevolent contacts, this threshold is all too easily reached. The schizophrenic's partial emotional regression and his withdrawal from the outside world into an autistic private world with its specific thought processes and modes of feeling and expression is motivated by his fear of repetitional rejection, his distrust of others, and equally so by his own retaliative hostility, which he abhors, as well as the deep anxiety promoted by this hatred.[7]

Fromm-Reichmann coined the term *schizophrenogenic mother*, but the more general idea that bad mothering was the source of the psychological disorders of children was not, of course, entirely new. In the United States, during and immediately after World War II, there had been a particular efflorescence of preoccupation with the notion that neglectful, narcissistic and/or overbearing mothers were centrally responsible for the psychological maladjustments particularly of the American male. For instance, novelist and essayist Philip Wylie, in his best-selling diatribe *Generation of Vipers* (1942), argued that a parasitic cult of "momism" had emotionally crippled countless boys and young men.[8] In 1946 psychiatrist Edward A. Strecker, a past president of the American Psychiatric Association, published a widely discussed lecture (colloquially known as "the Mom lecture") in which he thoroughly condemned any woman who infantilized her sons with her "smother love"—an outrage, Strecker dramatically intoned, that needed urgently to be addressed "for the welfare of the nation."[9] And in 1947, in their best seller *Modern Woman: The Lost Sex*, psychiatrist (and *Glamour* magazine columnist) Marynia Farnham and journalist Ferdinand Lundberg further argued that any woman who worked outside the home was inevitably going to damage her children because she communicated to them she felt nothing but "distaste for her role" as mother and because "no matter how much or little of it she betray[ed]," her children would not be able to "escape the confused impression" that she did not truly love them.[10]

It is no doubt accurate, as Fromm-Reichmann's biographer Gail A. Hornstein contends, that Fromm-Reichmann never intended for her passing reference to a "schizophrenogenic mother" to feed a postwar frenzy that "bad" mothers caused mental illness. Hornstein has insisted that Fromm-Reichmann never blamed mothers for her patients' schizophrenia, and indeed often worked together with mothers to assist them in healing their children.[11] Likewise, Fromm-Reichmann's most famous patient, Joanne Greenberg, who had been committed to Chestnut Lodge in 1948—just around the same time Fromm-Reichmann published on the concept of the schizophrenogenic mother—later sought to emphasize in *I Never Promised You a Rose Garden* (1964, published under the pen name Hannah Green), a thinly fictionalized account of how Fromm-Reichmann treated her schizophrenia, that Fromm-Reichmann wished to relieve Joanne's mother in particular of any feelings of guilt or responsibility for her daughter's illness. Of her relationship with her daughter, the mother in the novel tells the psychiatrist: "I told her often how much I loved her. She never felt unprotected or alone."[12] And while there may be a strong echo here of what Julie's schizophrenogenic mother told

R. D. Laing ("I've always tried my best to be a good mother to her"), Greenberg made clear that *this* mother should be taken at her word. Not once in Greenberg's documentation of her character's psychosis (or her uneven road to recovery) are the parents judged responsible.

Fromm-Reichmann's gesture to the "schizophrenogenic mother" concept did, however, benefit from its timing. Here was a psycho-dynamic concept for the source of mental illness at the dawning moment of the Cold War era, precisely as women were being actively encouraged to return to their "traditional" roles as wives and mothers. Thus this new sourcing of mental illness as neither biochemical nor genetic but rather familial and social became not only a means to bind women to their "appropriate" roles as mothers and homemakers but also to trau-matize the mothers of mentally ill children yet further.

Psychodynamically oriented psychiatrists seized on the new concept. "It is the subtly dominating mother who appears to be particularly dan-gerous to the child," wrote a psychiatrist in 1949 after careful examina-tion of a group of twenty-five mothers of adult schizophrenic patients at Johns Hopkins Hospital in Baltimore.[13] In 1950 another report ef-fectively stirred together Strecker and Fromm-Reichmann when it noted how damaging were *"covertly rejecting mother[s]"* who ("probably [in] a reaction-formation against unconscious hostility") feast "parasitically on their children and who aim, through babying them, to prevent them from ever becoming independent."[14] Or as a leading psychoanalyst put it most categorically in 1953: "A schizophrenic is always one who is reared by a woman who suffers from a perversion of the maternal in-stinct."[15] An impressive series of clinical studies conducted throughout the decade overwhelmingly confirmed this hypothesis.[16]

And yet none of the scholarly studies allowed a conviction that schizo-phrenia could strike any person victimized by bad parenting to evolve into a critical assessment of what exactly constituted *good* or *normal* parenting. Nuclear families might now be recognized as potential sites for the incubation of mental disorders, but this did not lead to a conclu-sion that the line between normal and abnormal might inescapably also become recognized as at best a blurred one. Any implicit recognition—at least not until 1963 or thereabouts—that the allegedly "normal" nuclear family might in fact by default be a psychically damaging institution re-mained unexplored and unexamined. Psychiatric and clinical researchers in the course of the 1950s argued with ever-greater force and intensity that children in any family might fall victim to schizophrenia if the fam-ily suffered from poor communication skills; but a position that *all fami-lies* basically suffered from these same problems was quietly sidestepped and remained unsettled. The refusal to see (or to acknowledge) this conceptual predicament is striking; after all, these same researchers made so much of the fact that individuals had above all an obligation to be forthright and direct with one another. The methodological dilemma their findings provoked became the proverbial elephant in the room for researchers of family therapies for schizophrenia.

Despite the at once intrinsic and largely unaddressed difficulties their investigations raised for them, psychiatric studies into the familial etiology of mental illness fairly blossomed for more than a decade after 1948 as medical researchers continued to confront a series of dead-end frustrations in their pursuit of an organic basis of schizophrenia. The decade's growing enthusiasm for a social etiology of mental illness led to a small mountain of scholarly articles by family researchers, each with its own set of concepts, and each based on years of intensive direct observation as well as hundreds of hours of interviews with families with a schizophrenic member. The earliest texts to make a case for the familial origins of schizophrenia emerged from concrete clinical and direct participant-observation ethnographic experiences not only of psychiatrists but also of anthropologists and sociologists who worked either with asylum inmates or with families of whom one member had been institutionalized. Beginning in the mid-1950s, these research teams began to publish the results of their research, and soon began to cite and refer to one another in what also quickly became a much broader and intensive conversation between and among teams of researchers, which, in turn, spurred new excitement for further research. There can be little doubt that the 1950s were a heady time for clinicians devoted to a paradigm that saw the family as the source of madness.

If schizophrenia meant that patients spoke only gibberish, what good could it possibly do for psychiatrists to strive to understand them? Fromm-Reichmann carefully demonstrated that Freud's position that schizophrenia was not treatable with psychoanalysis required revision and that on the contrary "it was possible to deal with schizophrenic communication as meaningful and potentially understandable and to establish workable relationships between the psychoanalyst and the schizophrenic."[17] However, Fromm-Reichmann's focus was principally the psychotherapeutic process. Although she acknowledged the need for psychiatrists to decode the garbled speech of schizophrenics, she was more intent on how psychiatrists might manage treatment once contact had been established, and she only gestured to the concept that schizophrenic communication disorders might principally be the result of familial communication disorders.[18]

It was left to others to pursue the question of how to unravel the mysteries of the schizophrenic's incoherence in light of familial dysfunctionalities. The psychiatrist Don D. Jackson had trained with Sullivan and Fromm-Reichmann at Chestnut Lodge in the late 1940s before moving to Palo Alto, where he continued experimental research into schizophrenia. In 1954 Jackson began to speak at professional psychiatric meetings on the concept of "family homeostasis," arguing that a patient's emotional disorders could not be properly evaluated without additional analysis of "the closed information system" that was the patient's family unit. Jackson contended that families naturally sought balance and resisted change in their relationships with one another, and so, therefore, emotional concerns for any family member produced difficulties for everyone else in the family circle. He provided this clinical example:

> The paternal uncle of a woman patient had lived with her parents until she was 10 when he married. Her mother's hatred of him was particularly overt; his presence seemed to deflect some of the mother's hostility toward her husband away from the husband, and the brother gave moral support to the father. Following this uncle's departure, four events occurred that seemed hardly coincidental: The parents began openly quarreling, the mother made a potentially serious suicide attempt, the father took a traveling job, and the patient quietly broke out in a rash of phobias.

Jackson proposed the necessity for psychotherapists to conceive of an emotionally disturbed patient "as only an instance in a field of force that extends from intrapsychic processes to the broadest aspect of the culture in which he lives," beginning with investigations into the patient's immediate family.[19]

Also in 1954 Lyman C. Wynne began to experiment at NIMH in Bethesda by combining psychotherapy of a schizophrenic patient with twice-weekly meetings with parents, as well as staff observation of patterns of family interaction. Wynne and his colleagues speculated that what went wrong in the families of patients who developed acute schizophrenia in late adolescence or young adulthood was that the natural process of individuation and the formulating of an autonomous identity did not lead to positive growth and evolution in familial relations but were instead experienced as threatening. As a result, what emerged were relations of "pseudo-mutuality," in which a powerful investment in the *appearance* of ongoing connection covered over actual conflict and growing alienation, in which, in short, the divergence of interests between parents and child was denied rather than openly acknowledged.[20]

But the most promising mid-1950s contribution to intrafamilial investigations into the etiology of schizophrenia emerged from research into communication disorders initiated not by a medical doctor but rather by anthropologist Gregory Bateson at Stanford University and the Veterans Administration Hospital in Palo Alto. Bateson's team (Jay Haley and John Weakland, along with Don Jackson as a psychiatric consultant) extensively tape-recorded and filmed schizophrenic patients; the goal was to decode—never to dismiss—what the recorded patients were saying on their tapes.[21] The breakthrough came only when the Bateson team began to consider more seriously the question of whether individuals might be *educated* to states of madness. In sum, the Bateson team asked: Could madness be a trained response to a confused familial communication system?

The answer came in 1956 in "Toward a Theory of Schizophrenia," an essay that introduced the hypothesis that it was not a single traumatic experience that triggered mental illness but rather a *repeated* pattern of being presented with nonoptions. They named their theory "the double bind" because, in their view, the subsequent schizophrenic had too often been enjoined by a parent or sibling to obey directives to which there could be no correct reaction. Classic examples were the "no-win" commands: "Don't be so obedient!" or "Be spontaneous!"[22] But rarely were the injunctions so blatant. For instance, the authors detailed the case of an unloving mother who expressed hostility to her child through coded and indirect speech: "Go to bed, you're very tired and I want you to get some sleep." The researchers commented: "This overly loving statement is intended to deny a feeling which could be verbalized as 'Get out of my sight because I'm sick of you.'"[23]

In short, and over and over, in the Palo Alto group's view, children who received mixed messages that placed them in situations impossible to resolve successfully were said to be most liable to develop schizophrenia. On the one hand, a mother communicated: If you do x (or do not do x), I will punish you (by withholding love). And on the other hand, the mother indicated (often nonverbally) that the former injunction should *not* be interpreted as a threat of punishment. For the preschizophrenic victim of the double bind, however, the dynamic was by no means banal, but rather took on an ugly life of its own; the child learned to interpret his entire universe in double bind patterns, and thenceforth "almost any part of a double bind sequence may then be sufficient to precipitate panic or rage."[24] (In fact, the authors thought that the hallucinatory voices heard by many schizophrenics were the forms taken by these contradictory commands.) Above all, the victim lost his grip on reality because he was not permitted to speak the truth without the ever-present jeopardy of losing a parent's love. To maintain sanity, the authors suggested, a child had to feel safe to comment critically on the incompatible messages he was receiving. But this was precisely what the double bind prevented.

The authors acknowledged that the interpersonal double bind dynamic they outlined also occurred within normal families as well as in countless ordinary work relationships, and they suggested that other experts' tendency to treat schizophrenia as utterly different from "normal" forms of "human thinking and behavior" was problematic. "In our approach we assume that schizophrenia involves general principles which are important in all communication and therefore informative similarities can be found in 'normal' communication situations."[25] Nonetheless, at no point did Bateson and his colleagues take this crucial insight as an occasion to critique what counted as normal. On the contrary, they clearly assumed that the vast majority of families were able to openly address multiple levels of meaning in their communications with one another—and proceeded to produce mentally well children. Only a minority of families succumbed to double binds to such a degree that madness ensued.

The new concept of the double bind coursed through the family research community with the resounding impact that scholarly articles almost never have. In breadth and range the effect this slim essay by Bateson's team was to have proved almost incalculable. There were certainly those who challenged the applicability of a double bind hypothesis to the etiology of mental disorders.[26] But to a remarkable degree, clinical groups across the United States quickly scrambled to keep up and to incorporate the Palo Alto group's ideas into their own findings.

The overwhelming tendency in competing studies on schizophrenia and family life during the 1950s was to present original evidence that served to reinforce and to expand upon the essential accuracy of a double bind hypothesis. At Yale University, a team led by psychiatrist Theodore Lidz began arguing in 1957 that the schizophrenic's family could foster "untenable emotional needs, and frequently offers contradictory models for identification which cannot be integrated."[27] Lidz and his colleague Stephen Fleck, a psychoanalyst, noted that clinical histories of schizophrenics revealed that these patients virtually always emerged

"from homes marked by serious parental strife or eccentricity."[28] Two
years later a research team led by psychiatrist Murray Bowen at NIMH
observed that parents of a psychotic child were often "separated from
each other by an emotional barrier which, in some ways, has characteristics of an 'emotional divorce.'"[29]

The problem of what constituted normalcy did begin to nudge its
way into discussions, but those discussions seldom got very far. It barely
occurred to familial etiology-focused researchers during the 1950s, and
even the early 1960s, that a family with a schizophrenic member might
appear pathogenic to observing professionals because those professionals had confused cause and effect—in other words, that a sick child was
the *impetus* for parental conflict or peculiarities, and not the other way
around. Only the most occasional critic of the family therapy approach
seemed to note immediately this additional methodological dilemma.[30]

Not that researchers were completely unaware that they had some in-
terpretive problems on their hands. Among the many striking aspects of
Wynne's clinical investigations at NIMH was his conclusion that there
but for the grace of good fortune and chance went each and every family.
Wynne and his colleagues were quick to state in 1958 that "we do not
mean to imply . . . that pseudo-mutuality *in itself* is productive of schizophrenia."[31] And subsequently, Wynne did worry over this feature of his
findings ever more self-reflexively. All families engaged in "self-rescuing
operations," Wynne elaborated, the consequences of which were that
the "underlying unsettled business is 'settled' or fixed in a kind of align-
ment that forestalls further exploration of the relationship." Introducing
the new concept of "pseudo-hostility," Wynne additionally suggested
that family members not only covered over unacknowledgeable differences with pseudo-mutual rituals, but also sometimes attacked one another aggressively as a way of warding off some even deeper despair or
danger (for example, the threat of rejection from a child might be managed by an immediate descent into spousal squabbling). In such families
pain caused only more pain, hostility led only to more hostility. Here,
too, Wynne conceded that also "within the families of nonschizophren-
ics there are of course extensive conflicts and defensive operations,"
but—he rushed to stress—"not, we believe, involving the same degree
of amorphousness and fragmentation, or the same intense reliance on
pseudo-mutual and pseudo-hostile mechanisms that disguise but help
perpetuate the underlying problems."[32] In short, Wynne stumbled repeatedly over exactly the insight he chose not to pursue.

So: What was the difference between a healthy family and a sick one?
As of 1961 no one had a clear answer to the question.[33] The move from

worrying over where exactly the differences between schizophrenogenic and nonschizophrenogenic families might lie to using an awareness of their commonalities to launch a critique of what counted as normal in society remained incomplete.

In the meantime, research into the family origins of schizophrenia continued. In 1957 family studies were being conducted by psychoanalyst Iván Böszörményi-Nagy at the Eastern Pennsylvania Psychiatric Institute.[34] The next year research began under the direction of Nathan Ackerman of Columbia University at the Family Mental Health Clinic in New York; in 1960 Ackerman opened his influential Family Institute, also in New York. In 1958 Don Jackson founded the Mental Research Institute in Palo Alto, which remained a major clearinghouse for investigations into the family origins of emotional disorders for the next several decades. In 1962 the Family Institute and the Mental Research Institute cofounded *Family Process*, a major new journal in the field of family therapy. (Another former member of Bateson's research team, Jay Haley, served as the journal's first editor.[35]) By 1963 Harvard, too, had joined the fray, and the Family Research Project there was reporting on its work as part of the Community Mental Health Program at the university's School of Public Health.[36]

By the early 1960s, research into the family and environmental origins of mental disorders appeared to be underway almost everywhere, and both a clear perspective and a durable set of perturbing problems were beginning to assert themselves. A consensus was consolidating that parents were blameworthy. When Nathan Ackerman at Columbia bluntly noted in 1958 that "psychiatric patients come from disordered families," there was little doubt that he already spoke for many.[37] Moreover, that same year Ackerman proved practically prophetic when he connected family therapy to greater concerns by writing: "The structure of family echoes disordered values in the larger pattern of human relations. Family and society are organically intertwined. Do we have a sick society?"[38] And it was this last question—as well as the puzzle of its possible relationships to the difficulties of parenting—that came within a matter of only a handful of years to direct discussions within and beyond psychiatric circles.

The theories put forward were utterly jumbled and cacophonously contradictory. Yet the central tenet—that madness had a familial and social rather than a biochemical origin—truly had a remarkable ripple effect. So much so that Ackerman could declare confidently in 1970, looking back on the "radical shift" in attitudes toward mental illness over the course of the prior decade: "The revolutionary turmoil of our day has forced upon us the recognition of the extraordinary dependence of the operations of personality on the social environment."[39]

Although it was conducted by scholars or physicians in clinical settings, this new research into the family processes that spurred mental illness into being also began to find a popular audience far beyond academic and medical circles. The new trend of seeing mental illness as linked to disastrous family relations soon made its appearance in dramatic film. Notably, the stirring and critically acclaimed *David and Lisa* (1962), based on actual clinical case studies, not only blamed an emotionally abusive mother (and feuding parents) for a teenage boy's mental illness but also promoted the theory that the therapy mental patients required most was love—a view that could have been drawn directly from Laing's *The Divided Self*. Eleanor Perry (whose screenplay earned her an Academy Award nomination) made the point explicit in an interview with the *New York Times*:

> In these times of nihilism and the threat of the Bomb, something miraculous is going on between human beings. People can really care and feel for the suffering of others; they can believe in each other and place a true value on the individual. That's what we're trying to say in this picture: there is a powerful healing quality in the love and trust between human beings.[40]

Rather remarkably, in a case of life imitating art imitating life, in her 1964 memoir, a young woman named Morag Coate cited the deeply cathartic experience of watching *David and Lisa* as prompting her complete recovery from recurrent bouts of schizophrenia. (Laing wrote the introduction, endorsing Coate's account and commenting: "I am grateful to her for returning to us, and for letting us know, vividly, yet with such discretion, what it was like."[41])

Also remarkable—if unfortunate—was how Betty Friedan chose to make use of familial theories of schizophrenia in *The Feminine Mystique* (1963), the text considered so foundational to the later women's liberation movement. Seeking to advance the rights of women to a meaningful and autonomous existence, Friedan cited evidence of a rising incidence of schizophrenic and autistic children as proof of the mind-warping damages done to women obliged to be stay-at-home mothers, and therefore also of an urgent need to allow women to pursue careers outside the home. Noting that "the human organism has an intrinsic urge to grow," Friedan observed how often "a woman who evades her own growth by clinging to the childlike protection of the housewife role will—insofar as that role does not permit her own growth—suffer increasingly severe pathology, both physiological and emotional." To underscore this logic, Friedan focused on how "mothers with infantile selves" in turn raised "even more infantile children," and how "at its most extreme," these "mothers with infantile selves" produced "schizophrenic children" or "'autistic' or 'atypical' children, as they are sometimes called"—children "arrested at a very primitive, sub-infantile level" who "have not organized or developed strong enough selves to cope even with the child's reality."[42]

Concepts relating to the familial roots of schizophrenia introduced in specialized psychiatric journals had also by the early 1960s begun to be approvingly cited in a range of widely read and well-respected periodicals for general readers. In 1962 and 1963 *The Atlantic, Scientific American,* and *The Nation* each announced and legitimated the new trend of thinking about schizophrenia as related to emotionally damaging interpersonal interactions. The essay in *The Atlantic* stated it baldly: "In sum, schizophrenia may be perceived as one kind of attempt to handle the human fear of being unloved."[43] In 1961 *Time* magazine reported favorably on research conducted by Lyman Wynne at NIMH. Adopting wholesale the theory that mental illness could be produced by disturbed familial relationships, *Time* provided an excerpt of a conversation between a mentally ill child and her parents:

> DAUGHTER: Nobody will listen to me. Everybody is trying to still me.
> MOTHER: Nobody wants to kill you.
> FATHER: If you're going to associate with intelligent people, you're going to have to remember that "still" is a noun and not a verb.

Quoting Wynne, the *Time* reporter concluded that a child in a family like this one would understandably have "'an underlying feeling of meaninglessness and pessimism about the possibility of finding meaning in any experience or behavior.' And that, [Dr. Wynne] added in effect, is enough to drive anybody crazy."[44] (Ultimately, the circle would be completed in 1971 when film director Ken Loach with a screenplay by playwright David Mercer fictionalized "The Ghost of the Weed Garden" and the story of Julie—renamed Janice—from *The Divided Self.* Highlighting the toxic qualities of Janice's home environment, Loach's movie was grimly titled: *Family Life.*)

III

Understanding the intricacies of the evolving research agendas and expert discussions can assist us in grasping more fully the often rapturous reception accorded R. D. Laing's writings on madness and the family throughout the 1960s. The growing cadre of investigators committed to a familial analysis of mental illness counted among Laing's earliest admirers in the United States. As Paul Watzlawick of the Mental Research Institute effused in the inaugural issue of *Family Process* in 1962, Laing was "one of those rare psychiatrists who combine clinical experience and intuition with a gift for methodic research and a wide range of knowledge in many other fields, such as philosophy, sociology, anthropology, literature etc."[45] And that same year Laing returned the compliment, venturing to the United States to present his research to leading American theorists in the field—Gregory Bateson, Don Jackson, and Lyman Wynne among them.

These American researchers had good reason to greet Laing as a kindred spirit. Like them, Laing arrived at his theories about schizophrenia from medical observation. In the mid-1950s, Laing had speculated that the regimented environment of the Glasgow mental hospital in which he worked might itself be having a deleterious effect on its inmates. He arranged to establish "a rumpus room" where time was unstructured, and patients and staff could sit together as peers. The results amazed Laing:

> They were no longer isolates. Their conduct became more social, and they undertook tasks which were of value in their small community. Their appearance and interest in themselves improved as they took a greater interest in those around them. These changes were satisfying to the staff. The patients lost many of the features of chronic psychoses: they were less violent to each other and the staff, they were less dishevelled, and their language ceased to be obscene. The nurses came to know the patients well, and spoke warmly of them.[46]

Setting himself in a lineage with Harry Stack Sullivan, while applying philosophical concepts from existentialism and citing icons of Western high culture like Samuel Beckett, Franz Kafka, Søren Kierkegaard, and Jean-Paul Sartre, Laing proposed that the state of insanity was provoked when an "inner self" withdrew as a means of survival from a world without affirmation. But as Laing phrased it, survival under these circumstances was paradoxical: "It can be stated in its most general form as: *the denial of being, as a means of preserving being.* The schizophrenic feels he has killed his 'self,' and this appears to be in order to avoid being killed. He is dead, in order to remain alive" (163, emphasis in original).[47] *The Divided Self* was a deeply pessimistic and despairing book, arguing principally that what we call madness was a feeling of extreme loneliness; insanity was a result of being misunderstood or neglected. "The schizophrenic is desperate, is simply without hope," Laing wrote. "I have never known a schizophrenic who could say he was loved" (39). A feeling of having one's self detached from one's body, a sense of the meaninglessness of existence, a feeling of irrelevance—this was (according to Laing) the human condition.

If *The Divided Self* was as much a contribution to existentialist philosophy as it was to psychology, and if it preeminently theorized the relationship of the self to the wider society, Laing's subsequent work turned to a close study of family dynamics. Putting the matter plainly in interpersonal terms in 1961, Laing observed that "schizophrenics are *par excellence* sensitive to a failure to be recognized as human beings by others," and that "psychosis is often a desperate effort to hold on to something" meaningful and genuine. What a schizophrenic needed in order to regain health was not medical treatment but the authentic confirmation of his or her self. Honest and direct interactions were key to improved mental status, but such interactions were frequently in short supply within families. An early proponent of Bateson's double bind theory, Laing drily remarked on how family members often communicated problematically with one another: "Some people undoubtedly do have a remarkable aptitude for keeping the other person tied in knots."[48] This was a theme to which Laing would return time and again in the years ahead.[49]

Laing's *Sanity, Madness, and the Family: Families of Schizophrenics* (1964), coauthored with psychiatrist Aaron Esterson, challenged the entire notion of schizophrenia as a biologically rooted pathology and also criticized the idea of the schizophrenic as somehow vastly different from normal human beings. The authors argued that the condition labeled by other experts as schizophrenia was often the result of disturbed interactions within families. They contended that the "'symptoms' that are universally regarded in the psychiatric world as 'caused' by a disease, i.e., an organic pathological process, probably largely determined by genetic, constitutional factors"—among them "catatonic and paranoid symptoms, impoverishment of affect, autistic withdrawal and auditory hallucinations, confusion of 'ego boundaries'"—were in fact better understood as the *outcome* of the patient's "inter-experience and interaction with her parents." They also made a frontal assault on the role and the self-understanding of the conventional psychiatrist, stating that psychiatrists who presumed the very existence of schizophrenia as an already established fact were operating from "a mistaken starting-point." And it was here that Laing and Esterson suggested that the designation "schizophrenic" was also a way of policing and enforcing social conformity. Among other things, Laing and Esterson described a schizophrenic as a person "acting in a queer way, from the point of view usually of his relatives and of ourselves."[50] Their goal was to understand the patient's *own* perspective on his or her experiences, and to study them within the matrix of multiple familial relationships. For Laing and Esterson, persons deemed "schizophrenics" were simply doing their level best to preserve a sense of self in the face of lovelessness, neglect, and aggression.

Interestingly, the authors were quite self-reflexively aware that they could be read as inappropriately parent-blaming, yet they rejected that potential criticism. They wrote:

> It might be argued as regards our historical reconstruction that her parents might have been reacting in an abnormal way to the presence of an abnormal child. The data hardly support this thesis. Her mother and father reveal plainly, *in the present*, that what they regard most as symptoms of illness are what we regard as developing personalization, realization, autonomy, spontaneity, etc. On their own testimony, everything points to this being the case in the past as well. Her parents felt as stress not so much the loss but the development of her self.[51]

Such a remark gives an important glimmer of insight into how young radicals rebelling against their families could have found Laing's work on madness relevant to themselves.

Over time, however, and certainly by 1964, Laing became increasingly intrigued to mimic (his version of) the inner workings of a schizophrenic mind. This meant that feelings of persecution and paranoia, for instance, as well as articulations of fractured logic, were no longer off-limits as avenues of authorial expression. Nor were these represented as what only diseased minds experienced. By 1964 Laing began not just to write about madness but also more fully to embody the subject of his study. He appeared eager to resist the facade of his own sanity, revealing instead a fuller, deeper self in all its incoherent, fervent glory. While this might have seemed an awful risk, one fraught—to put it mildly—with the possibility of professional humiliation (or excommunication), it was a calculated risk. Laing's work, even at its most obtuse and darkly conspiratorial, and even as it approached self-parody, still managed to hold these lesser qualities in tension with a wild moral desire to celebrate freedom—both personal and societal.

Thus readers of Laing were required to come equipped to tolerate ever-higher levels of inconsistency and ambiguity to appreciate his method—although perhaps this was the point. Writing in 1964, for instance, Laing invoked the concepts being formulated in the context of family process research in the United States—including Bateson's and Wynne's—and at his own Tavistock Institute before launching a far greater critique:

> Socially, this work must now move to further understanding, not only of the internal disturbed and disturbing patterns of communication within families, of the double-binding procedures, the pseudo-mutuality, of what I have called the mystifications and the untenable positions, but also to the meaning of all this within the larger context of the civic order of society—that is, of the *political* order, of the ways persons exercise control and power over one another.[52]

And that same year, in a lecture at the Institute for Contemporary Arts in London, Laing went further still, arguing "that we are effectively destroying ourselves by violence masquerading as love."[53] This became a big theme for Laing, even as it moved him ever closer to the land of slippery logic and simplistic melodrama:

> Only by the most outrageous violation of ourselves have we achieved our capacity to live in relative adjustment to a civilization apparently driven to its own destruction. Perhaps to a limited extent we can undo what has been done to us, and what we have done to ourselves. Perhaps men and women were born to love one another, simply and genuinely, rather than to this travesty that we call love. If we can stop destroying ourselves, we may stop destroying others.[54]

Or as Laing also noted in 1965 (paraphrasing Martin Heidegger):

> We psychotherapists are specialists, as they say, in human relations. But the Dreadful has already happened. It has happened to us as well as to our patients. We, the therapists, are in a world

in which the inner is already split from the outer, and before the
inner can become outer, and the outer become inner, we have to
re-discover our "inner" world. As a whole generation of men,
we are so estranged from the inner world that there are many
arguing that it does not exist; and even if it does exist, it does
not matter . . .

Under these circumstances, our relationships with our patients are our re-search. A re-search, a search, constantly reas-
serted and reconstituted for what we have *all* lost, and which
some of us can perhaps endure a little more easily than others, as
some people can stand the lack of oxygen better than others, and
our re-search is validated by the shared experience of experience
[sic] regained in and through the therapeutic relationship in the
here and now.[55]

The family therapists of the 1950s had stumbled over the question of
what constituted the normal if all families shared characteristics that led
to mental illness. Laing resituated the puzzle at the level of society, believing that theorizing the social would lead to answers that the biochemical
closed off (since the social at least was subject, he hoped, to change). But
as it happened neither Laing nor any of his admirers were able finally to
theorize social change at the level of the individual psyche. Laing never
clarified the mechanisms that interconnected individual psyches and political systems. Instead he appeared unabashedly to have arrived at the
limits of his own capacities for understanding and—spouting florid gen-
eralities—saw madness in everyone everywhere. "Our alienation goes
to our roots," Laing wrote in 1967. "At all events, we are bemused and
crazed creatures, strangers to our true selves, to one another, and to the
spiritual and material world."[56] By the later 1960s, Laing's growing affection for aphoristic language translated into vague political analysis at
best.

Yet Laing's theories nonetheless continued to receive enthusiastic en-
dorsements from a cadre of well-respected psychiatrists—Harvard's Robert Coles and Yale's Robert Jay Lifton among them. Coles praised Laing
as "an exceptionally courageous psychiatrist who is willing to plumb
his own depths and challenge head-on the hypocrisy and duplicity of his
own profession and the larger society of which it is so prominent a part.
I can only hope that he will be heard and heard respectfully."[57] Lifton
voiced similar praise, especially for *The Divided Self.*[58] And throughout
the decade, Lyman Wynne, possibly the most highly respected authority

on the treatment of schizophrenia in the country, strongly championed Laing's ideas on the familial origins of mental illness.[59]

The task of articulating answers to fundamental questions was left to others. What was it that put persons on a collision course with psychosis? How did political arrangements in a particular society exert an impact on an individual's mental health?

One well-regarded thesis was that problems in families were the result of cruelties pervasive in American culture as a whole. Anthropologist Jules Henry had observed mentally ill children while working with Dr. Bruno Bettelheim at the Sonia Shankman Orthogenic School in the 1950s, and also had lived with families in which one child was psychotic (although institutionalized and not living at home). In *Culture against Man* (1963), Henry veered back and forth between attacking American society as a whole for its superficiality and aggressiveness and sharply criticizing the parental dysfunctions that he was convinced were the main triggers for child psychosis. Several years later Henry would put the two halves of his theoretical framework together in a different way and argue that the deceptions that flooded through American society were spilling like sewage into the most intimate of human interactions. But in 1963 he was still more intent on insisting that parents were most immediately responsible for madness in their little children. Henry, too, acknowledged that *all* families displayed some combination of harmony and misery. And he conceded as well that it was difficult to tell whether the preponderance of suffering over contentment in families with a psychotic child was "a consequence of the disaster" or had been "there before." Nonetheless, in his detailed elaboration on case studies of individual families, Henry expressed certainty that it was above all parental lovelessness and narcissism—an inadequate capacity to nurture and give affection, and a tendency either to treat children as if they were not there or as though they were a burden—that constituted the "roads to madness."[60]

Throughout the 1960s Henry continued his years of intensive ethnographic fieldwork with families with a mentally ill child as he also became more overtly political. What served for Henry as the bridge between his ethnographic research and a broader social critique of American life was what Henry called the problem of "sham." Henry stated unequivocally that "by the time he is 6 years old or so, the child has probably learned that he will be shot if he does not believe with all his heart and soul that sham IS truth." But this was only a microcosm of the destructive impact of shamming on the United States as a whole. Henry also wrote:

> An outstanding example of social sham on a large scale in our society is the condition of the Negro, who lives like a rat, being told he lives in a democracy and that everything is being done to improve his lot; and the Ghetto riots are the expression, on a social scale, of the underlying schizophrenic dialectic. The hostility of the Negro erupts in shooting in the presence of sham, while the clinical schizophrenic, having learned that he dare not erupt, goes mad, and may shoot himself. On the international scene, of course, the biggest sham is the war in Vietnam, where the United States, while proclaiming to the world that it is building a nation, is destroying one.[61]

Yet—as with Laing—an indecisiveness about the process by which a sick society produced sick individuals remained. For instance: "It is clear that our civilization is a tissue of contradictions and lies," Henry sharply noted in 1967, and therefore "the main problem of psychiatry is not to cure mental illness but to define sanity and account for its occurrence." Among other things, what Henry meant was that given how hypocritical the world was, it was amazing that anyone was sane at all. And in 1963 Henry had contended that the United States stood apart from the rest of the world in its capacity to induce psychosis in its citizenry. "In this we are secure in our riches," he observed.[62]

Was it tragic that society demanded that the individual engage in shamming? Or was the cruel but inevitable tragedy the fact that some individuals apparently could not learn to sham? In 1963, and sounding rather Laingian as he addressed the topic of education, Henry bitterly observed that "the school metamorphoses the child, giving it the kind of Self the school can manage, and then proceeds to minister to the Self it has made."[63] By 1967 Henry was noting that "in schizophrenogenic families sham and confusion infest every aspect of life, so that the people in it draw a crooked breath, so to speak." Yet Henry also observed that "shamming" was a defining characteristic of contemporary life. "For we all live every day by sham," he stated, "anyone who fights against it, makes life unbearable."[64] In *Pathways to Madness*, published posthumously in 1971 (he died in 1969), and focused again more fully on family interactions, Henry concluded that children quickly learned from their deceiving parents that "they must not let them see that they see through them." Furthermore, the child who "makes shamming a natural

part of his life by seeing his parents practice it," grows up with "a graduate degree" in sham, and then will proceed to "use his skill at deception
against the world and be most dangerous with those he says he loves."[65]
Right through to the end of his career, in short, Henry remained seriously confounded. Yet at the same time he remained partial to authoritative assertions that habits of dishonesty were transmitted from generation to generation—and with disastrous political consequences. It is
perhaps no surprise that Laing became a fast champion of Henry's work,
in early 1964 promoting Henry's ideas about how schools crushed individual creativity in the name of education and analogizing from this
to the deleterious dynamics within families.[66] And although he would
never acquire the cult status of a Laing, Henry became an important and
highly esteemed influence on radicals of the younger generation. Invited
by Laing to address an international New Left audience at the Dialectics
of Liberation conference in London in 1967, for example, Henry once
again linked together the war in Vietnam, the plight of black children in
ghettos, and the ways in which parents' emotional "desertion" produced
"autism" in children.[67]

IV

In the 1950s there had certainly been significant advances in the biomedical *treatment* of mental illnesses, from the discovery of new antipsy-
chotics to two classes of antidepressants and a range of minor tranquilizers. The antipsychotic Thorazine alone was prescribed more than two
million times within the first year of its availability in 1954.[68] However,
in the years that followed, the biomedical model for the *source* of mental
disorders began to be harshly accused of being both insufficient as ex-
planation and unsatisfactory as methodology. By the end of the 1960s,
researchers who subscribed to the biomedical model for the etiology of
mental illness were acknowledging that their studies had not yielded results supporting their position. In the second half of the 1960s, for instance, a clinic at the Tulane University School of Medicine, which had
previously postulated that schizophrenia resulted from a biochemical disorder whose prevalence could be measured in family members, revealed
that their data, "while demonstrating a familial trend," was "not sufficiently definitive to allow a specific genetic interpretation." The authors
confessed "that environmental factors might also play a significant role"
in the etiology of the disorder.[69] A further study by the same clinic went
so far as to suggest (in a striking echo of Laing and Esterson's theoretical position) that the prevalence of raised plasma protein among chronic

schizophrenics might actually be an *effect* of "environmental influences early in life."[70] Increasingly over the course of the decade, psychiatrists who favored a biomedical model came under ever-greater pressure to admit that their approach toward mental illness had been flawed and that mental disorders (particularly schizophrenia) were not principally due to somatic imbalances, but rather should be traced to social conditions. The search for a specific biochemical trigger for schizophrenia remained stalled, even a sympathetic critic acknowledged, not least because it had been driven by circumstantial evidence and clinical hunches.[71]

A special session at the American Psychiatric Association annual meeting in 1968 established to debate competing concepts of mental illness dramatized signs of the changing times. Speaking in defense of medical science was Roy R. Grinker Sr., director of the Institute for Psychosomatic and Psychiatric Research and Training in Chicago (and co-author two decades earlier of the landmark study, *Men under Stress*), who rejected a view that mental illness "is not a disease and therefore physicians are not necessary." Conceding the tremendous degree to which the prevailing view currently was "in reaction against the 'disease' concept in psychiatry," Grinker nonetheless cautioned that "the pendulum has swung too far away" from "concepts of syndromes and accurate diagnostic criteria." In an attempt to seek a conciliatory tone, Grinker concluded that "for the good of all concerned there should be a moratorium on debates, conflicts, and exhortation by armchair psychologists as well as parochial psychiatrists."[72] Yet this plea to set aside divisive differences and focus on cooperation fell mainly on deaf ears.

Speaking for the opposition, George W. Albee, professor and chair of psychology at Case Western and author of *Mental Health Manpower Trends* and other government-sponsored studies documenting the dearth of adequate psychiatric personnel in mental hospitals across the country, derided the biomedical model of mental illness in uncompromising terms. As Albee put it acerbically: "This model, which occupies the center of our clinical stage, places the identification of forces in the individual before consideration of the hostile and damaging forces in his world; it demands that we try to fix him, treat his disease (as we do other diseases), and then send him back to the continuing horrors of his world." Albee was wholly dismissive of the voluminous medical literature devoted to proving an organic etiology for mental illness, observing that the findings of these hundreds of pages of densely written scientific text could be summarized with a single sentence: "We haven't found anything yet, and we're still looking." The truth of the matter was that "there is no convincing evidence that schizophrenia is an identifiable disease," Albee intoned with all the assurance of someone who understood how much the tide had shifted in his favor.[73]

By the later 1960s, advocates of a social model of mental illness got additional impetus for their inquiries into the nexus between individual psychology and social conditions from psychiatrists concerned with social justice. Widely admired liberal psychiatrist Robert Coles went so far as to speculate in 1967 that there would never be an "end to mental illness" due to advances in medical research because "'mental illness'" (he himself put the words in quotation marks) was "a social problem involving the family, the nursery, the neighborhood, the nation and its economic or political condition." To treat the sickness of the individual, psychiatrists had first to concede the sickness in society. So when the ghetto dweller who suffered daily hunger or the concentration camp survivor who experienced Auschwitz felt the depths of despair, this was "a legitimate despair," Coles wrote; it was morally wrong for a psychiatrist to be "'treating'" that individual's "human capacity to suffer not 'illness' but feelings." It was overdue for doctors (like himself) to accept the limits of their trade, Coles continued, because "murder, war, racism, concentration camps, and genocide are what science has conspicuously failed to prevent in this century," and because "nothing, I repeat nothing, that anyone engaged in psychiatric research might find will make us as human beings invulnerable to repetitions, in future centuries, of such sins." Despite the growing popularity and prevalence of tranquilizer use among men and women in America, and unable to foresee the blockbuster future of psychopharmacology, Coles rhetorically—and scathingly—inquired: "What pills will ever dissolve the anxiety and fear that go with life itself?"[74]

Through this era of revolt and resistance, the potent brew of ideas advanced by Laing and his cohort achieved increasing popularity and influence, as Laing himself achieved an odd sort of stardom. By 1965 Laing was internationally heralded as the counterculture's principal psychiatrist—the man who hobnobbed with members of the Beatles in London, cavorted with psychedelia guru (and former Harvard University psychologist) Timothy Leary in New York, and treated film actors like Sean Connery (when he freaked out over the fame he achieved as secret agent James Bond). At the same time, Laing established left-wing political credentials, publishing in 1964 a social critique of insanity in the influential journal *New Left Review*.[75]

The 1960s turned out to be remarkably receptive to gloomy theories about how insanity constituted an inner deadening in defensive response to the pain of life. In 1967 Laing published *The Politics of Experience*, a treatise on madness and society that sold several hundred thousand paperback copies in the United States alone. In 1970 the cover of the *New York Times Book Review* posed the provocative question, "Must man first go mad in order to be sane?," as it offered a most generous assessment of Laing's career, noting how his work "has shaken just about everyone and everything it has touched."[76] In 1971 *Life* magazine provided a multipage photo spread on a man it called "one of the best known and most controversial psychiatrists since Freud," while *Esquire* magazine followed suit a few months later with a fawning interview under the unsubtle title, "After Freud and Jung, now comes R. D. Laing."[77] By the time he conducted a lecture tour of US college campuses in 1972, Laing had become an iconic figure; his lectures were like rock concerts, and adoring fans proudly displayed bumper stickers: "I'm mad about R. D. Laing."[78] That same year as well, there was a highly touted documentary film based on Laing's therapeutic work, and Dick Cavett interviewed Laing on his popular television program. Thus when it was rumored that Laing was in active negotiations with NBC to produce a twenty-six-part television series on the intertwined themes of madness and despair, the report was considered completely credible—though the series never materialized.[79] Small wonder that author Angela Carter would write retrospectively: "I suppose that R. D. Laing's *The Divided Self* was one of the most influential books of the sixties—it made madness, alienation, hating your parents . . . it made it all glamourous."[80]

By the time psychiatrist (and Laing associate) David Cooper published *The Death of the Family* (1970), a relentless blast at family life, he was really preaching to the choir in the counterculture and New Left:

> The power of the family resides in its social mediating function. It reinforces the effective power of the ruling class in any exploitative society by providing a highly controllable paradigmatic form for every social institution. So we find the family form replicated through the social structures of the factory, the union branch, the school (primary and secondary), the university, the business corporation, the church, political parties and governmental apparatus, the armed forces, general and mental hospitals, and so on.[81]

The mere fact that the *New York Times Book Review* devoted a full page to articulating overall admiration for what Cooper had to say sug-

FIGURE 6 John Haynes's photograph of R. D. Laing, "philosopher of madness," as he sits in a tree on Hampstead Heath. From *Life* magazine, October 8, 1971. Reprinted with the permission of John Haynes.

gests just how influential this critique of the nuclear family had become. So did the way the review summarized what it saw as Cooper's key contention: "The family is our Catch-22 since it is the primary weapon by which we are bound to the insanities of normal life in a modern society."[82] The normative Cold War origins of early theorizing about familial dysfunctionality had not prevented the New Left and counterculture from reversing the lessons of that research into something usable for their own radical purposes. For activists in the 1960s, and for many on the political sidelines as well, what mattered about those psychiatric investigations into the familial causes of mental illness was that they appeared above all to legitimate their revolt against—and revulsion at—their own families.

3

Suffering from Contingencies

The interpretative scheme of the total institution automatically begins to operate as soon as the inmate enters, the staff having the notion that entrance is *prima facie* evidence that one must be the kind of person the institution was set up to handle. A man in a political prison must be traitorous; a man in a prison must be a lawbreaker; a man in a mental hospital must be sick. If not traitorous, criminal, or sick, why else would he be there?　　**Erving Goffman, 1961[1]**

I

A woman lives unhappily with an emotionally unstable husband. Finding a boyfriend, she wishes only at this point to escape her marriage, and she consequently arranges to have her husband committed to a mental hospital. A psychologically erratic parent lives at home with her adult children. When those children decide they now want to move away and live on their own, they have their parent removed to a psychiatric facility. An unruly teenage girl disrupts her parents' home life. Yet it is only when the girl indicates a new sexual interest in someone her parents find inappropriate that they seek the counsel of a psychiatrist who has the girl committed. Many mentally unwell individuals are living outside asylums; but they remain tolerated, if uncomfortably so, until such time as the circumstances of persons closest to them are transformed in some regard and toleration wears thin. Only then do these same individuals find themselves carted off—involuntarily—to mental institutions.

In Erving Goffman's *Asylums* (1961), the inmates are nameless, faceless. They have no detailed stories per se; there are no case studies. They are brought into view for a moment—a mere sentence or two. We never learn with any specificity through what process they were led to be committed. They never emerge from the shadows of the text as individuals. Goffman may be well known as a sociologist who was especially fascinated with the dramaturgical aspects of interpersonal existence, but actual persons seldom make an appearance in *Asylums*. Yet at the same time, and despite the utter anonymity of what we may refer to as its cast of characters, the text presumes a remarkable degree of identification with the anguish of these undifferentiated inmates. And its stance is uncompromising: The inmates suffer in a mental hospital that has morally and therapeutically failed them.

R. D. Laing located the etiology of mental illness in the repetitive emotional injuries of the nuclear family. The family was a place of cacophonously conflicting emotions that too often engaged in the double binding of an individual—usually a child—who could be driven to madness in the process. Goffman's turn toward a social diagnosis is quite dissimilar from the one discussed in the prior chapter.

Asylums does not locate the origins of mental illness in repetitive childhood traumas. Whereas in Laing's *The Divided Self*, the mental patient suffers from an absence of genuine love, in Goffman's *Asylums*, the mental patient suffers from circumstances over which control has been lost. In Goffman's account, persons close to the emotionally unwell individual collectively choose to act for reasons all their own. The targeted individual has become too much of a nuisance, is difficult, is unsocial or antisocial. Previously everything had been managed. But now there was nothing else to be done. Now the psychiatrist tells the wife or husband or mother and father or sons and daughters that the asylum is their best option for their spouse or child or parent. For Goffman, in short, the source of "mental illness" is a matter of personal betrayal. While "society's official view is that inmates of mental hospitals are there primarily because they are suffering from mental illness," one might instead say—as Goffman put it with his trademark deadpan sobriety—"that mental patients distinctively suffer not from mental illness, but from contingencies" (135).

Goffman's *Asylums* has often been interpreted as a sort of intellectual blueprint for the nightmarish vision of the mental hospital found in Ken Kesey's countercultural classic, *One Flew Over the Cuckoo's Nest*

(1962), not least because both became inspirations to a subsequent psychiatric survivors movement. However, in Kesey's *Cuckoo's Nest* the mental states of Chief Bromden, Billy Bibbit, and Dale Harding deteriorate due to Nurse Ratched's sadistically enforced prohibitions on all positive or pleasurable experience; to regain (and maintain) sanity, Kesey rhapsodized that what a person most requires is love (an analysis quite consistent with Laing's perspective). A distinctive feature of Goffman's *Asylums*, by contrast, is its emphasis not on love (or its absence) but rather on the all too indiscriminate reasons by which *any* individual suddenly finds him- or herself locked inside an asylum, betrayed by his or her most intimate relations, stripped bare, and terrifyingly vulnerable. Nowhere in *Asylums* do we encounter an antiauthoritarian rebel like the larger-than-life Randle Patrick McMurphy who courageously takes on "the system," motivates his fellow inmates to heal themselves, and dies a martyr's death. Instead Goffman's text chooses to linger on abjected and specifically *nonheroic* inmates. In a sense, *Asylums* and *Cuckoo's Nest* register as complementary rather than comparable early 1960s manifestos against the public mental hospital.

Quite a few of the interlocking concepts advanced in Goffman's *Asylums*—on psychiatric diagnoses as determined by social factors, on the damages done to individuals by the power relations within institutions, on psychiatric practices as forms of "social control," but above all on the malleability of the human mind and the means by which selves could be "modified" and "reformed"—were being actively discussed and debated from the beginning of the Cold War. *Asylums* was very much a product of Cold War culture—and in a double sense. On the one hand, Goffman's work may be placed in a lineage with a preexisting tradition of psychiatric reform efforts evolving in complex interrelationship with an accumulation of sensational exposés produced in the postwar era on the horrendous circumstances in American asylums and the variously beleaguered or valiant psychiatrists who worked in them. Key texts included Mary Jane Ward's autobiographical best-selling novel, *The Snake Pit* (1946); Albert Q. Maisel's photojournalistic essay in *Life* magazine, "Bedlam 1946"; Albert Deutsch's influential survey, *The Shame of the States* (1948); and Mike Gorman's report, "Oklahoma Attacks Its Snakepits," in *Reader's Digest*, also in 1948.[2] These texts were generally not at all hostile to psychiatrists, but rather (as scholarship has observed) "were focused instead on the stinginess of state governments and the indifference of the American people."[3] As of the early 1960s, the reform efforts stimulated by these exposés were already beginning to bear some fruit, in terms of improved psychiatric institutions as well as in a fledgling movement for deinstitutionalization, and yet many abuses continued, and sordid conditions persisted.

On the other hand, however, *Asylums* may also be situated in relationship to a histrionically anticommunist anxiety endemic to—even constitutive of—the Cold War 1950s. This ever-metastasizing anxiety circled around the threats that "brainwashing" posed to democracy in America, and the malicious potential of psychiatrists to manipulate the psyches of those in their charge. Just as the origins of 1960s critiques of the nuclear family originally lay in remarkably normative Cold War–era preoccupations with "schizophrenogenic mothers," so too the widespread and distinctively left-leaning 1960s preoccupation with the insidious power of ideology and with the vulnerability of the self to malignant social forces can be traced back to right-wing hysteria over communist strategies for "mind control" and other forms of "coercive persuasion." This chapter will position *Asylums* in preexisting debates about brainwashing, and then will explore how Goffman came to use the ideas associated with brainwashing in his urgent attempt to facilitate imaginative identification with inmates of American mental hospitals. The publication of Goffman's text marked a key moment in the ideological turn by which an originally right-wing paranoia about mental vulnerability could be put to use for progressive politics.

II

"Brainwashing" was a new concept in the 1950s. Named "menticide" by New York psychiatrist Joost A. M. Meerloo and "brain warfare" by Allen W. Dulles, director of the Central Intelligence Agency, the methods that typically came to be called "brainwashing" grew specifically out of concerns regarding the psychological tortures inflicted upon American prisoners of war in Korea to extract false confessions.[4] The word "brainwashing" had only been introduced into English by journalist Edward Hunter in 1950, who said it was a translation from Chinese of *hsi nao*, which literally meant "cleansing of the mind."[5] Hunter, a fervid anticommunist who had served during World War II in the Morale Operations Service of the Office of Strategic Services, a precursor to the Central Intelligence Agency, kept himself in the news on this issue throughout the decade, testifying to the House Committee on Un-American Activities in 1958 that the aim of "communist psychological warfare" was "the penetration of our leadership circles by a softening up and creating a defeatist state of mind." What the communists hoped to achieve by brainwashing American citizens, Hunter argued, was "the liquidation of our attitudes on what we used to recognize as right and wrong, what we used to accept as absolute moral standards."[6] The ultimate communist goal was to take over the United States through psychological methods.[7]

Joost Meerloo's early contributions to these debates proved especially influential. In 1954 he published his wholly terrifying assessment of brainwashing for the *New York Times Magazine*. Invoking the authority of his own experiences at the hands of Nazi interrogators while a member of the resistance movement in occupied Holland, but adapting the resulting insights to the case of communist efforts to convert American prisoners, Meerloo described the inevitability with which victims succumbed to aggressive indoctrination techniques. And Meerloo (influenced by Pavlovian ideas) challenged readers who doubted the implications of his argument that the modern science of psychiatry ought to be held accountable:

> But the circus trainer can tame lions! And the tyrant can tame people and their minds! Modern psychology itself has delivered into his hands various instruments which he has craftily learned to apply in achieving his perverted goal of thought control. . . . Liberty and mental freedom are no simple ideals we can take for granted, or grasp at in a mood of rebellion. They have to be thought through. Their natural and artificial limitations have to be known. If man is unaware of new mental pressures threatening him in this aftermath of war, he will become an easy and willing victim, howling with the wolves in the woods.[8]

Much of this pessimism concerning the ability to effectively resist indoctrination was due to a prevalent paradigm in the 1950s for how best to understand the psychological impact of brainwashing on a prisoner's mind. As two prominent psychiatrists wrote in 1956 in a detailed and thorough review of the evidence concerning "brainwashing" techniques in the Soviet Union and in communist China, totalitarian indoctrination strategies reflected a sophisticated understanding of how to infiltrate the workings of the human mind:

> Although the Communist management of prisoners was not designed by psychiatrists or neurophysiologists, and those who carry out this management do not have formal psychological training, nevertheless the interrogator does deal with the prisoner

> by using many of the same methods which the physician uses in
> the management of his patients. He allows the prisoner to talk at
> length about his family and his life. This produces in the prisoner
> a warm and dependent relationship toward him.

As a consequence, they concluded, it was "not at all incomprehensible" how some prisoners subjected to communist indoctrination strategies passed through "a state of total defeat" before they arrived at an experience that shared "many of the features of a religious conversion."[9] Or as Meerloo had ominously cautioned in 1951, through a reliance upon the "several tools" of "modern psychiatry," the dictator is able to place "his own thoughts and words into the minds and mouths of the victims he plans to destroy or to use for his own propaganda."[10]

These concerns were not completely empty of substance. During the Korean War captured American soldiers did make radio broadcasts that parroted communist propaganda critical of the United States. Some POWs did collaborate with the enemy; a handful of POWs did refuse to be repatriated to the United States. (Yet while reports asserted that collaboration was distressingly widespread, this was, in the final analysis, not proven to have been true at all.) By the mid-1950s, there were especially heinous allegations that POWs had signed false confessions claiming knowledge of classified American plans to use biological weapons against China. Even though the evidence for a major problem turned out subsequently to be flimsy at best, "Why did many GI captives cave in?" became at the time a soul-searching question of national import.[11]

The ideological impact of anxieties generated by the brainwashing controversy proved almost inestimable. Brainwashing called the essence of American identity into question. There was a pressing fear that Americans lacked the psychological toughness and emotional backbone required to resist such methods; too many American POWs were believed to have suffered from a disgraceful condition dubbed "give-up-itis."[12] As a prominent army psychiatrist who interviewed nearly a thousand former soldiers held captive by the Koreans bluntly stated in 1956: "The behavior of many Americans in Korean prison camps appears to raise serious questions about American character."[13]

There were grave suspicions that torture methods refined through the use of psychiatrists' most sophisticated insights into the human mind could undermine the entire American way of life. Modern psychiatry was responsible for placing into enemy hands strategies now being used to destroy American democracy. Was it possible that brainwashing was "psychiatry spelled backwards," as one critic phrased it?[14] Was American psychiatry in an adversarial relationship to the goals of a democratic society? By the mid-1950s, this vision of psychiatry as linked to the dissolution of dearly held American values was far from marginal. And now things had gone too far; even an attempt to establish a "school of survival" where American soldiers' psychic spines might be strengthened should they be subjected to brainwashing was concluded to be "no help."[15]

Psychiatry could do no good, even while it had already done a good amount of potential harm. By the late 1950s it was almost an article of faith that Pavlovian notions about animal behavior could easily be applied to human beings. As a well-respected text on the subject of mind control concluded in 1957: "Though men are not dogs, they should humbly try to remember how much they resemble dogs in their brain functions."[16] The apogee of Cold War anxieties about "brainwashing" came in 1959 with Richard Condon's paranoid thriller, *The Manchurian Candidate*, which imagined communist captors programming a former POW to do whatever they trained him to do (though afterward be unable to remember what he had done).[17] The novel was a huge bestseller. Cold War alarmists believed that the fragility of selves when subjected to coercive indoctrination was proven fact.

Social scientific and medical research into brainwashing directly challenged conspiratorial conclusions about its efficacy. An early move among investigators was to emphasize that human minds could be healed, and that "thought reform" was not irreversible. Subsequently, these commentators also turned the lens around and began to question just how benign the American government's ideological efforts might be.

The new mood was summarized by Albert D. Biderman, a sociologist working for the Air Force who interviewed Americans who had been subjected to indoctrination in Chinese prisoner of war camps. Biderman announced categorically that the very concept of "brainwashing"—he himself put the term in quotation marks—needed to be "debunked." In an essay from 1962, Biderman reviewed books published the prior year by MIT social psychologist Edgar Schein (*Coercive Persuasion*) and Harvard Medical School psychiatrist Robert Jay Lifton (*Thought Reform*). These books (which had been preceded by a number of important articles) fundamentally challenged the idea that brainwashing was possible. Biderman's take was that for a full decade journalists as well as a number of ill-informed scholars had been riling the American public with over-the-top accounts of how "the techniques of analyzing human behavior might fall into the hands of unscrupulous but powerful individuals

and organizations who would thereupon mold people as they pleased
and rob individuals of their independence and identity." Consequently,
these accounts had established in the popular imagination an image of
"brainwashing" as (in Lifton's sarcastic summary) "an all-powerful, irresistible, unfathomable, and magical method of achieving total control
over the human mind." In Biderman's view, hysteria about "brainwashing" would not have taken such hold in America without the combination of a Cold War–fostered "diabolical view of Communism" *and* eth-
nocentric racism toward the "strange" and "bizarre" "Oriental."[18]

Without a doubt, Schein and Lifton were debunkers. Each in their
own way, but both based on direct encounters with Americans who had
been subjected to coercive indoctrination methods by their communist
captors, sought to develop more differentiated analyses of the painful
damages done by forced interrogation techniques. But they also worked
to identify the limits of coercive thought reform. In his precursor articles Schein (who had worked for the military and interviewed repatriated American POWs shortly after their release) objected to the analysis
of Joost Meerloo and others because they sought "to conceptualize the
process of brainwashing in terms of a simple conditioning or learning
model."[19] The Pavlovian model, in Schein's view, simply did not work.
Nor did susceptibility to the pressures of indoctrination lie in a particular individual's weakness. Rather what was unique—and uniquely effective—about Chinese communist indoctrination was the way it systematically combined a whole range of techniques for putting pressures
on individuals. As Schein put it: "It is my opinion that the process is
primarily concerned with social forces, not with the strengths and weaknesses of individual minds." Schein did not dispute that "some men collaborated because their egos were too weak," and they were "primarily
motivated by fear," but he was most interested in the inventive variety of
strategies the Chinese used to encourage not only collaboration but also
lasting conversion among less weak individuals.[20] Moments of friendli-
ness, encouragement to cooperation, promises of rewards, a divide-and-
conquer strategy that separated POWs by rank and by color, withholding of news from the West coupled with a barrage of "heavily biased"
procommunist literature, gradual steps taken to ensure a shift in frames
of reference, opportunities for discussion: It was all of these techniques
together that made indoctrination successful.[21] Yet even though Schein
believed that indoctrination did sometimes succeed (although he offered
a more complex account of its effectiveness), he was no less concerned
about how the prevailing assumptions about "brainwashing" created
a climate in which people were getting "carried away with hysteria."

Yes: Communists had "a different ideology," one that was "not consonant with the democratic ideology." But communist strategies would seem less "terrifying" if Americans reminded themselves that the techniques used by the Chinese were not unfamiliar to Americans, and had their counterparts in education, advertising, and the histories of religious conversions.[22]

Robert Jay Lifton's objections, too, were both scientific and political. Having extensively interviewed and evaluated POWs repatriated from North Korea, Lifton found that these men certainly experienced adjustment problems; most were withdrawn, many felt guilt, some expressed anger, and nearly all displayed "patterns of defensive isolation." Lifton did not seek to underestimate or minimize the torture associated with communist thought reform. He documented how prisoners were broken down. He spoke of "an *annihilation of identity*" characteristic of the entire indoctrination process, as well as the "emotional assaults" upon the victim, assaults that resulted in the victim being "stamped with another identity." He also spoke of "soul surgery."[23] But Lifton found as well that the harm could be reversed. The very fact that these men were returned "home by ship" and thus experienced a "delayed homecoming, with the opportunity to live together and form these strong group ties, was nonetheless of definite value." Lifton concluded that the men all appeared responsive to therapeutic treatments, and that it remained unclear to what extent Chinese thought control experiments would result in long-term psychological damage. What ultimately happened to the psyches of these men, he indicated, depended a great deal on the psychiatric care they would subsequently receive.[24]

At the same time, Lifton also wished to understand better how "thought reform" could and might exist in nontotalitarian environments. In 1956 Lifton observed that Chinese communist thought reform could be thought of as "almost a caricature of things we can encounter in our everyday life in various phases of our existence."[25] And in 1961 he would retrospectively observe how McCarthyism in the United States— with its "cult of confession and repentance; a stress upon self-betrayal and a bond of betrayal between accusers and accused; the creation of a mythological doctrine (the State Department was being overrun by Communist 'subversives' who were in turn responsible for 'losing China'); and the demand that victims take on a new identity in accordance with this myth"—"became a poor imitation of its declared enemy."[26] Democratic America was not immune to totalitarian impulses. Lifton had observed at a symposium held during the annual American Psychological Association meeting in 1956:

Every society makes use of similar pressures of guilt, shame, and confession, and of milieu control, as [a] means of maintaining its values and its organization. We must ask ourselves where we—inadvertently, and in less extreme form—could also be applying these in excess, to mould uniform identities, and to make men think and act in the conforming fashion. We are confronted with the problem of any democratic society—that of maintaining a balance which limits these forces sufficiently to allow its people a sense of individual freedom, creativity, and human dignity.[27]

It was this view that would come to have unanticipated effects far beyond the scope of analyses of exploitative psychological experiments performed by the communist Chinese. If some kind of thought reform existed in all social environments, including the democratic United States, then the question became: Who experienced mental coercion in the United States in a manner that most resembled the indoctrination processes in totalitarian societies? The answer, according to Erving Goffman, was the mental patient.

III

In October 1956 Goffman and Lifton had the opportunity to compare notes when both participated in four days of symposia on the topic of "persuasion" in the fields of medicine and health. Organized by the Josiah Macy, Jr. Foundation and held in Princeton, New Jersey, the meeting brought together about two dozen participants and invited guests from a range of medical, scientific, and social scientific backgrounds. It was an unusually impressive and wide-ranging assembly of scholars and researchers.[28]

It was clear from his presentation that in 1956 Goffman had already settled on the four central concepts for the book he was beginning to write on the mental hospital. He first mapped the tenets for "total institutions." He spoke of how new inmates to total institutions invariably experienced "mortifications of the self" and how these mortifications involved "a kind of 'degrading process'" that resulted in a "resocialization and reconstruction of the self along a new basis." He spoke also of "the moral career of mental patients," describing how the mental patient took on "a stigma" that "he will have for the rest of his life, namely, the identity of being a mental patient or an ex-mental patient." He spoke of how the inmate in an asylum made "secondary adjustments," creating "something like an underground" society where the inmate can "move in a relaxed, self-respecting way" and where "he cannot be tyr-annized." And finally, Goffman briefly discussed "the psychiatric view of the world" inside the mental hospital where "each item of conduct" by a patient was "rationalized" by staff as yet another sign of the pa-tient's mental illness. Designated as "sick," in turn, the inmate assimi-lated "a 'psychiatrized' self."[29] (All these ideas would appear intact and unchanged, structuring the four chapters of *Asylums*, which Goffman published five years later.)

Most notable, however, was that in 1956 Goffman also said he had been reading the literature "on brainwashing in Red China," and that this reading "no doubt entered into the way in which I conceptualized my material."[30] Even before Lifton presented his research on Chinese communist thought reform, Goffman and Lifton—as well as other par-ticipants—had commented repeatedly on comparable aspects in their analyses. When Lifton said that "the Chinese Communists view thought reform as a thoroughly uplifting, harmonizing, and therapeutic experi-ence," he noted that "there are sharp analogies, sometimes disturbing ones perhaps, to some of the work that Dr. Goffman has presented."[31] And Goffman, too, linked the circumstances of persons in communist in-doctrination camps and persons involuntarily committed to mental hos-pitals in the United States:

> One is presumably there for one's own good. I think it is impor-tant to get that point. Presumably the treatment in all concentra-tion camps wasn't for one's own good, but in the thought reform process, it is presented in the guise of being for your own good, even though you don't know it yet that it is for your own good. You are not sufficiently aware of what is good for you. Thus it does not feel completely hostile.[32]

A preoccupation with brainwashing proved to be no minor ingre-dient in Goffman's analysis of the mental hospital. A year after the en-counter with Lifton in Princeton, for instance, Goffman was stating how "progressive mental hospitals" and "brainwashing camps" *both* offered "the inmate an opportunity to live up to a model of conduct that is at once ideal and staff-sponsored—a model felt by its advocates to be in the best interests of the very persons to whom it is applied." And while citing evidence from Lifton as well as Schein on recently repatriated prisoners of war, Goffman concluded that "one mode of adaptation to the setting of a total institution is that of *conversion*."[33] That the inmate in the to-tal institution capitulated to his environment—and that the experience of life inside the institution made wildly dissimilar individuals within it behave in astoundingly similar ways—was, Goffman said in 1959, and would repeat again in *Asylums*, "thus a tribute to the power of social forces." Goffman found it remarkable not only that the dynamics within the institution could stamp on "an aggregate of persons a common fate and eventually, because of this, a common character," but also "that this social reworking can be done upon what is perhaps the most obstinate diversity of human materials that can be brought together by society."[34] And—in yet another adaptation of a concern with communism—in *Asylums* Goffman would make definite links between how US mental institutions treated their inmates and how totalitarian societies treated their intellectual dissidents. Reference to Polish intellectual Czesław Miłosz's writing on "the captive mind" underscored the extent to which Goffman intuitively believed that there was little meaningful difference between the situation of persons caught in these two (only seemingly) vastly divergent social universes (320).

Yet to arrive at this view Goffman did not only reverse conservative fears of what communists might do to Americans to explore what Americans were doing to their own most vulnerable citizens. He also engaged in aggressively selective readings of the more liberal psychiatric and psychological studies he cited, invoking their authority while turning their analyses on their head. Lifton, for instance, had analyzed "brainwashing" only to *revalidate* the need for psychiatric practice and treatment, not to undercut that need; persons traumatized by "thought reform" processes *required* group and individual therapies. Schein had made comparable arguments. What Goffman derived from these studies by experts on indoctrination techniques and psychological torture, however, was that they confirmed how the self might be radically reconstituted if locked (literally) in a total environment. For Goffman these studies underscored the flimsiness of the self when confronted with social coercion. Goffman utilized insights that defended psychiatric treatment to critique psychiatric treatment.

In this way Goffman also argued that the dangers of thought control emanated less from the communist sphere and more from the United States' own government. He held that psychiatrists were not healers, but rather were mechanics of coercion; their work did not enable autonomy but rather defended social norms. He believed that mental hospitals punished deviants and nonconformists; they policed selves. By the early 1960s, and after years of study, Goffman's disrespect for psychiatry was full-blown. The portrait of psychiatric practices in *Asylums*—in complex relationship to the Cold War climate in which it was produced—was unforgiving.

IV

Goffman's analysis of the self as constituted (and repetitively reconstituted) by social forces had not originated with his project on the insane asylum. Goffman had argued much the same in his prior research on "deference" and "demeanor" in social encounters.[35] In *The Presentation of Self in Everyday Life* (1959), based on his PhD dissertation of 1953 (on a farming community on one of the smaller of the Shetland Islands), the self did not exist in any pure or defined sense, but was performed and produced in relation to a complicated matrix of ever-shifting interpersonal cues and social circumstances. "The self, then, as a performed character, is not an organic thing that has a specific location, whose fundamental fate is to be born, to mature, and to die; it is a dramatic effect arising diffusely from a scene that is presented, and the characteristic issue, the crucial concern, is whether it will be credited or discredited."[36] Although Goffman's *Asylums* was marketed (and indeed also received by reviewers and scholars of the history of sociology) as a study of life in a "total institution," it should really also be understood as a continuation of Goffman's investigations into the nature of the self.[37]

Goffman's confrontation with the situation of the mentally ill fundamentally complicated the conception of the self he had developed in his work on the Shetland Islands. In *The Presentation of Self*, Goffman had developed a practically postmodern notion of the self as entirely (or at least almost entirely) constituted by social interactions and circumstances (and this notion of the self certainly made an appearance in *Asylums* as well). Yet in an attempt to impress upon the reader the searing pain caused by involuntary incorporation into an institution that claimed to—but all too often did not—heal, Goffman tended intermittently also in *Asylums* to presume a preexisting self and then to detail the damages to which it was subjected. At other points Goffman stressed how much a self required social supports for sustenance. And still at other moments, Goffman sought to detail the ways individuals managed to rescue a partial sense of themselves in resistant opposition to the demands of the institution (arguing that the self was "a stance-taking entity" that emerged *against* something—in this case the pressures placed upon it [320]). At yet further moments he implied how epistemologically destabilizing it inescapably was for a self to have all one's resistances *and* compliances routinely interpreted by staff and doctors as signaling need for continued mental care. In spite of Goffman's authoritative assertions that an aim of *Asylums* was "to develop a sociological version of the structure of the self" or (at another point) to develop an "institutional approach to the study of the self," the interesting effect was to foreground how enduringly *insoluble* was the question of human selfhood (xiii, 127). The nature of the relationships between selves and social forces, relations and settings remained almost impossible to discern.

Both the impatient search for more adequate metaphors to express the consequences for individuals institutionalized in a mental hospital and the mutually incompatible versions of selfhood parading through the pages of *Asylums* give an indication of just what an unusual text this was for a sociologist to write. It was not that sociological concepts were absent from the book. On the contrary, *Asylums* can be positioned in relationship to developments within the discipline of sociology during the postwar era. Sociologist Everett Hughes had first introduced Goffman to the idea of the "total institution" in 1952 while Goffman was still a graduate student at the University of Chicago.[38] Goffman's eventual description of mental illness as preeminently a social construct yet one with quite potent effects on individuals' self-understandings would owe much as well to the work of sociologist Edwin Lemert, whose *Social Pathology* (1951) had argued that persons treated as deviants took on the role assigned to those behaviors, and that the role regulated and modified their behaviors. (Strikingly, in 1946 Lemert had written specifically about how legal commitment to an insane asylum functioned as a form of social control.)[39] Sociologist Howard S. Becker, who attended graduate school with Goffman in Chicago, extended the ideas of Lemert, Hughes, and others by using the concept of "career"—which typically characterized persons in legitimate occupations—also to describe how persons who broke social rules (like marijuana users) adjusted in a sequential process over time to their new role as designated deviants. And Becker also proposed—as he later wrote in 1963—that "the central fact about deviance" was that "it is created by society," adding "that *social groups create deviance by making the rules whose infraction constitutes deviance*, and by applying those rules to particular people and labeling them as outsiders."[40] These sociological concepts proved critical to Goffman as he conducted his own ethnographic fieldwork on the inner world of the asylum.

At the same time Goffman offered no programmatic suggestions for reform of the mental hospital. This was highly unusual in scholarship on psychiatric hospitals. He paid little attention to sketching the daily routines of the inmates or the staff. He did not explain or outline the specific structure of the institution. It can often be difficult from Goffman's writing on the asylum to arrive at any kind of clear picture of the institution. Instead, as has been remarked, "Goffman conveys a 'tone of life'" in *Asylums*.[41] Goffman's was an especially expressive account of an unusual and extreme experience and, as such, it threw off the formulas and formalities of sociological research. The effect on the reader could be disorienting. And yet it also made the writing more emotionally involving.

Directly related to this point was that not much in Goffman's writing on mental hospitals exclusively applied to the lives of psychiatric patients. At every step Goffman's method considered ethnographic evidence gleaned from fieldwork and worked that evidence into insights that might readily be grasped in terms "universal" to being human. Thus Goffman's restless style of presenting ideas—full of colorful digressions, telling anecdotes, and lively literary quotations—proceeded more in the fashion of imaginative nonfiction than sociological analysis. Ideas were often expressed axiomatically. Examples taken almost at random are:

- It is not very practicable to try to sustain solid claims about oneself (164–65).
- To engage in a particular activity in the prescribed spirit is to accept being a particular kind of person who dwells in a particular kind of world (186).
- When existence is cut to the bone, we can learn what people do to flesh out their lives (305).

Although his work was rooted in participant observation, then, both this aphoristic quality of Goffman's writing and its tendency to abstract from the particular to the universal gave an intimation of its larger purposes. On the one hand, *Asylums* aimed to create opportunities for readers to *identify with* patients in a mental institution, to stop seeing those deemed crazy as somehow radically other from those deemed normal. On the other hand, the case study of the insane asylum in *Asylums* became an occasion for *theorizing more generally* about interhuman relations, the peculiarities of contained settings, and the structure of the human self (and the relationship among the three).

In an additional set of moves Goffman sought to express just how dreadful and degrading the entry into the enclosed universe of the hospital could be. Upon entry, patients were violated in multiple ways: their personal possessions were taken away, to be replaced by undifferentiated institutional objects; their body was stripped, often in front of members of the opposite sex; and their innermost thoughts were invaded and the facts of their most discreditable past behaviors were recorded for endless future perusal by strangers. In short, patients could no longer control information flow about themselves. Not only did Goffman spell out how these "territories of the self are violated," but he also worked to communicate the visceral intensity of what he called "contaminative exposure": the dissolution of boundaries between the patient and his fellows as well as his surroundings. In a striking choice of illustrative quotation, Goffman used not an example directly from a mental hospital but rather from a boarding school (in this case George Orwell's). The quote was replete with disgusting eating utensils encrusted with accumulated sour porridge, food filled with unidentifiable gross objects, slimy wash basins and always slightly damp and smelly towels, and filthy lavatories exuding their stench onto the corridors, thus once again cannily creating opportunities also for those readers who could not conceive of themselves as potentially put away as crazy nonetheless to be able to imagine the palpable grotesquerie of a squalid environment (23–27).

B eyond the meditations on human nature that were a major component of *Asylums*, there were other strands of argumentation that can be read as more deliberately ideological. There is no question that the book was meant as a powerful indictment of the institution of the mental hospital. And one of the most striking aspects of *Asylums* was its recurrent juxtaposition of the conditions of psychiatric patients in mental hospitals with those of inmates in Nazi concentration and death camps. This was not an innovation; journalist Albert Deutsch had observed in 1948 how conditions on a mental hospital ward were starkly reminiscent "of the pictures of the Nazi concentration camps at Belsen and Buchenwald."[42] Yet Goffman simply took this point as foundational.

Nazism emerged as a lurking presence throughout Goffman's book, surfacing in sentences and asides and footnotes at the most seemingly odd moments. In a typically abrupt and almost non sequitur sequence of assertions, Goffman described a scene from the insane asylum in 1950s America, making it abundantly clear that (with the slightest shift in language) it might as well be a description from Nazi-occupied Europe:

> Prisoners and mental patients cannot prevent their visitors from seeing them in humiliating circumstances. Another example is the shoulder patch of ethnic identification worn by concentration camp inmates. Medical and security examinations often expose the inmate physically, sometimes to persons of both sexes; a similar exposure follows from collective sleeping arrangements and doorless toilets. An extreme here, perhaps, is the situation of a self-destructive mental patient who is stripped naked for what

is felt to be his own protection and placed in a constantly lit se-
clusion room, into whose Judas window any person passing on
the ward can peer. (24)

Nazism figured as well in the constant surveillance and the relentless
regulations of the mental hospital. It figured in discussions of the stratifi-
cations within inmate society. And it figured in descriptions of how mental hospital patients—like concentration camp inmates—were forced to
scavenge through garbage for any scrap of edible food (213). It was a
major reference point in a discussion of "the betrayal funnel" composed
of kin and experts that slowly relieved inmates of their human rights
through a process that ensured their cooperation because they realized
only too late what was happening to them. Here, and however astonish-
ingly, Goffman invoked the terrible fact that gas chambers were "fitted
out like delousing rooms, and victims taking off their clothes were told
to note where they were leaving them" (141). And Nazism was directly
referenced when Goffman asserted that an obligation during group therapy meetings that inmates discuss intimate matters (like an affair with
another patient) had its parallel in the sadistic demand that Jews in concentration camps watch their loved ones be beaten to death by SS officers
(33–35). Goffman also linked cruelty among inmates to behavior in concentration camps, and he invoked the whippings Nazis sometimes forced
inmates in the camps to give one another (23). It is hard to avoid the conclusion that Goffman felt that elements of fascism still persisted—not
abroad in Germany but rather at home within mental hospitals in the
United States.

V

In 1956, during the presentation of his findings about his year of fieldwork at St. Elizabeths Hospital, Goffman informed the distinguished
group of scholars and intellectuals gathered in Princeton: "If we want to
be completely explicit about all of these things and try to get this matter settled once and for all, let this be admitted: When I refer to the fact
that mental hospitals are terrible places, I feel they are."[43] Yet this position could hardly at this moment be considered a popular one. Many
accounts in the second half of the 1950s found much to applaud and
commend about state asylums. They may have been snake pits—even recently—but much had changed in just a few years. By the mid-1950s reports announced that psychiatric hospitals had made considerable strides
toward the successful treatment of "America's No. 1 health problem."[44]

And much of this fresh enthusiasm for the capabilities of asylums to address mental illness stemmed from the development of new and effective medications.

In the mid-1950s newly discovered drugs began to reshape daily existence on wards across America in dramatic ways. When Thorazine (or chlorpromazine) arrived on the market, it was immediately heralded as a godsend—posting sales of $75 million in its first year—thanks to large state hospitals like Pilgrim State in New York that prescribed the drug to every one of the 15,000 inmates.[45] That same year, the *New York Times* also reported that the drug reserpine—which was a chemical extracted from an Indian snakeroot plant—was yielding "frequently astounding" results in the treatment of schizophrenic patients.[46] A major six-part series in 1956 on a state mental hospital in Columbus, Ohio, for the *Saturday Evening Post* (which reached three million subscribers) quoted a doctor who candidly effused: "These drugs are not going to empty the hospital—this is not an antibiotic of the mind—but they sure do help us."[47] As the series noted, doctors at the Columbus institution no longer resorted to insulin coma therapy; they also no longer performed lobotomies on patients. However, the series also acknowledged that many patients at Columbus State continued to receive EST (electroshock treatments). "EST is still our mainstay," said the hospital's superintendent, acknowledging that EST remained cheaper than other treatments.[48]

The revolution in antipsychotic drugs also made an appearance in popular culture. Worlds apart from *Asylums* was prolific best-selling novelist (and medical doctor) Frank G. Slaughter's *Daybreak* (1958), a melodrama about life inside a state asylum that offered unqualified glorification of the new "wonder drugs." Situated in the recent past, *Daybreak* focused on the travails of a kindly brain surgeon who must race to find a cure for schizophrenia before his hospital's corrupt superintendent insists that he perform a lobotomy on a young, gifted and catatonic female patient. (The superintendent believes that lobotomies would create a slave work force and thereby reduce the hospital's operating costs.) The kindly surgeon—smitten with the beautiful schizophrenic—discovers the antipsychotic drug reserpine just in the nick of time —a discovery described (in an author's afterword) as "*the most sensational medical discovery of modern times.*"[49] Written as if sponsored by the pharmaceutical industry, *Daybreak* ends happily with the successful healing of the young woman's schizophrenia via drug therapy, the disclosure of the superintendent's diabolical plans, and the touching declaration of love by the noble surgeon for his beautiful (and newly sane) patient.

Even the very same asylum in Washington, DC, where Erving Goffman conducted his fieldwork, and which he unflatteringly labeled a "total institution," was singled out as the finest state mental hospital in the
nation. "As a taxpayer, you own and support one of the world's best
centers for treating mental illness," gushed *Harper's* in 1956 about St.
Elizabeths Hospital. "The average citizen regards 'asylums' with horror
and shrinks from the idea of sending a member of his family to one,"
but St. Elizabeths was, in fact, "a pacesetter in its field" and "a glowing
example of how a mental hospital can be run." St. Elizabeths no longer
performed lobotomies; it had also drastically reduced its use of electroshock. And it was said that tranquilizing drug therapies had made all the
difference (though St. Elizabeths was also witnessing "great success with
psychodrama"). As an inmate who had been committed to several mental hospitals before he arrived at St. Elizabeths testified: "This hospital
offers a patient every opportunity for recovery, if he can—or will—take
advantage of it."[50] This was clearly not the asylum according to Goffman.

How do we square Goffman's account in *Asylums* with more mainstream accounts? For one thing, even as drug therapies raced through
American mental hospitals, altering permanently the paradigm for how
to treat the mentally ill, Goffman chose to make scant mention of their
use—and there was no direct mention of chlorpromazine or reserpine
or the perceived therapeutic value of either. Goffman indicated only
that "the forced taking of drugs" kept wards quiet at night and thereby
allowed a reduction in staff (381). Goffman also acknowledged how
lobotomy was "now sharply declining in American hospitals," which
corresponded to the fact that since its peak year in 1949, the rate of lobotomies had dropped sharply throughout the 1950s.[51] But Goffman
also indicated that psychiatrists continued to rely in the later 1950s on
insulin coma therapy, even though psychiatrists had generally come to
consider the use of insulin coma therapy to be antiquated. As a psychiatrist announced, "were insulin coma a new treatment invented in 1958,
it would have no hope of catching on in the way it did" when it had first
been introduced nearly a generation before.[52] And Goffman further implied that the administering of EST remained "widespread"—perhaps
accurate for some hospitals (like Columbus State), but not true on a
national level (382). Statistics from the years 1958 and 1960 revealed
a sharp reduction in its frequency.[53] In addition, although there was an
experimental movement to eliminate both the locked wards and locked
entrances of mental hospitals in the second half of the 1950s, *Asylums*
made no mention of these developments.[54] In short, *Asylums* achieved its

central aim of disparaging the mental hospital by sidestepping pertinent facts about changes already underway.

Yet at the same time Goffman was hardly out of sync with broader trends within sociology and the social sciences when he heaped scorn on the mental hospital. In 1949 psychiatrist Alfred H. Stanton and sociologist Morris S. Schwartz had posited that psychiatric treatment for mental patients was often based not on premises that ensured patients' well-being, but rather "explicitly" and "solely on the grounds that they make the patients easier to manage."[55] And in their definitive study, *The Mental Hospital*, published in 1954, Stanton and Schwartz sought exceptionally vivid language to express the sheer awfulness of existence as a mental patient:

> It is hard to keep in mind what it means subjectively to be a mental patient; to be so fearful that each aspect of the environment represents a threat to one's existence; to experience the world as unreal and to see the "outside" as just a flimsy structure with no substance; to live with the feeling of restraint and being closed in, or suffocated, and to feel rebellion and resentment at this and be unable to express it in any effective way; to experience utter, desperate, and unrelieved loneliness, with no hope of change; to feel that in the entire universe there is no person that will ever understand one; to believe that one's actions have no effect and that one is not affected by the actions of others.[56]

And in the later 1950s two sociologists bluntly concluded that "it appears more likely that large mental hospitals produce more alienation than they treat."[57]

Despite announced improvements in asylum life, more disturbing views of asylums also continued to acquire popular currency into the 1960s. Not only Kesey's novel but also many other novels and films began to exploit and dramatize the sad and strange lives led inside mental hospitals. Dariel Telfer's *The Caretakers* (1959) set a high bar in terms of its lurid representation of the asylum as a place rife with sexual abuse and psychic mistreatment of its inmates. By comparison, J. R. Salamanca's bestseller, *Lilith* (1961), was relatively tame in its depiction of a manipulative bisexual nymphomaniac (but then again, its setting was based on the liberal and privileged Chestnut Lodge). In director Samuel Fuller's graphic and surreal *Shock Corridor* (1963) the mental hospital was where an ambitious journalist must go in order to solve a murder case—only to be driven insane by the place. And in Frank Leonard's *City Psychiatric* (1965), drawn from the author's experiences as an attendant at Bellevue mental hospital in New York City, the asylum was the inner circle of hell. Reeking with the stench of feces and urine, Leonard's asylum was where patients became so much debris and capable staff members were fired for struggling to maintain humanity on their wards.[58]

By the time Frederick Wiseman, an attorney with a Yale law degree, and John Kennedy Marshall, an anthropologist with graduate training from Harvard University, received permission in 1966 to film inside the Massachusetts Correctional Institution for the Criminally Insane in Bridgewater, the horrors of the asylum were old news. Yet their *Titicut Follies* emerged nonetheless as the most remarkable and emotionally shattering documentary about an asylum ever made. Drawing on Goffman's strategy, the film repeatedly compared Bridgewater to a Nazi concentration camp. This was evident in the brutally casual power exercised by guards in their treatment of the (often pitifully naked and deliberately humiliated prisoners); in the perverse and obsessive interest shown by the in-house psychiatrist in the sexual predilections and compulsions of a young pedophile (probing with voyeuristic and leering persistence the pedophile's attraction to young children despite having a steady girlfriend); and in a conversation between guards about the way the smell of "gas" (presumably used to kill vermin) clung to their clothes for weeks despite their best efforts to air them out. Bridgewater was, *Titicut Follies* suggested, the reincarnation of Dachau in America.[59]

As the 1960s progressed, an idea that conditions within insane asylums represented an instantiation of fascistic tendencies continued to spread. The psychiatric survivors movement and its supporters in the New Left and counterculture would frequently avail themselves of such an analogy. By the later 1960s it would be no longer much remembered that for a decade "brainwashing" had been primarily conceived of and feared as something that could be done to ordinary US citizens by the communist Chinese or Soviets. Many young people instead started from a conspiratorial premise that brainwashing was what was being done to ordinary American citizens by their own government and US corporations. In this new—and now progressive—form of paranoia, the abuse of mental patients by psychiatrists and the power of capitalist ideology to pervert Americans' capacities for self-recognition and accurate understanding of reality were each emerging as exemplary instances of the hideousness of psychology and psychiatry in general.

4

The Therapeutic State

Organized psychiatry's search for the "causes of mental illness" thus reminds one of the drunk who looks for his house key under the street light—not because that's where he dropped it, but because that's where the light is.

Thomas S. Szasz, 1970[1]

I

On Memorial Day in 1957 Edith Louise Hough received a visit at her District of Columbia apartment from her former fiancé. A graduate of Radcliffe College, Hough was mourning the recent death of her father, and the ex-fiancé—who had just married another woman three weeks earlier—wished to offer his condolences. Hough, however, located her pistol and wrapped it in a towel. She then proceeded to shoot her ex-fiancé four times before she fired a final bullet directly into his temple as he lay dying on her couch. Following her arrest Hough was found not mentally competent to stand trial on the charge of first-degree murder. She was committed to St. Elizabeths Hospital, where she remained for the next year. In May 1958 the hospital certified that Hough could stand trial; the trial ended with an acquittal by reason of insanity—and Hough was returned to St. Elizabeths. Yet it was a matter of only months before hospital staff determined that Hough posed no danger to the community. She was allowed to leave the hospital nearly every day to visit the city for several hours in the company of her seventy-five-year-old mother unescorted by a hospital attendant. In October of 1958 the psychiatric hospital recommended the conditional release of Edith Hough so that she might find employment, declaring that this was an important aspect of her rehabilitation. However, other psychiatrists who examined Hough disagreed, calling the decision to release her "very risky," and testifying that Hough, who was in her early forties at the time, was "a sick little girl" who suffered from "high grade paranoid schizophrenia." The plea for release was denied, and a second appeal for release in 1959 was also denied. It was additionally determined that it had been "illegal" to allow Hough to leave the hospital for day trips without a court order. Yet by 1960 Hough had nonetheless managed successfully to assume an office job in downtown Washington, and in 1961 she petitioned once more for her release. This time psychiatric testimony observed that Hough understood she had been insane at the time of the murder; psychiatrists also noted that Hough had not demonstrated psychotic symptoms for three years. And so in July 1961, or approximately four years after killing her former fiancé in cold blood, Edith Hough was released from the asylum so that she might live at home with her mother.[2]

The strange case of Edith Hough was a minor episode in the history of jurisprudence with respect to discussions surrounding the insanity defense and procedures for criminal commitment to a psychiatric hospital. It offered no genuine precedent and might have been forgotten completely were it not for a scathing commentary on the case provided by psychiatrist Thomas S. Szasz. Written in 1960 after Hough's two initial appeals for release had been denied but before her final appeal was approved, Szasz's essay mocked the legal process from start to finish. If Hough was "insane" and "dangerous" at the time of the murder, how was it determined that she was no longer "insane" or "dangerous" and could now stand trial? If competent to stand trial, how could it be decided that she was innocent by reason of her "mental illness"? If legally innocent, how could it be determined that Hough remained "dangerous" to the community and needed to be held indefinitely in a psychiatric hospital? If not legally innocent, why was Hough not sentenced to a prison for a specific term?

It was not just that Edith Hough had effectively gotten away with murder that most distressed and outraged Szasz. It was also the incipient signs of a creeping despotic regime reflected by a presumption that Hough required continued "hospitalization" not because of what she had done in the past but because of what she allegedly remained capable of doing. As Szasz observed, Hough was continuing to be held "as a *preventive measure*!" As Szasz added:

> Let us not forget that this social act has, and with good reason, been regarded as the hallmark of the totalitarian state. The legal restraint of a person justified by *what he might do* (in the future) is there used with the explicit aim of social reform. . . . Let us at least entertain the possibility that by engaging in certain modifications of social living—for this is what we are doing—we run the risk of squandering the greatest asset of our Nation and its distinctive form of government, namely, the autonomy, integrity, responsibility, and freedom of the individual.[3]

By this point in his career, Szasz—who had first come to prominence as an expert on psychosomatic disorders—had been questioning the unstable boundaries between psychiatry and the law for several years. Since at least 1956 Szasz had been arguing that it was inappropriate for a psychiatrist to testify in court as an "expert arbiter who must decide whether a person is 'ill' within or outside the rules which society sets for illness."[4] Szasz aggressively began to pursue several interwoven arguments concerning abuses of psychiatric practice. In 1957 Szasz proposed that psychiatric classifications of mental disease were effectively meaningless, and that even terms like "schizophrenia" merely enabled society to "explain" an "entity" that did not exist.[5] Questioning the legitimacy of psychiatrists' evaluations of defendants' mental competence, he argued that same year that the insanity plea ought to be abolished entirely.[6] In 1958, in the first article (of many) he published in a law journal, Szasz further argued that when psychiatrists participated in criminal proceedings as expert witnesses, they essentially served as moral salves on the guilty conscience of the populace. As Szasz asserted, "if punishment of those who violate social roles engenders guilt" (and he certainly believed it did so), then that guilt "should not be obscured by pseudopsychiatric considerations of 'mental illness.'"[7] And also in 1958 Szasz began to argue strongly that the involuntary commitment of individuals to mental hospitals constituted a fundamental breach of their civil liberties—and that involuntary commitment should be abolished as well.[8]

In taking these positions, and taking them quite so early, Szasz has long been identified as a renegade and an iconoclast, a forerunner and progenitor of the antipsychiatric attitudes that would soon come to sweep through the counterculture, the psychiatric survivors movement, as well as various radical therapy and radical psychology movements.

All of these sought to discredit the status quo of psychiatric practices and procedures due to their alleged mistreatment of individuals labeled "mental patients." Szasz would be vigorously denounced and dismissed by some of his peers, but he would also garner considerable prestige—at least for the duration of the 1960s, during which time he would be taken quite seriously as a powerful and radical voice for social change and ethical reconsideration—and not solely on the political left. Szasz's often savage critique of psychiatry on the one hand, and his passionate libertarian defense of "the autonomy, integrity, responsibility, and freedom of the individual" on the other hand, found an audience that traversed conventional left-right divisions. His populist mix—openly hostile to the presumed arrogance of the medical professional—served Szasz well. He was asked to testify before a Senate subcommittee on the constitutional rights of the mentally ill. He wrote regularly for the *New York Times*, reviewing books in addition to publishing a seminal piece on the "the myth of mental illness" in the newspaper's influential Sunday magazine. His ideas would come to permeate not only psychiatric discussions but also legal ones in both scholarly venues and popular periodicals. He published dozens of articles on a truly impressive number of subjects— psychiatry, psychoanalysis, psychotherapy, psychology, neurology, law, criminology, education, political affairs, and secular humanism—and in an impressive range of leading journals (including *Harper's* and the *New Republic*). The same year (1973) that he would be interviewed on PBS television (by conservative journalist William F. Buckley Jr.), he would also be profiled in *Penthouse* magazine.[9] He would, in short, become recognized—and not without justification—as one of America's best-known and most influential living psychiatrists.[10]

By the early 1970s it would no longer be required to acknowledge Szasz's name in connection with his ideas, so "universal" and widely accepted had they by this time become. An essay in *Psychology Today* could, in 1973, open with these sentences: "Once we had grand inquisitors. Now we have psychologists."[11] And yet there would then be no mention whatsoever that Szasz had written much the same three years earlier: "Just as the Inquisition was the characteristic abuse of Christianity, so Institutional Psychiatry is the characteristic abuse of Medicine."[12] What might once have been understood as beyond the pale with respect to attacks on the mental health professions would come within only a dozen years to be understood as orienting insight.

How did this process of change come to pass? Through what mechanism had Szasz's radical skepticism—especially his argument that psychiatry was not a legitimate branch of medical science at all because there was nothing scientific about it—traveled from the furthest edges to the very center of social thought about the political meanings of mental illness in the United States? This chapter situates the positions of Thomas Szasz more firmly within their historical context as a means of illuminating first of all the remarkable extent to which his ideas reflected popular cynicism about psychiatry already circulating widely during the mid-1950s. The chapter further emphasizes that Szasz's most powerfully original and unorthodox contributions, rooted in his deep and abiding enmity toward the power he perceived psychiatry as wielding in jurisprudence, must be placed within preexisting debates in the legal and psychiatric professions ongoing since at least 1954 (when the introduction of new rules for the legal process of determining the criteria for pleading an insanity defense were established by the US Circuit Court of Appeals in the District of Columbia). But the chapter will also explicate how the often highly problematic and morally ambiguous ethical values articulated by Szasz nonetheless could have enormously important and beneficial effects—not only for the advocacy of disability rights but also for the nascent movements to achieve feminist aims and gay and lesbian equality before the law.

II

Not everyone considered the rise of a new therapeutic culture in the 1950s to be a necessary good. Psychological insights could also muddle common sense, as psychiatrist Jerome D. Frank indicated in 1957 when he observed how parents who devoured dozens of books and articles on child psychology sometimes lost sight of their own best instincts. Frank wrote that children were not "infinitely fragile and sensitive objects, to be blighted by a look or a word." On the contrary, Frank (himself a father of four) argued that "anger directed at a child's shortcomings is good for his self-esteem and contributes to his emotional growth: it implies that he *can* do better." As Frank indicated, parents should not necessarily hesitate "to smack Junior for fear of damaging his delicate little psyche."[13] Additionally, the sociologist Philip Rieff suggested sardonically in 1959 that Americans in the 1950s had begun to rely rather too indiscriminately on psychiatry to remedy the slightest nick and scratch of life:

> All experience is symptomatic now. People seek treatment because they sleep poorly, or have headaches, or feel apathetic toward loved ones, or because they are dissatisfied with their lives.

Patients complain of the boredom and vacuity of their inner freedom, and desire to learn how to fill it by means of strategies that
guarantee more direct satisfaction. In response to the increasingly diffused complaints of patients, psychoanalysis has had to
grow more openly didactic. Conversely, because of its increasingly ideological bent, psychoanalysis may be said to be partly
manufacturing its own clientele. As the aristocratic Roman sum-
moned his philosopher when he was ill, as the Christian went to
his pastor, so the dispirited modern visits his analyst.[14]

Yet further critiques of the torrent of therapeutic discourse were far
less tolerant, venting instead both bitter resentment and suspicion at the
postwar psychologization of American culture. In 1954 the popular general interest magazine, *Coronet*, had run an alliteratively (and oddly il-
literately) titled article, "Psychiatry Is for Psuckers." The article deliberately stoked newly formulated but eventually profoundly consequential
fears that psychiatry functioned as a method for delimiting the autonomy of individuals *and* for excusing their self-indulgence:

Every hour on the hour, thousands of American lives are being
needlessly ruined. Every year, increasing numbers of well-meaning
people, seeking to improve their way of life through psychiatric
means, fall into the clutches of psycho-quacks. Instead of getting the ethical help they desire, they often lose independence of
thought and action, sacrifice mental and emotional health, and
pay huge sums of money to those who do them serious harm.

What psychiatry accomplished, the *Coronet* piece further contended,
was the destruction of families and the weakening of community life.
The process within therapy sessions was absurd. "The subject knows
that he is supposed to say anything that comes into his mind. The more
bunk he concocts, the more pleased is his psycho-seer." And yet at the
same time the psychotherapeutic encounter was increasingly an activity
in which one had to participate simply so one could say one had. ("Today, in some social circles, you had no standing unless you are having or
have had some form of psychotherapy.") The outcome of psychotherapy, however, was that the patient learned "all sorts of psycho-phony
excuses for his shortcomings and anti-social conduct."[15]

Suspicion of the new therapeutic culture during the 1950s could also
flip into outright paranoia. Critics of psychiatry from Delaware to Cali-

fornia declared that "mental health" campaigns were "a Communist plot" and "a sinister Marxist weapon!": "Mental hygiene is a subtle and diabolical plan of the enemy to transform a free and intelligent people into a cringing horde of zombies."[16] Anti-Semitism lurked near the surface as well. At a 1956 Senate hearing, one invited witness opined: "Psychiatry is a foreign ideology; it is alien to any kind of American thinking. . . . I think it is important to realize that almost 100 percent of all psychiatric therapy is Jewish and that about 80 percent of the psychiatrists are Jewish. . . . I am opposed to any nation who attempts to usurp American nationality."[17]

There were also those who argued that psychiatry was a more home-grown means to stigmatize and suppress *conservative* political dissent. In 1956 anti-mental-health extremists argued that a bill passed in Congress for the construction of a new psychiatric hospital in Alaska represented "a plot to establish a concentration camp for political opponents of the Eisenhower Administration!"[18] And in 1957 a strikingly bizarre piece in the widely read conservative journal, *American Mercury* (where William F. Buckley Jr. had worked as associate editor before founding the far more influential *National Review* in 1955), also mapped the conspiratorial intentions of contemporary American psychiatry. Those who were advocating on behalf of the improved mental health of Americans had found their "activities are lubricated by generous streams of money," much of it federally funded. This might have been for the common good, the article suggested, were it not that these same leaders of "the mental health crusade" as well as all those conducting research in the "Behavioral Sciences" (the words appeared in quotes in the article) tended "to talk one thing and mean another." Here again political paranoia arose. As the article ominously observed of these mental health crusaders:

> Ostensibly, their goal is a nation free of destructive mental illness. Actually, the goal of some of the most vocal mental healthers is a nation which is made to their ideological image. This social-minded fringe of the mental health army equate mental illness with refusal of the individual to accept the social pattern which they, in their omniscience, seek to impose. To such propagandists, the accusation of mental ill health is a killing weapon with which to destroy a troublesome non-conformist. . . . It is conceivable that the charge of mental illness may be used as a convenient political or ideological weapon to discredit or imprison anyone who deviates from the established popular norms.[19]

Which brought *American Mercury* to discuss the curious case of Ezra Pound. At the time the poet had been held at St. Elizabeths Hospital for more than a decade on the grounds that his support for Mussolini's fascism had demonstrated his mental incompetence to stand trial on charges of treason. But what *American Mercury* saw in the Pound case was a miscarriage of justice. "If guilty, he should have been entitled to the ordinary procedures and recourses of our criminal court system." Indeed, the rhetorical question raised by the Pound case was that if the charge of insanity could be thrown at "the famous Pound," what chance did "any obscure individual" have "if he happened to get himself on the unpopular side of an issue which was invested with deep running popular political emotion"? As the article also went on to argue, if "would-be mind-controllers and brainwashers who see in mental health an inviting opportunity to remake human personality along Left-Liberal lines" were allowed to run the roost, then "the insanity charge can become a barbed weapon against dissent in any controversial national situation. Mental health enforcement can become a substitute for the citizen's legal rights." And what most enraged *American Mercury* was what it saw as the stark hypocrisy of a group like the American Civil Liberties Union, which had refused to defend Pound even though many among its membership had chosen to turn a blind eye to the evil acts of Joseph Stalin. "Pound's legal error," the *American Mercury* coolly concluded, "was that he chose the wrong dictator."[20] The circulation of such attitudes helps to explain how Szasz could become popular on the political right. But no less striking is the parallelism (albeit with directly opposite political implications) between the worries expressed by these right-wing commentators about psychiatric suppression of dissent and the critiques of psychiatry that subsequently would be formulated within the New Left and the counterculture.

III

When should a person who had committed a criminal offense be judged not guilty by reason of insanity? For more than a hundred years by the 1950s, the law had been clear only in its vagueness. Under the M'Naghten rule, first proposed in Great Britain in 1843 and later in the 1880s adopted in most jurisdictions in the United States, persons were held not responsible for their actions if they had suffered "a defect of reason" at the time their criminal actions occurred, and thus had not comprehended that what they had done was morally wrong. An incapacity to distinguish right from wrong became the standard legal test for insanity until it was modified in 1929 by the "irresistible impulse" doctrine, which held that insanity may be exculpatory if individuals had neither the cognitive capacity to adjudge "right" from "wrong" *nor* the ability to exercise control over their criminal acts. And this remained the test for criminal insanity until the 1950s.

In 1945 the United States Navy medically discharged Monte Durham on the grounds that he suffered from a "profound personality disorder." Two years later, after pleading guilty to interstate auto theft and while on parole, Durham attempted suicide. He was committed to St. Elizabeths Hospital. After his discharge Durham broke his parole by writing bad checks and was again committed to St. Elizabeths before being transferred to a prison. Upon his release Durham again wrote bad checks, and was again sent to St. Elizabeths. After his discharge Durham was arrested for housebreaking, whereupon at his pretrial hearing he was sent for a fourth time to St. Elizabeths—where he remained for more than a year until he was evaluated as competent to stand trial. The *Durham v. United States* trial in 1954 resulted in the so-called Durham rule, written by Judge David L. Bazelon of the Court of Appeals for the District of Columbia, who would come to be considered "one of the giants of mental health law."[21] The Durham opinion represented the first major reassessment of the criminal responsibility of the mentally ill in more than seventy years.

In his decision in *Durham v. United States*, Judge Bazelon rejected both the M'Naghten rule and the "irresistible impulse" test for insanity. Judge Bazelon held that existing standards for determining the mental fitness of defendants to stand trial were obsolete given "enormous developments in knowledge of mental life." As Bazelon wrote:

> We find that as an exclusive criterion the right-wrong test is inadequate in that (a) it does not take sufficient account of psychic realities and scientific knowledge and (b) it is based upon one symptom and so cannot validly be applied in all circumstances. We find that the "irresistible impulse" test is also inadequate in that it gives no recognition to mental illness characterized by brooding and reflection and so relegates acts caused by such illness to the application of the inadequate right-wrong test. We conclude that a broader test should be adopted.

In sum, the Durham decision required that a jury, based on expert testimony from psychiatrists, must determine not only whether the accused "suffered from a mental disease or defect" but also whether the crime was "the product of such mental abnormality."[22]

Many in the psychiatric and legal professions greeted Bazelon's new Durham rule with lavish praise. For years leading psychiatrists and legal scholars had argued publicly for the rejection of the M'Naghten rule, seeing it as untenable due to shifting medical conceptions of mental illness. For instance, in 1952 the American Psychiatric Association had reclassified both psychopathic and sociopathic personalities as a disease (rather than a nondisease) category in DSM-I—a fact that observers saw as giving particular urgency (and even inevitability) to a legal need to rethink the existing test for insanity. The new Durham rule was understood as a sign of great progress. As one psychiatrist wrote in assessing the positive impact he believed the Durham rule would have with respect to the psychiatrist who appeared as an expert witness to determine the mental competence of a defendant to stand trial, "the chief merit of the new rule is that it permits him to present his testimony in concepts that are familiar to him and that actually exist in mental life. He will be thinking and talking as a medical psychologist, rather than as a theologian or a metaphysician."[23] And another psychiatrist gushed how the Durham opinion "must be considered truly momentous and Judge Bazelon's opinion a vital turning point in the history of forensic psychiatry," adding that it represented "a bold, gigantic step in the direction of enlightened instead of formalistic justice, of humanism instead of bureaucratic obedience to a legal formula."[24] In 1956 the liberal Supreme Court justice, William O. Douglas, likewise applauded the Durham opinion, labeling it "imaginative" while suggesting it was "long overdue." Douglas also effused: "At last—at long last—we are on the road to distinguishing in the law between wilful people and sick people and in protecting society in a civilized way against the actions of both classes."[25] And in 1961 the American Psychiatric Association acknowledged Judge Bazelon's contribution, giving him the Isaac Ray Award for his contribution to the psychiatric aspects of jurisprudence.

Yet there were also those who argued strenuously that the new Durham rule would inevitably do far more harm than good. For these dissenters one concern raised by the Durham rule was how it seemed quite likely to diminish the extent to which persons guilty of criminal offenses—newly reconstituted as "helpless victims of disease"—would be held responsible for their actions.[26] Others expressed concern over the inherent haziness of the words "disease" and "defect" that were central to the rule; as one legal scholar noted, "it is difficult to see how any abnormalities that have a psychical dimension can be excluded from the meaning of the terms."[27] And the celebrated psychiatrist Frederic Wertham—best remembered for his postwar campaign against "the psychopathology of comic books" (but a crucial advocate for the plaintiffs in the *Brown v. Board of Education* decision in 1954 as well)—also strongly criticized the new rule.[28] While Wertham took aim at Bazelon, concluding that it was "doubtful" that the judge's new test for insanity would improve "the present unfortunate state of forensic psychiatry," he saved his sharpest criticisms for members of his own profession, noting that the Durham decision potentially opened the door for "psychoauthoritarianism" because it gave "undemocratic leeway to the partisan and/or bureaucratic expert, and, on account of its wording, lends itself to grave abuse."[29]

However, the sharpest and most eloquent early critique of the Durham rule may have come from a young Washington lawyer named Edward de Grazia (who had previously worked, however coincidentally, for a time at Bruno Bettelheim's Sonia Shankman Orthogenic School for children in Chicago, and who would later be applauded for his successful defense of William Burroughs's novel, *Naked Lunch*, against charges of obscenity). De Grazia argued that the Durham rule "is intended to, and very probably will, allow psychiatrists greater freedom to contribute to the courtroom solution" with respect to criminal responsibility, and this was precisely its problem. Psychiatrists tended to see criminal behavior as "symptomatic" of "mental disease," and therefore it would "be expected that few psychiatrists will hesitate to find the necessary causal connection between the crime and the disease, once they have determined the disease to exist, knowing a crime has been committed." De Grazia, in short, had identified another sort of faulty logic infecting the legal system's increasing reliance on psychiatric expert testimony: When a person commits a crime, that person may be judged mentally ill on the basis of having committed a crime. The illness must be the reason for the crime or the crime would not have been committed in the first place. Or as de Grazia stated the problem, "The average psychiatrist's attitude toward criminal behavior seems to embody, as a basic assumption, that such behavior is prima facie evidence of mental disease."[30] Therefore, de Grazia argued, the evaluation of a criminal by the psychiatrist was neither medical nor scientific, but must properly be recognized as a product of more purely subjective criteria.

Moreover, de Grazia strenuously questioned whether it was more desirable to be deemed "insane" than "guilty." After all, what fate awaited persons committed to the asylum? What "therapy" did they receive? How was it determined when they were "cured"? As de Grazia wryly noted, Monte Durham had been released from St. Elizabeths as "cured" on three separate occasions—after receiving insulin coma and electroshock treatments—and yet "none of these cures, however, seemed to cure him of his disposition toward crime." De Grazia also ardently attacked the practice of shock therapy, noting that it was "widely used today" even as "little is known about how shock treatment works" and "even less is said about how the patient feels." In sum, de Grazia added, none of the developments heralded by the new Durham rule boded especially well for the defendant advised to consider the insanity plea, especially a defendant who "might not wish to forego the certain austerity of prison for the uncertain luxury of a hospital for the insane." (This turned out to prefigure quite remarkably the terrible and fatal lesson Randle Patrick McMurphy came too late to learn in Kesey's *One Flew Over the Cuckoo's Nest*.[31])

The most celebrated skewering of the insanity defense in the 1950s emerged from unlikely circumstances. In 1952 on Michigan's Upper Peninsula a lieutenant in the United States Army had entered the Big Bay Lumberjack Tavern and, before a roomful of witnesses, shot and killed the tavern's proprietor. It was an open-and-shut case. Yet at trial defense attorney John D. Voelker argued that his client could not be held responsible for his actions that fateful night because the lieutenant had suffered temporary insanity at the time of the murder due to the fact that when his wife returned home she told him that the proprietor at the Big Bay Lumberjack Tavern had just beaten and raped her. Voelker put a psychiatrist on the stand as a witness for the defense. The psychiatrist concurred that in his expert opinion the lieutenant had been insane on that night and thereby could not be considered accountable for his actions since he neither had consciously planned to kill the tavern owner nor could remember having done so. The prosecution countered with their own psychiatrist who testified that the defendant was absolutely sane that fateful night and had no prior history of mental illness.

The jury sided with the defense and acquitted the lieutenant by reason of temporary insanity. And the judge, citing that the exonerated man's mental disorder had been temporary, did not wish to commit a decorated war veteran to an overcrowded mental hospital. He thereby ordered that the lieutenant be released from custody immediately. Having shot and killed a man in front of a crowd of witnesses, the lieutenant strolled out of the courtroom a free man.

In 1958 Voelker, now a justice on the Michigan Supreme Court, published *Anatomy of a Murder*, his thinly veiled fictionalized record (under the pseudonym "Robert Traver") of the Big Bay murder case. The next year, director Otto Preminger released his movie version of the case. Both as fiction and as film, *Anatomy of a Murder* satirized the alleged medical science of psychiatry. A plea of temporary insanity represented a loophole in the law, and in both novel and film it was fully apparent that the defense attorney identified the plea as having little to do with ethics or reality; it was simply a workable legal strategy. In the novel, when the lawyer first proposed an insanity plea to his client, the lieutenant objected that "this insanity business" was "pretty damned unscientific." He elaborated:

> Well, we can't prove insanity without a medical expert, you tell me. Yet you and I have already decided I was insane, we know that we're going to plead insanity—you tell me it's the only legal defense I've got. And even I can see that now. In other words you a mere lawyer and I a dumb soldier have between us decided that I was medically and legally insane. Having decided that, we must now go out and shop around for a medical expert to confirm *our* settled conclusion.

To which the attorney replied: "The present outlook and ritual of the law on legal insanity is almost as primitive and nonsensical as when we manacled and tortured our insane. I agree with you." The lieutenant pursued the question: "And supposing our chosen psychiatrist, when we find him, says I'm not nuts?" His lawyer candidly replied: "In that event, we keep shopping around, as you say, till we can live-trap one who does."[32]

Americans were clearly tickled and titillated by *Anatomy of a Murder*'s mockery of psychiatry and its often luridly graphic account of rape (or was it consensual infidelity?) and retribution. The novel found a remarkably receptive popular audience and became one of the biggest blockbuster publishing events of the decade. Sales of over a million copies in hardcover and three million copies in paperback kept the book on best-seller lists for more than a year. The film received seven Academy Award nominations, including for best picture, best actor, and best adapted screenplay.

IV

In the writings of Thomas Szasz, civil libertarian, legal and psychiatric perspectives on the Durham rule *and* both populist and rarified intellectual arguments against the incursion of therapeutic thinking into everyday lives of ordinary Americans found coalescence. Szasz believed that psychiatrists and other mental health professionals were like astrologers in the sense that they too theorized at extraordinary length about processes that had no basis in reality. Planets did not determine human behavior, and Szasz asked his readers to consider how there was just as little truth in the idea of mental illness. He granted that psychiatrists who thought of themselves as investigative, curious social scientists like anthropologists or sociologists might potentially have some value, especially if they shared their expert knowledge freely with others. But psychiatrists who engaged in the business of sorting other people into categories or used their authority to manipulate and coerce other individuals into participating in whatever role-playing a particular society endorsed were henchmen for the state.

Szasz had two core passions. He was disturbed by the way the incursions of psychiatry into the realm of the law caused the entire system of taking responsibility for adjudicating right from wrong to break down. Szasz was also outraged that the mental hospital functioned "as an extra-legal system of social control" that imprisoned persons who had broken no laws, and in 1960 he called for "a Bill of Rights for the 'mentally ill.'"[33] On both counts, psychiatry, Szasz was beginning to suggest, posed a grave threat to civil liberties in a democratic society. He would make this explicit in 1962 when he called psychiatrists "ecclesiastic witchhunters," and in 1963 when he wrote that "psychiatrists are permitted to do what no one else may do—namely, deprive Americans of their constitutional rights."[34] Ever more forcefully, Szasz pushed the case that the blurring of the boundaries between psychiatry and law signaled the encroachment of totalitarianism into American democracy.

One early advocate of Szasz's ideas was sociologist Erving Goffman, who acted as if he had found in the psychiatrist a sort of intellectual soul mate. When Goffman explained in *Asylums* that mental illness and mental health were labels that had only a marginal basis in social reality, he quoted Szasz:

> More precisely, according to the common-sense definition, mental health is the ability to play whatever the game of social living might consist of and to play it well. Conversely, to refuse to play, or to play badly, means that the person is mentally ill. The question may now be raised as to what are the differences, if any, between social non-conformity (or deviation) and mental illness.

The radical answer, according to Szasz (and again approvingly cited by Goffman) consisted "only of a difference in our *attitudes* toward our subject."[35]

What is ironic, however, is that the seemingly similar perspectives of Goffman and Szasz toward mental illness resulted from diametrically opposed attitudes toward the suffering of the mentally ill. Confronted by the afflictions he witnessed within the "total institution" of the mental hospital, Goffman had radically amended his prior conception in which a human self was not much more than an effect produced by social interactions; in *Asylums*, Goffman posited a preexisting self that could (and was) subjected to suffering. Yet Szasz took a drastically different view; seeing the pain of the mentally ill did not cause him to acknowledge that pain but rather to question its legitimacy. For Szasz the "pain" that an individual expressed was a culturally bound conception, and one that could not be taken at face value and on its own terms. "Pain" (and it was often his choice to place the word in quotation marks) had most frequently to be interpreted as an expression of a demand an individual wished to place (whether consciously or not) upon his or her social environment. As Szasz wrote in 1957:

> The communicative meaning of "pleasure" may be compared and contrasted with the communicative meaning of "pain." The latter usually expresses an accusation directed toward a significant person or a demand for some sort of help from him. . . . Whereas *"pain" is a command for action, "pleasure"* (which may be equated here with contentment or happiness) *calls for no action.* The ego's essential experience and wish is for *no change* from the existing situation. Insofar as this affect communicates a command (or a wish), it is a command for the persistence of the *status quo.*[36]

Thus "pain" in Szasz's world had always to be interrogated. He considered it to be often a form of connivance.

In *The Myth of Mental Illness: Foundations of a Theory of Personal Conduct* (1961), Szasz's controversial ideas reached a large—and largely receptive—general audience. Among other things, Szasz here expressed utter hostility for the idea that mental illness might have a physiological source, asserting that "the notion of a person 'having mental illness' is scientifically crippling."[37] Szasz also, however, explained that it was not solely the psychiatrist who deserved the rap for the social invention of "mental illness." Szasz spread the blame. He noted that just as every comic needed a straight man, so "a schizophrenogenic parent requires schizophrenic offspring," and an agoraphobic wife required "a certain kind of 'protective' (controlling) husband, and so forth" (290). But his

most essential point was that all human beings were—deep down—
always responsible for their own actions, and every life was the result
of decisions an individual had made.[38] Cheating, lying, and other forms
of deceit were elaborate techniques used by the weak to gain advantage, and "mental illness," in his view, was simply another means of
subterfuge. As Szasz wrote, "impersonation in general and lying in particular are employed as strategies for self-advancement" (270).[39] Szasz
emphasized the extent to which psychiatrists participated in the games
their patients played; hysterics and other psychiatric patients "imperson-
ated the sick role" in "accordance with the rules of the medical game,"
while "concomitantly, psychiatrists and psychoanalysts, by accepting
the problems of their patients as manifestations of 'illness,' commit a
complementary act of impersonation: they impersonate physicians and
play the role of the medical therapist" (306).

The potential for using Szasz's fulminations—as the basis *both* for
useful critiques of the preening pretensions as well as the normative impact of psychiatry *and* as the basis for an unwillingness to confront the
possibility that mental illnesses could be either organic or simply mys-
terious but nonetheless quite real in origin—was apparent. Szasz's core
claims had two incompatible implications that neither his book nor any
of his later work would ever successfully reconcile. Nor were these to be
reconciled by either his numerous critics or his many enthusiasts, all of
whom tended to rivet onto one or the other strand of Szasz's thinking.

On the one hand, there was Szasz's perspective—immensely useful
for a range of subsequent politically critical projects—that the label of
madness served as a means to punish nonconformists. ("Those who cannot play the game of 'social normality' are assigned to the game of 'psychiatric illness'" [293].) In addition, Szasz believed that environment
and education, and, in general, "the effects of postnatal experiences" far
outweighed the "role of biological characteristics" (229). He expressly
repudiated the idea that whites were superior to persons of color or that
men were superior to women; the pertinence for later antiracist and feminist work was clear.[40]

On the other hand, and as previously mentioned, Szasz had an intense preoccupation with the idea of personal responsibility. He interpreted mental illness as a (albeit often unconsciously deployed) strategy
for evading responsibility and/or exercising power in the games of interpersonal interactions. It was in keeping with this strand of his thinking that Szasz continued to write eloquently about the legal profession's
increasing use of the insanity defense and the ever-growing meddling of
psychiatrists in judicial decisions. He had argued in 1958 that this trend

made a mockery of the rule of law and "runs counter to our entire concept of the ethics of a secular democratic society."[41] But it was also in keeping with this strand that Szasz was able to dismiss the very idea of mental illness as anything other than a label or a ruse. For example, in detailed readings of the work of Jean-Martin Charcot and subsequent experts on hysteria and on psychosomatic symptoms, Szasz laid out his position that playing at being mad allowed individuals to control their situation. Helplessness and illness were mere tactics of domination (even as "ill" persons may well have hidden their own motives also from themselves). For Szasz—in at least this one way a classic Freudian—"'symptoms' at once hide and express" what is really going on in human interactions (297).[42] And what was really going on was always a game of power. Thus Szasz could offer this incredible (and incredibly insensitive) formulation: "In the hysterical transaction, disability is used as a coercive maneuver to force others to provide for one's needs" (198).

Yet Szasz also had his moments of powerful identification with those individuals deemed to be mentally ill and confined in asylums, and in the years that followed, Szasz offered increasingly incendiary commentary on the state of psychiatry and the psychiatric institution. In 1962, for instance, Szasz asserted (in a manner that also echoed Goffman):

> To be called mentally ill is like being called a Negro in Alabama or a Jew in Nazi Germany—or to be called a schizophrenic in a courtroom. You are finished, unless somebody defends you. You can't stand trial, you have no rights, you can't get out of the hospital. Everybody is protecting you. Even the District Attorney is protecting you. . . . Everybody all of a sudden wants to help, and you have no more enemies. Someone said, "Protect me from my friends, and I will take care of my enemies." The so-called patient has no enemies; everyone wants to help.[43]

And in 1963 Szasz was making summary statements like this: "Psychiatric hospitals are, of course, prisons."[44]

Perhaps unsurprisingly, the collective weight of his opinions brought its own set of consequences. Szasz became the bête noire of American psychiatry; his milder critics merely characterized his writing as "tendentious and wildly misleading."[45] His harsher critics were vicious and personal in their attacks; Szasz was labeled "a bird that fouls its own nest," and was caricatured as somehow typically Hungarian in his outlook.[46] They additionally characterized Szasz as "irresponsible, reprehensible, and dangerous" and his writings as possibly a form of right-wing propaganda.[47] In 1964 law professor Henry Weihofen condescendingly said (with Szasz in attendance) during an address to the American Psychiatric Association annual convention: "The fears about what goes on in mental hospitals that Dr. Szasz fosters are seized upon by the right-wing extremists with whom he has been playing footsie."[48] And in late 1962 the commissioner of the New York Department of Mental Hygiene sought to bar Szasz from teaching his seminar on psychotherapy at the Syracuse Psychiatric Hospital; his case was placed under investigation by order of Governor Nelson Rockefeller. These actions led in turn to a statement of protest from the American Association of University Professors.[49]

Yet even as he was a polarizing figure, Szasz managed to accrue powerful allies and influential admirers. Conservative William F. Buckley Jr. was a booster for Szasz, seeing fit in 1963 to publish him in *National Review*. At the other end of the spectrum, the progressive Supreme Court justice, Arthur J. Goldberg, praised Szasz in 1964 for having made "an eloquent plea for the right of the mentally ill" and having called attention to "the abuses—existing and potential—of human rights," also specifically in self-defined "enlightened mental health programs and procedures."[50] And psychotherapist Jay Haley, part of the original Bateson group in Palo Alto that devised the double bind theory (and now editor of *Family Process*), went out of his way to defend Szasz from his critics, observing in 1965 that "instead of being indignant, we should rejoice to find a clear and thoughtful intellect in this profession."[51]

Controversies neither slowed Szasz down nor diminished the intensity of his convictions. If anything they fueled his mission. Szasz soon broadened the scope of his libertarian pursuits, arguing for the inherent legality of suicide, stating how "in a free society, a person must have the right to injure or kill himself."[52] Suicide, as Szasz put it in an essay for the *New York Times Magazine* in 1966, "should be recognized as a basic human right."[53] And Szasz also began to apply ideas he gleaned from the perceived failures of psychiatry to advocate for concerns seemingly unrelated to the rights of mental patients. Prominent among these were publications as early as 1962 in defense of a woman's unrestricted right to birth control as well as to an abortion.[54]

V

Many ideas about psychiatry and the law that Thomas Szasz promoted with distinctive flourish and tireless zeal came shortly to undergird a wide range of left-liberal social critiques during the 1960s. An important example was "the Therapeutic State," a concept Szasz introduced in 1963, elaborating that it represented "the major implication of psychiatry as an instrument of social control." In any Therapeutic State, Szasz wrote, the supposedly magnanimous and humanistic goal of society was to ensure individuals who were adjudged unable to care for themselves "the right" to have care provided for them. Certainly this was the case in the USSR, which had developed an "explicitly 'therapeutic' program" for dispensing with disobedient citizenry. "As a result," Szasz noted, "the criminal trial in the Soviet Union focuses on establishing whether or not the defendant was a 'bad boy,' not on whether a crime was committed." And this had begun to happen in the United States. As Szasz warned: "There has been a slow but steady drift in American law toward considering not only persons formally discredited by psychiatrists, but everyone, a little bit 'insane,' hence 'irresponsible' and in need of governmental 'therapy.'"[55]

During the 1960s, the concept of the Therapeutic State gained ground. And many who promoted the idea reflected a direct indebtedness to Szasz's conspiratorial take on psychiatric power. Notable among these was psychiatrist Ronald Leifer, who had done his residency training under Szasz's supervision in Syracuse, and who decried the expansion of "community psychiatry"—ostensibly a liberalizing maneuver to expand services to the populace—as in effect "the extension of coercive mental health practices" that would in reality only result in fostering involuntary treatments while serving further as an extralegal means of broadening the power of the state to intrude in people's lives.[56]

Even more significant were the contributions of law professor Nicholas N. Kittrie, who utilized the concept of the Therapeutic State to promote a rather more tempered—if equally vigorous—critique of how psychiatric methods functioned to erode civil liberties. Like the liberal jurist Arthur Goldberg, Kittrie also found in Szasz's framework a valuable means by which to criticize the expansion of psychiatric authority within the legal system. Since 1960 Kittrie had argued that the compulsory treatment of mental patients represented a possible infringement of due process.[57] By 1966 Kittrie had adopted the phrase "Therapeutic State" as his own, contending that more and more classes of individuals (for example, alcoholics, drug addicts, juvenile delinquents) were accountable not to criminal jurisdiction, but rather were subjected to "new types of borderland proceedings, lodged between the civil and criminal law." As Kittrie observed, this new approach was being "carried out in the name of the new social aims of therapy," even if in reality it often resulted in indeterminate periods of incarceration and yielded unclear or ineffective results. While the official goal was, in other words, "rehabili-tation," these new proceedings were more accurately resulting in "less judicially cumbersome and more individualized and informal programs of social control."[58] As Kittrie argued forcefully in 1971: "Surely the right to live one's life free from bodily and psychological alteration is ba-sic to our scheme of society. The ability to remain as you are is clearly a right suggested by the general pattern of the Bill of Rights."[59]

The statements and actions of Bruce J. Ennis, staff attorney for the American Civil Liberties Union and director of the Mental Health Law Project in New York, further challenged the sheer arbitrariness of the law when it came to issues of mental illness. Testifying before the Sen-ate in 1969, and referencing the scholarship of both Szasz and Goffman, Ennis said:

> Our society is remarkably, though properly, reluctant to confine persons solely because of what they might do in the future. Prob-ably fifty to eighty per cent of all ex-felons will commit future crimes, but we do not confine them. . . . Of all the identifiably dangerous groups in society, only the "mentally ill" are singled out for preventive detention, and . . . they are probably the least dangerous as a group. . . . Why should society confine a person if he is dangerous and mentally ill but not if he is dangerous and sane? . . . For every man who, if at liberty, would take his life, or assault his neighbor, there are thousands in confinement who would not. For every man who, if at liberty, would embarrass or destroy his career, there are thousands whose careers are de-stroyed because of confinement.[60]

In 1972 Ennis published *Prisoners of Psychiatry* (with an introduction by Szasz), a terrifying set of case studies about individuals who had not been convicted of any crime but whose lives had nonetheless been devas-tated by diagnoses of mental illness. The opening case related the story of Charlie Youngblood—an African American and a veteran injured during boot camp—who in 1968 had become so frustrated by the Vet-eran Administration's repeated refusals to grant him disability benefits that he had made a phone call to the Justice Department in Washington, DC, and said of the attorney general that he would "break his ass" if nothing was done about his claim for benefits.[61] The secretary became so upset that she contacted the FBI who, the next day, sent agents to ar-rest Youngblood on charges of threatening to harm the attorney gen-eral. Declared incompetent to stand trial, Youngblood was slated to be indefinitely committed to a mental hospital when he contacted Ennis. (After two years of court battles, all charges against Youngblood were dropped, and he did receive his VA disability payments.)

Experiences like those of Charlie Youngblood's led Ennis to conclude in 1974 that the "expert" judgments offered by psychiatrists during commitment proceedings were often worse than useless. They were no more reliable—or valid—a means for assisting judges or juries with determining a defendant's potential "dangerousness" or assessing a defendant's need for hospitalization than simply "flipping coins in the courtroom."[62] In an effort to promote a more just legal system with respect to the treatment of the mentally ill, Ennis and the Mental Health Law Project in 1973 and 1974 published a three-volume (1,500-page) handbook, *Legal Rights of the Mentally Handicapped*, an indispensable and pioneering resource for advocates in the just-emerging field of disability rights.[63]

During the later 1960s and early 1970s, perspectives on the civil rights of individuals deemed "insane" generated an impressive amount of legal scholarship. "Mental illness" began to appear in this scholarship within quotations marks, as it did for instance in a discussion of how attorneys might better protect the rights of individuals faced with involuntary commitment.[64] Legal scholars began openly to assert (as one did in 1965) that "inalienable rights without which no citizen would consider living are denied mental patients, and these patients with various mental maladies become referred to as 'inmates' who are 'institutionalized' in 'mental prisons.'"[65] There were discussions of how best to restructure medical practice with respect to informed consent.[66] And legal scholars began to ask the question: "Are psychopaths merely 'nonconformists'?"[67]

Despite the criticisms from the medical world, then, the ideas promoted by Szasz became integral to a revolution in thinking about the complicated relationship between psychiatry and the law. Even when he was not directly cited, the presence of Szasz was palpably evident. This was clear, for instance, when a community health expert observed in 1968 that accused felons had more legal protections—such as right to counsel—than persons facing allegations that they were mentally ill.[68] It was no less clear when Harvard law professor Alan M. Dershowitz wrote also in 1968 that the legal status of persons confronted with prospects of involuntary commitment was untenable because the courts had seen their authority usurped by the psychiatric profession. According to Dershowitz, courts sat "merely to review decisions made by psychiatrists," psychiatric decisions that frustrated Dershowitz because he saw them as based on criteria so vague and "so meaningless as even to preclude effective review."[69] The following year (and anticipating the opinions of Bruce Ennis) Dershowitz further questioned the value of expert testimony of psychiatrists, observing that "among every group of inmates presently confined on the basis of psychiatric predictions of violence, there are only a few who would, and many more who would not, actually engage in such conduct if released."[70] Dershowitz had unquestionably studied Szasz.[71]

Even Judge David L. Bazelon began to carefully seek a means by which he could reverse his prior decision on the interrelationship between psychiatry and the law. The father of the Durham rule wished by the 1970s to find a way to disown his progeny—a task that had been made easier by the rejection of the rule in several federal courts and by the assessment in 1967 that the rule amounted to "a disaster whose lessons have yet to be learned."[72] And so in 1972 Bazelon officially abandoned the Durham rule, having himself become disillusioned by the ambivalent role played by psychiatric expert testimony.[73] Looking back in 1974, Bazelon reflected his frustration when he noted that the Durham rule "had failed to take the issue of criminal responsibility away from the experts."[74]

It is difficult not to surmise—despite the indirect means by which he chose to declare it—that Judge Bazelon was admitting that Thomas Szasz had been right all along. In 1975, a mere dozen years after Szasz had made a similar claim, Bazelon went so far as to observe how "the medical model of 'sickness' could be and was perverted" in *both* the Soviet Union and America. "We do not like to compare ourselves to the Soviet Union in this regard," Bazelon wrote, "but I am sad to say that psychiatrists in the United States, wittingly or unwittingly, react to the institutional pressures of their employers in a manner which is analogous in principle, at least, to behavioralist professionals in the Soviet Union."[75] What had been considered in the early 1960s revisionism of the most outrageous variety had by the early 1970s emerged as the new orthodoxy.

The revolution Szasz promoted in legal thinking about the mentally ill spread also in more unusual legal directions. He was prominently and extensively cited in a law review essay from 1968 on the need to reevaluate the practice of using psychiatric testimony in workmen's compensation cases to determine whether workers were telling the truth about their pain.[76] He was cited in law articles that analyzed how (or if) the potential mental illness of a parent should be adjudicated in child custody proceedings, as well as how (or if) courts may require professional psychiatric counseling for married couples in divorce proceedings.[77] He was referenced in a 1968 legal brief (on behalf of appellant Timothy Leary) on the use of psychedelics with respect to religious ritual and freedom.[78]

And then there was Szasz's important connection to the newly evolving legal discussion of women's and gay and lesbian concerns. Feminist and gay and lesbian legal scholars located in Szasz invaluable intellectual and cultural support on a whole range of social issues. It was becoming common sense, as one law essay noted in passing, that "the myth of mental illness" served "as a justification for the subordinate social status of women."[79] An essay in defense of the right of lesbian mothers to child custody cited Szasz among those who subscribed to a "nonsickness" view of homosexuality.[80] (This made perfect sense; Szasz had written cuttingly in 1963 about the real reason legal sanctions against homosexuality persisted: "Legislators are notoriously wary of trying to repeal laws prohibitive of sexual conduct. It is bad politics to do so."[81]) And Szasz was cited in a law review essay critical of judges who denied alimony to feminist or lesbian mothers. This essay summarized its position in terms Szasz would certainly have found congenial: "Law and psychiatry collaborate to produce a definition of mental illness that suggests the social position and political needs of the formulators."[82] The designation "mentally ill," in short, was increasingly understood to have a political function.

The world of ideas pressed by Thomas Szasz took hold far beyond the reaches of the intelligentsia. By the early 1970s several groups within the counterculture and the New Left were protesting the treatment of mental patients. The Radical Therapist Collective praised Szasz's contributions to the critique of traditional psychiatry.[83] The Insane Liberation Front adopted wholesale the Szaszian perspective when it demanded "an end to the existence of mental institutions and all the oppression they represent."[84] The ex-psychiatric patients affiliated with the publication *Madness Network News* repeatedly cited Szasz as a key progenitor.[85] An anthology titled *Radical Psychology* excerpted the writings of both Goffman and Szasz, and while it criticized them both as "the least politically radical in the book," it nonetheless also praised them for seeing "mental illness and psychology as forms of ideology."[86]

Activists and members of the counterculture found confirmation in the widely circulating concepts concerning the socially coercive power of the psychiatrist. The psychiatrist was "a person who in essence plays the role of a policeman," as a pseudonymous commentator who wrote frequently on issues pertaining to mental illness stated in an underground newspaper from San Francisco in 1970.[87] "Therapy today has become a commodity, a means of social control," stated the Radical Therapist Collective in its manifesto. "We reject such an approach to people's distress." The manifesto concluded: "We must realize that many people called 'mentally ill' have been socially traumatized by our society. While we do not pretend that all mental suffering is socially caused, we are alert to the social and political roots of much of it. These roots can no longer be ignored—they must be dealt with in a significant way."[88] As a mental patient who called herself Pandora wrote in 1970 of life in Oregon's Dammasch State Hospital, the asylum where she was involuntarily committed: "This is a state holding institution much like other holding institutions (schools, prisons)." All the institution sought was to "make the patients more manageable, smoother, and shinier!" There was "no interest in 'curing' you or rehabilitating you (no more than, say the average prison), even according to some perverted definition of sanity!" And Pandora energetically asserted: "There is no medical definition of sanity! It's all a myth!"[89]

Such condemnatory assessments of psychiatric abuses were hardly limited to the counterculture or New Left. In 1964, Karl Menninger, considered "the dean of American psychiatrists," cautioned that because "a label can blight the life of a person even after his recovery from mental illness," psychiatrists had to acknowledge that their use of medical terminology, "instead of helping to comfort and counsel and heal people . . . often cause[s] despair."[90] By the later 1960s and early 1970s, there was broad popular sentiment that psychiatry could not and should not be interpreted as an ideologically unbiased profession. *Psychology Today* in 1969 noted how unscientific psychiatrists invariably turned out to be, so that "the psychiatrist who is politically liberal, psychoanalytically oriented and deeply concerned with social justice will be more likely to find a given offender nonresponsible than the psychiatrist who is more politically conservative, more biologically oriented and more concerned with individual rights and privileges."[91] (That same year two psychiatrists had even testified before a District Court in Florida that a hippie suffered from mental illness because he advocated free love and drug use.[92]) In 1974 the *New York Times* would assert how "sociopath" had become "a catchall word for public nuisances, which tells less about the character of the individual so labeled than about the predicament of the labelers."[93] That the reputation of psychiatry was under attack from multiple quarters was further evidenced by the cult status accorded philosopher Robert M. Pirsig's best-selling (if frequently obscurant) memoir, *Zen and the Art of Motorcycle Maintenance* (1974), with its allusions to the author's legal (and involuntary) commitment to a mental hospital, his medical diagnosis as "schizophrenic," his extensive experience with electroshock treatments, and his rejection of psychiatry as a model for grasping the essence of his (or anyone else's) humanity.[94]

As for Szasz, and however perversely, he had in the meantime moved into the orbit of L. Ron Hubbard. The founder of the Church of Scientology and no stranger to paranoid delusions, Hubbard was certainly Szasz's equal in his uncompromising criticisms of psychiatric practices. In 1969 Hubbard published his treatise, *Crime and Psychiatry*, in which he blamed psychiatrists for—of all things—"soaring crime statistics." Like Szasz, Hubbard advocated a value system based on personal responsibility, a system he believed psychiatrists actively subverted and undermined. And adapting the term *crime* in yet another way, Hubbard fumed that "crimes of extortion, mayhem and murder are done daily by these men in the name of 'practice' and 'treatment.'" And: "There is not one institutional psychiatrist alive who, by ordinary criminal law, could not be arraigned and convicted of extortion, mayhem and murder. Our files are full of evidence on them."[95] That same year Szasz and Hubbard cofounded the Citizens Commission on Human Rights, a nonprofit "human rights advocacy group" that has sought for more than forty years to investigate and expose "psychiatry's abusive and coercive practices."[96] In 1971 Szasz helped as well to establish the Libertarian Party, ensuring among other things that the party "called for a halt to government-psychiatry mind control operations."[97] These aspects of Szasz's career were, and have remained, less widely known and acknowledged by the counterculture and New Left at the time and by scholars in more recent years.[98]

VI

As the discussions of R. D. Laing, Gregory Bateson, Erving Goffman, and Jules Henry among others in chapters 2 and 3 indicate, psychiatrist Thomas Szasz was far from the sole public intellectual in the 1950s and 1960s to advocate openly on behalf of the position that the condition known as madness had above all to be viewed through the lens of a social diagnosis. Madness did not exist outside of social relations—interpersonal, familial, or institutional. Yet each of these thinkers pressed for a different emphasis with respect to the meanings of what "caused" madness.

What distinguished Thomas Szasz from this cohort was not just the provocative lengths to which he was willing to pursue his opinions. He also had a complete disinterest in the view that an etiology of "mental illness" could be located within abnormal familial patterns and an indifference toward the idea that institutions could literally drive individuals crazy. Szasz instead called for the "abolition" of "mental illness" as a category of human self-knowledge.

Yet the absolutism Szasz advocated came bundled together almost inevitably with a set of serious theoretical difficulties and moral ambiguities—many of which I have also sought to outline in this chapter. Szasz effectively denied the reality of "pain." He scoffed at the notion that persons truly suffered from their afflictions, believing instead that "suffering" was a form of "malingering."[99] He had little use for the actual experiences of the mentally ill. He had no patience at all for the possibility that psychiatry could (or might desire to) reform itself in order to become better aligned with more humane (and humanistic) procedures and policies. To Szasz, efforts at psychiatric "reform" were cosmetic adjustments made to mask further the corrosive and intrusive power of American psychiatry, in other words, to make psychiatry function as a more efficient tool of social control bludgeoning the civil liberties of Americans. This has been the perspective Szasz has been arguing (and arguing and arguing) with grueling consistency for more than half a century.

At the same time, Szasz's all-or-nothing ideological stance pressed his opponents, especially within the psychiatric profession, to delineate their defense for a host of medical procedures and legal practices—like electroshock treatments or like the mechanisms by which persons were involuntarily committed to an asylum or by which they were counseled to plead insanity in a courtroom.[100] As this chapter has also sought to outline, the absolutism of Szasz additionally mobilized social and political activism within the legal system: on behalf of the rights of the mentally ill; on behalf of women's rights; on behalf of the rights of gays and lesbians; on behalf of drug addicts, juvenile delinquents, hippies, and anyone else society deemed to be living and acting outside social norms and conventions. In these respects, it remains remarkable to contemplate the upheavals within the social and cultural landscape to which the ideas Szasz promoted during the 1960s and 1970s were to contribute.

What Szasz managed to advance was a new common sense that the emperor—that is, the professional psychiatrist—wore no clothing. Psychiatry bore the most indirect relationship to medical science, or so Szasz insisted. And his unapologetic and uncompromising outrage—voiced at a moment when there was an already-existing, widely available, and broadly populist discourse of discontent over the rise of psychiatric authority in the United States—was soon to be taken by many as both morally righteous and ethically urgent.

Part Two: The Revolution in Feeling

5 The Insanity Trip

What is called insane denotes that which in the determination of a particular society must not be thought. Madness is a concept that fixes limits; the frontiers of madness define what is "other." A mad person is someone whose voice society doesn't want to listen to, whose behavior is intolerable, who ought to be suppressed. . . . In every society, the definitions of sanity and madness are arbitrary—are, in the largest sense, political.

Susan Sontag, "Approaching Artaud" (1973)[1]

I

Preoccupation with madness intensified just as the Vietnam War escalated. The war made it appear as though the world had turned upside-down, with the categories of "normal" and "abnormal" entirely inverted. Countercultural critics of the war were filled with anguish at the idea that dropping napalm could constitute sanity, and they were no less stunned that they were the ones pathologized as unstable and deviant by the US government and the war's supporters. No surprise that Joseph Heller's *Catch-22* (1961) became ever more popular as the war dragged on. Heller's novel had transposed the double bind theory to a war zone in which the sane soldier could not be found psychologically unfit to complete a highly dangerous mission because only a sane soldier would ever request to be declared unfit—while also the insane soldier had to complete the mission since he would never make such a request. (There was no way out.) Yet many in this time also came to believe that "madness is purification," that deliberately going crazy could be a way to achieve greater mental and emotional health and well-being, that breaking down (with or without the help of lysergic acid diethylamide commonly known as LSD) was also a key to breaking through.[2] There were, in short, many reasons for "the insanity trip" (to borrow Susan Sontag's rueful phrase) to acquire such prominence during the Vietnam War era.[3]

Identification with the supposedly liberatory elements of derangement and mental illness swept through the popular arts and academic disciplines, leaving little untouched in its wake. In addition, however, cross-identification with the mad could also become a way of articulating a kind of existential despair. The despair was widespread, and had already been in evidence during the Summer of Love and what was considered the peak of flower power.

This was especially clear at the two-week-long Dialectics of Liberation Congress organized in July 1967 in London by psychiatrists R. D. Laing and David Cooper and their associates. Gregory Bateson, Jules Henry, Paul Goodman, Herbert Marcuse, Stokely Carmichael, Allen Ginsberg, Julian Beck, and Paul Sweezy were all in attendance. The Congress was the decade's major international gathering of the counterculture and radical left's leading intellectual luminaries. (Even Erving Goffman had been invited—but declined to attend.) Many participants advanced antipsychiatric theories. It nonetheless became quickly apparent that no one had any answers. The celebrity speakers conflicted about almost everything, from the benefits and demerits of political violence and the potentials of drug use to how best to change the world. A sense of hopelessness hung over the entire proceeding.

Beat poet Ginsberg may have been the most eloquent on the need to fundamentally rethink the project of being human. He noted that all across the planet life forms were swiftly being decimated by the actions of *Homo sapiens*. He intoned that the ideal response to such dire eventualities was to attend closely to the wisdoms of shamans and spirits. One had to undergo "deconditioning," Ginsberg said, in order to recognize that we all project ugly fantasies onto others—fantasies fueled by hatred and paranoia that keep us alone and separate from the communalism of human existence. Ginsberg called on the audience to join him in "totally neutralizing all negative affect" and to "demonstrate tranquility" toward all. But he also mused that "the world is a madhouse and everybody's nuts," and that it was quite possible that "the whole fucking shithouse" could soon go "up and clunks."[4]

It appeared profoundly true to many radicals during the second half of the 1960s that society had gone crazy and that the only sane response was to resist the madness—and risk being labeled mentally ill for doing so. At certain times such contentions took on great ethical urgency, as for instance when nonviolent Catholic activists Philip and Daniel Berrigan, protesting the Vietnam War, argued with tremendous moral power that the burning of Vietnamese children (with Dow Chemical's napalm) constituted an act of madness—not their own burning (with homemade napalm) of draft files at Selective Service offices in Catonsville, Maryland.[5] And when the Trappist monk Thomas Merton wrote with savage sarcasm of war and torture in "A Devout Meditation in Memory of Adolf Eichmann," madness was also very much on his mind:

> Torture is nothing new, is it? We ought to be able to rationalize a little brainwashing, and genocide, and find a place for nuclear war, or at least for napalm bombs, in our moral theology. Certainly some of us are doing our best along those lines already. There are hopes! ... Those who have invented and developed atomic bombs, thermonuclear bombs, missiles; who have planned the strategy of the next war; who have evaluated the various possibilities of using bacterial and chemical agents: these are not the crazy people, they are the *sane* people. The ones who coolly estimate how many millions of victims can be considered expendable in a nuclear war, I presume they do all right with Rorschach ink blots too. On the other hand, you will probably find that the pacifists and the ban-the-bomb people are, quite seriously, just as we read in *Time*, a little crazy ... perhaps we must say that in a society like ours the worst insanity is to be totally without anxiety, totally "sane."[6]

At the same moment cult films like Swedish director Ingmar Bergman's *Persona* (1966) and French director Philippe de Broca's *King of Hearts* (1966) were (each in its own way) reflections and further popularizations of R. D. Laing's ideas about the socially manufactured nature of madness, as they also advanced antiwar sentiments. Far more comic though no less earnest was an attempt in 1967 by antiwar activists "to form a ring of exorcism sufficiently powerful to raise the Pentagon three hundred feet," as journalist Norman Mailer recorded the scene. An inspired lunacy informed antimilitarist commitments: "In the air the Pentagon would then, went the presumption, turn orange and vibrate until all evil emissions had fled this levitation. At that point the war in Vietnam would end."[7]

Yet the Vietnam War was about more than dropping bombs from planes. The war also brought the topic of intimate human violence into sharp relief as a category for widespread social and political analysis. How had it been possible for "ordinary" and seemingly sane young American men at My Lai in March 1968 to engage in the rape, torture, and mass killing of unarmed South Vietnamese citizens?[8] How could these men obey orders—as they subsequently claimed at their trial they had done—when they must have understood those orders to be so horrifically unconscionable? Or was this not about obedience at all, but rather about voluntaristic, even enthusiastic, cruelty?[9]

Nor was the My Lai massacre taken to be atypical. On the contrary, as philosopher Herbert Marcuse commented, the guilt America felt about My Lai was "the guilt of a society in which massacres and killing and body counts have become part of the normal mental equipment."[10] Those within the antiwar movement came quickly to accept the bitter conclusion as well that it was absolutely possible to incite individuals to perpetrate the most horrendous atrocities on innocent persons.[11] At the same time many on the left and within the counterculture also came to accept that the US military was working to "brainwash" its soldiers to behave like sociopaths so that they might be more effective in combat and/or to remove all sanctions against immoral behavior (for the same reason). An emergent intuitive understanding (especially within the counterculture) that there existed a definite link between militarist actions and mental disease was most pointedly underscored in songwriter Arlo Guthrie's darkly satiric rendition of the rationale given for his having been rejected for military service—not because he'd shouted homicidal threats during a medical review to the army psychiatrist ("I wanna see blood and gore and guts and veins in my teeth. Eat dead burnt bodies. I mean kill, kill, kill, kill."), but because he'd had a prior arrest for littering.[12]

At times the argument was that true sanity meant resistance to the war and institutional racism and poverty. At other times the point was that what counted as sanity was evil, and craziness was the only appropriate moral response. Or, in yet a third variation, the contention was that society was making people crazy. For instance, in reflections from 1974 on the circumstances that led to his nervous collapse (and involuntary commitment to a mental hospital) three years before, a graduate of the University of California at Berkeley wrote:

> With atomic apocalypse hanging over our heads, and fascism around the corner, we felt that the Revolution had to happen

quickly or else there was no hope at all. And by Revolution we
also meant the birth of a New Man and a New Woman. But
few of us experienced the total personal transformation that
seemed so necessary so immediately. Women's Liberation, Gay
Liberation, Third World Liberation, Viet Nam, ecological devastation—the pressures were immense. And some of us sensed
something happening in Washington, D.C., that could only be
described as incipient fascism, but the rest of the country did not
take our fears seriously and we felt very isolated. (Now, with
"Watergate" exposed, I don't feel so alone.) In the face of all
this, following the Mayday demonstrations [in 1971], when the
impotence of the anti-war movement became intolerably obvious, I broke.[13]

Along related lines, as radical psychiatrist Joseph Berke wrote in the
early 1970s: "We're up against a whole society that is systematically
driving its members mad."[14]

   It is almost impossible to imagine these ideas taking root in the United
States without a seismic shift having already previously occurred in the
mainstream imagination about the potentially social nature of mental
illness. As problematic as it may in many ways have been, what the academic work on social theories of schizophrenia and the growing popu-
larization of the associated ideas through the 1950s and first half of the
1960s had facilitated was the powerful plausibility of social diagnoses
as well as a partial destigmatization of and growing fascination with insanity. Madness had also been gradually transformed into a condition
that could potentially strike anyone trapped in inhumane circumstances.
As Goffman's *Asylums* had most poignantly and persuasively made the
case, the insane person was a sane person who had fallen on rough times.
Or, in another version, and more strongly influenced by Thomas Szasz,
the designation of "mentally ill" could be understood as a means to police deviance. As psychologist Bert Kaplan put it in 1964, "abnormality
involves a negative relationship to prevailing social norms," adding that
most personal accounts by individuals deemed psychotic also "reveal a
core of rebellion and rejection of expectations regarding social participation."[15] Those who had been diagnosed as insane could be cast less as an
object of pity or disgust or fear and more as an object lesson. As Mitch
Snyder, head of the Community for Creative Non-Violence in Washington, DC, took to putting it in his passionate advocacy work on behalf of
the homeless: "A psychotic episode is a socio-political event and not a
medical event."[16]

It was the war in Vietnam that made its critics even more fiercely committed to a social diagnosis of mental illness, indeed, to turn the social diagnosis into a full-fledged political diagnosis. The issues of mental illness and militarism were not understood as distinct, but distinctly interwoven. It was in this context that psychiatrists became especially suspect, since they were seen as supreme apologists for the same social system that had produced (and would continue to produce) massacres like My Lai. As radicals politicized the category of mental illness, many psychiatrists who had been resistant to the social model insisted again more strongly on an analysis that located mental illness within the individual—and not society. In turn, radicals pinpointed psychiatry as a profession that played a key role in social control and coercion. From this perspective, too many psychiatrists did nefarious ideological work.

For radicals it became common sense to see psychiatrists as insidious norm-defenders and to see mainstream psychiatry as an enterprise that needed to be resisted strenuously. In 1970, for instance, Howard Levy, a military doctor locked up in a federal penitentiary for refusing to train Green Berets in medical techniques (on the argument that it violated medical ethics and furthered the war effort), wrote from his prison cell that "psychiatrists play an essential role in, firstly, defining standards of behavior which serve the needs of repressive institutions and, secondly, in enforcing adherence to these standards."[17] Or to state the matter more generally, as radical psychiatrist Richard Kunnes put it self-critically: "Psychiatric services help, allow, or force people to adjust to an often repressive system." And it was the *system* that was the problem: "Staying within his licensed, professional role, the psychiatrist may seldom consider that the economic and social system is 'sick,' instead of the individual patient."[18] Likewise, when the American Psychiatric Association held its annual convention in 1970, a radical newsletter distributed to attendees clearly linked the diagnosis of "mental illness" to larger political issues, noting that "we should be aware that we are serving to pacify our patients, and not to liberate them." Here again the war was never very far from anyone's mind. As the statement added: "Pacification in the sense that the word is used in Vietnam—keep the natives quiet, keep the natives supporting the existing power structure, keep the natives apart and isolated."[19]

By the early 1970s it was further taken to be simple truth by radicals both inside and outside of the disciplines of psychiatry and psychology that many mental health services advocated and supported by more conventionally liberal therapists were not beneficent but repressive. Key instances of this were community mental health programs. Liberals had championed these programs as the desirable outcome of federal efforts under President John F. Kennedy to deliver psychiatric and counseling services directly to poor and underprivileged neighborhoods that had traditionally little or no access to such services. In liberal terms community mental health programs represented a great step forward, especially in light of the evidence in several epidemiological research studies that persons from economically depressed backgrounds suffered far higher rates of psychiatric disorders than persons from affluent communities.[20]

Radicals disagreed, however, increasingly seeing in community mental health programs just more subtle forms of social control. Mainstream therapists who worked with young people had only been trained to "depersonalize them, adjust them, change them against their will, or blackmail them by withholding achievement."[21] Social workers and psychologists as well as psychiatrists and educators in these communities served as "soft police" who helped to enact "a form of oppression far more destructive than that of the armed occupier." Brute force alone would never be enough to suppress political dissent because "law and order" tactics were not politically expeditious as a means to win "the hearts and minds" of the people. Kinder and gentler approaches were also required. The aim of psychiatric interventions in underprivileged communities was to weaken militant action, often by channeling the fervor and rage of the militants toward more individualistic goals—such as personal advancement. "Therapy" meant "co-opting" militant action. From the radical perspective, therapeutic tools served to trick oppressed individuals not to advocate on behalf of their own liberation by suggesting offers of material and psychic rewards if they abandoned their activism. This was "the 'psychologicalization of discontent,'" as a radical psychologist declared at the Annual Meeting of the American Orthopsychiatric Association in San Francisco in early 1970. He concluded: "The problem of the ghetto is not one of psychopathology. To convince an individual in an oppressed community that the root of his problem is intrapsychic is to mystify him, pacify his legitimate and healthy anger, and surely, to oppress him."[22] In a repressive and unjust society, there would always be a role for the community psychiatrist.

II

In 1970 Michael Glenn, a United States Air Force psychiatrist stationed in Minot, North Dakota, together with a small group of individuals involved in social work, formed the Radical Therapist Collective, and soon thereafter started a journal called *Radical Therapist*. Within a short time the journal gained support from a variety of like-minded organizations around the country, including the Psychologists for a Democratic Society, Psychologists for Social Action, and the Radical Caucus of the American Psychiatric Association. The Radical Therapist Collective additionally joined forces with groups in the newly emergent psychiatric survivors movement, comprised of current and former mental patients who argued on behalf of mental patients' civil liberties, such as the right to challenge involuntary commitment and the right to refuse treatment. These mental patient liberation organizations included: the Insane Liberation Front in Portland, Oregon; the Mental Patients Liberation Front in Boston; the Mental Patients Political Action Committee (MP-PAC) in New York; as well as groups in cities that ranged from Vancouver in Canada to Harrisburg, Cleveland, Baltimore, Richmond, Minneapolis, Syracuse, Nashville, and Washington, DC in the United States. *Madness Network News*, a journal for the "anti-psychiatry/psychiatric inmates liberation" movement (whose motto was "All the fits that's news to print"), began publication in San Francisco in 1972. The radical therapy movement proved to be internally divided and would soon schism (between one faction that believed that therapy could serve the radical political process and a second faction that argued that therapy needed to be abolished completely). Yet everyone involved in the movement shared a basic ethical and political belief that mainstream practitioners misused psychiatric and psychological methods, which in turn was seen by radicals to confirm that there existed systemic ideological deficiencies within the "helping professions." All radical therapy activists were additionally on red alert to identify incidents of psychiatric and medical malfeasance.

In this last regard radical therapists often did not have to look too hard. There remained in the early 1970s indisputable manifest mistreatment of mental patients—abuses that had continued despite the reform efforts of the 1950s and 1960s. Several incidents in particular became especially notorious and were repeatedly marshaled as evidence for the radical therapists' case against mainstream psychiatry. For instance, radicals were aghast at the news in 1967 that a military psychiatrist named Lloyd H. Cotter had conducted behavioral experiments on patients diagnosed with schizophrenia at the Bien Hoa mental hospital in South Vietnam. Cotter's stated goal was to help these patients, but it was impossible for critics not to read in Cotter's report an utter disregard for the terror and suffering he must have brought them. In brief, Cotter had become enamored with "operant conditioning," a technique devised by psychologist B. F. Skinner that suggested that "positive" and "negative" reinforcements could encourage individuals to give up behaviors deemed undesirable.[23] Cotter had also read how psychiatrist O. Ivar Lovaas had withheld food from autistic children to promote a reduction in their antisocial behavior, and so decided he would starve his own "difficult-to-activate patients."[24] Some patients held out for five days without food before they succumbed to Cotter, but the doctor was in the end able to announce that every single patient had finally "volunteered for work." Yet this was not all. Cotter further administered to recalcitrant patients unmodified electroconvulsive treatments (a technique already illegal in the United States because it meant patients did not receive anesthetics or muscle relaxants and therefore ran a risk of fractured bones and compression injuries of the spine). Undeterred by the frank chance that he might injure his patients, Cotter announced that he'd given "several thousands" of these shock treatments, and that "our objective of motivating them to work was achieved."[25] And what kind of work exactly were these patients asked to do? It was work growing crops for a deployment of Green Berets stationed nearby. In no uncertain terms radical critics expressed disgust and horror that mentally ill Vietnamese were tortured to further the US imperialist cause in Southeast Asia.[26] (As psychiatrist E. Fuller Torrey scathingly remarked about Cotter's experiment: "It makes Kesey's novel read like the Bobbsey Twins."[27])

In late 1967 another case sparked indignation, this time involving three doctors at Harvard Medical School who had suggested that social and economic factors alone could not explain the violent rioting in Detroit that summer—riots that left forty-three dead, more than a thousand injured, and resulted in over seven thousand arrests. In an oft-cited essay, "Role of Brain Disease in Riots and Urban Violence," which appeared in the *Journal of the American Medical Association*, psychiatrist Frank Ervin and neurosurgeons Vernon Mark and William Sweet argued that while it was "well known" that "poverty, unemployment, slum housing, and inadequate education underlie the nation's urban riots," the "obviousness of these causes may have blinded us to the more subtle role of other factors, including brain dysfunctions in the rioters who engaged in arson, sniping, and physical assault." There was a strong need for clinical studies to be conducted "of the *individuals* committing the violence" to determine whether "brain dysfunction related to a focal lesion plays a significant role in the violent and assaultive behavior" of black ghetto dwellers.[28] There was additionally a need, the doctors added, to develop "reliable early-warning tests" to detect and screen for potentially violent offenders.[29] This last research agenda received major grants of more than $600,000 from the National Institute of Mental Health and the Justice Department's Law Enforcement Assistance Administration, monies designed expressly to study "the incidence of violent disorders in a state penitentiary for men; estimate their prevalence in a non-incarcerated population; and improve, develop and test the usefulness of electrophysiological and neurophysiological techniques for the detections of such disorders in routine examinations."[30] There had also to be established diagnostic detection centers that could help to prevent violent outbreaks. The first such center "for the study and reduction of violence" opened at UCLA in 1972 (and received more than a million dollars in state monies from California governor Ronald Reagan in 1973).[31]

Such events infuriated radical critics. *Madness Network News* criticized the individualizing notion of mental illness, noting angrily how a cultural belief in "the 'born criminal' has always been popular, touching on our deepest fantasies about the devil within us, and providing the perfect alternative to focusing on social ills."[32] And social ills were the key to understanding mental disorders. "People don't *have* mental illness," stated *Madness Network News*. "It's not like the flu. Mental illness is not a medical issue. It is a social issue."[33] At the same time the efforts of the Harvard Medical doctors also signaled to radicals that the state was fully prepared to use psychiatric practices not solely to repress behavior it deemed nonnormative but also preemptively to alter the behaviors of persons it had decided to label deviant—not unlike what Anthony Burgess had described in his dystopian novel, *A Clockwork Orange* (1962), and what director Stanley Kubrick had represented in his visceral film adaptation released in 1971.

The news from psychiatry only continued to get worse. In 1970, and most egregiously, there was the report on an infamous phenomenon known as "aversive therapy" and how it came to be utilized to "treat" homosexuality. At the annual meeting that year of the American Psychiatric Association, psychiatrist Nathaniel McConaghy discussed with aplomb the results of his clinical trials on gay men. McConaghy described how he had tested the "conditionability" of homosexual subjects, injecting them with a drug to induce nausea while they watched slides of nude or partially nude men. McConaghy also gave the men electric shocks while they watched these same slides, blandly announcing how each individual had "received a total of 1,050 shocks during treatment."[34] Like Cotter in the South Vietnamese mental hospital, McConaghy's self-congratulatory report noted that his therapeutic methods had been a success. His gay subjects had felt a little less gay after receiving their "aversive" treatments.

To say that announcement of McConaghy's experiments appalled radicals and gay rights activists would be an understatement. During

McConaghy's presentation at the American Psychiatric Association annual convention, shouts of "barbaric!" and "gay is good!" greeted him, and he was loudly accused of serving as a "tool of fascist psychotherapy."[35] He was also asked, "Where did you take your residency, Auschwitz?"[36] And yet, and despite the furor they had caused, the results of McConaghy's aversive therapy would shortly appear (as had Cotter's account of his experiments with Vietnamese mental patients) in the flagship *American Journal of Psychiatry*.

And last, though by no means least of all, there was the gruesome news in the early 1970s of prisoners in the United States who had been used as guinea pigs for painful and dangerous experiments. At the prison medical facility in Vacaville, California, prisoners deemed "incorrigibles" were subjected to electroshock and aversive therapies to modify allegedly disruptive behavior—therapies that the leftist magazine *The Nation* angrily and indicatively labeled "the clockwork cure."[37] Moreover, in *Ebony* magazine in 1973, it was reported how some purportedly uncooperative black prisoners were in particular being threatened with lobotomies. *Ebony* said that it was a "new threat to blacks" when "prisoners seem to be fair game for the psychosurgeon's knife." The fact that prison authorities had insisted that lobotomies were being performed "only when or if voluntary consent is obtained" was dismissed as an abomination since requests for "voluntary consent" in prison were invariably accompanied with sanctions against anyone who refused.[38] In 1974 there were additional reports in the *New York Review of Books* and elsewhere that prisoners at Marion Federal Penitentiary in Illinois, "who, because of racial or cultural backgrounds, political or religious beliefs, feel compelled to speak out against the inhumanities of the prison system" were being forced to undergo behavior modification experiments, and that prisoners who attempted to resist "treatment" were being "chained to steel beds until they changed their minds about cooperating."[39] Comparable behavioral experiments were also being conducted or were reportedly being planned at correctional institutions in Butner, North Carolina, and Springfield, Missouri.[40] What could "voluntary consent" mean to prisoners coping with such conditions?

Outrage at behavior modification emerged by the end of the 1960s as a kind of left-wing variant of what had been in the 1950s a right-wing preoccupation with communist brainwashing. The obsessive concern now became the expanding power of an at once aggressive and "therapeutic" state to intervene in (and interfere with) the consciousness of the vulnerable and disenfranchised. And the concern was unquestionably fueled by paranoia—that a state (in the 1950s the danger had been imagined as communist while in the 1960s it was capitalist and supposedly democratic) was fully capable of using psychological means to break the resistance of those cast as undesirables or deviants. As radical sociologist Phil Brown emphasized in 1973, *"psychological manipulation pervades all areas of society."* And Brown went on to cite an evocative welter of examples:

> Advertising psychologists aid the corporations . . . by brainwashing people into consuming harmful and/or meaningless products, with the promise of financial and/or sexual success if the correct products are bought. School psychologists push working class children into vocational tracks, while placing middle strata children into academic tracks. They counsel students against militancy, with thinly veiled threats of reprisal. Further, they gain students' confidence, then report their "antisocial" attitudes to the higher administration. Military psychologists polish the machinery of U.S. imperialism in Indochina and elsewhere, providing "adjustment" for antiwar GIs and counseling bomber pilots so they won't feel guilty about napalming Vietnamese. . . . Community mental health centers cool out ghettos, defusing militant activities with soft-sell therapy services. State hospitals jack people up on thorazine and give electroshock or lobotomies to working class people whose behavior would never be "treated" if they were wealthy. Psychology is a class rip-off: the subjects tend to be poor; those who reap the benefits tend to be rich.

In short, as Brown concluded with a flourish, "The indictment is endless, and the activities of psychology professionals become more abhorrent the more we open our eyes." For Brown and many others, psychology had become *"an ideology for the defense of the status quo"*—and one deeply dangerous to democracy.[41] Suspiciousness about the state's intentions was not seen as suspect by radical psychologists and psychiatrists, but rather as insightful. As leading radical psychologist Claude Steiner wrote prominently (and in all capital letters) in his 1969 manifesto for the radical therapy movement:

> PARANOIA IS A STATE OF HEIGHTENED AWARENESS. MOST PEOPLE ARE PERSECUTED BEYOND THEIR WILDEST DELUSIONS. THOSE WHO ARE AT EASE ARE INSENSITIVE.[42]

At its most extreme, the argument went further to state bluntly that psychiatrists and other therapy professionals served as handmaidens to a Nazi-like state apparatus. It was not just Nathaniel McConaghy who was accused of acting like a fascist. Psychiatrist Ronald Leifer suggested in 1969 that every single community psychiatrist was little more than "a spy or Gestapo agent" who exercised "surveillance over ordinary persons such as 'immoral' mothers, students, former mental patients, mental health clinic clients, welfare recipients, blue-collar workers and criminals."[43] Lawyer Edward Ben Elson, who provided legal counsel in Madison, Wisconsin, for dozens of individuals involuntarily committed to mental institutions, routinely referred to the operations of "Amerikan Psychiatry." As Elson observed in 1970: "The psychiatrists & the judges engaged in civilly committing the 'mentally ill' are behaving criminally, & if they don't stop what they've been doing, surely someone is going to punish them. If there is a God in heaven, they are surely going to get what's coming, like Adolf Eichmann did before them."[44] Along related lines, Phil Brown observed that "Behavior modification experts work out tortures to 'cure' deviants (read: gays, political activists, etc.); California's infamous prison system employs such experts at its Vacaville Adjustment Center for troublemakers in the prisons—the activities of the behavior modification experts at Vacaville sound remarkably like the 'medical research' of Hitler's concentration camps."[45] Likewise, radical psychiatrist Peter R. Breggin in 1973 tarred with a broad brush the abusive psychiatric treatment of mental patients, calling such treatment akin to "the final solution." And he added: "As a Jew and a psychiatrist I have long held a deep conviction that the attempted extermination of the Jews and the maltreatment of mental patients are somehow profoundly connected."[46] By this moment such views had become almost an article of faith for many in the New Left and counterculture.

III

Alternative community groups and "rap centers" were set up across the United States to deal with all sorts of emotionally intense eventualities that came from living in a messed-up world. These centers worked on theorizing and practicing a "new kind" of counseling and psychiatric treatment, dedicated (as the Radical Therapist [RT] Collective wrote in 1971) to the development of "a therapy that serves the people." The RT Collective motto announced: "Therapy means change not adjustment." To which the collective added with caustic bluntness: "When people are fucked over, people should help them and fight it, and then deal with their feelings."[47] In its manifesto the RT Collective identified the many ways persons were being "socially traumatized" by their circumstances: by the chemical destruction and pollution of natural resources and the environment, by the barrage of the mass media, by the tediousness of public education, by the war machine in Vietnam, and by the haunting gloom that hung over humanity from the threat of nuclear annihilation. As the RT manifesto concluded: "Unless we as therapists and people can look beyond 'professional' issues and approach the social and political roots of suffering, we act as unknowing agents for the established order."[48] Similarly, there was the philosophy toward mental problems promoted at the influential Radical Psychiatry Center (RaP) in Berkeley, directed by Claude Steiner: "People's difficulties have their source not within them but in their alienated relationships, in their exploitation, in polluted environments, in war and in the profit motive."[49]

Ann Arbor, Seattle, Atlanta, Cambridge, Chicago, Manhattan, Brooklyn, and Portland, Oregon, all established "counterinstitutional" therapy rap centers by 1970. As a way to break down the power hierarchy between client and counselor, these centers tended to emphasize the group encounter, which was also identified as a key to the processes of making social change. RaP in Berkeley, for instance, conducted workshops as well as discussion groups and training programs for radical therapists. It offered any number of group therapeutic exercises, such as the Trust Circle, which was intended to help the anxious individual "learn to trust the whole group in close contact."[50] It provided young people a place to crash for a couple of nights in case of emergencies, and it provided free drug counseling. Counselors came with training in law, psychiatry, and psychology and were dedicated to the process of helping others "get their heads together." The aim in all instances was strictly to avoid the conventional (and always disingenuous) "games" that radical therapists were convinced were typically being played in more mainstream therapeutic relationships—games that denied the existence of both power and politics. What radical therapists sought "should be an end to therapy programs as they now exist," pronounced Michael Glenn and Richard Kunnes, cofounding members of the RT Collective. They also proclaimed: "Everyone therapeutic, no one a therapist!"[51]

Considerable energy in radical therapy centers also went into strategies intended to politicize the deeply alienated persons who came through their doors. This too was in keeping with the ideas promoted by Steiner, who wrote the equation like this: "Oppression + Deception = Alienation." To which Steiner added a second equation: "Oppression +

Awareness = Anger."[52] Feeling alienated was bad and lonely, but it could also transform into something positive and political when it was understood as stemming from societal dilemmas. Spreading the news about a sociopolitical diagnosis was part of the healing process; breaking down boundaries between individuals was also essential. The formula Steiner emphasized was this: "Liberation = Awareness + Contact," where "contact" meant interpersonal relations that fostered inner strength and bonded persons together in communal opposition to their oppression.[53]

Radical Therapist captured well the movement's mood—and the purposefulness of radical psychological insights—in an autobiographical account it published in 1971. The author recounted how feelings of anguish had consumed his every moment, and how he had succumbed to "a very schizophrenic state—deathly insecure of nothing in particular but my reality in general." He had experimented with drugs, and while these "increased self-awareness," they also "made me painfully aware of the enormity of my problems." His depression had continued to deepen until the day he enrolled in a course at the free university on "the politics of mental illness." In this class he learned that alienated persons like himself "don't exist simply as individuals but in definite social contexts and their ideas and feelings are a product of their social experience." Recognizing that the solution to his problems was in accepting "human interdependence," he immediately began to improve. He grasped for the first time how his father and mother had been exploited in their lives, and how social and economic factors also exerted a "disastrous" impact on his own development. And this process of increased awareness also led to "a much deeper interest in and capacity for political struggle."[54] Certainly it can be easy to scoff at the sentiments expressed in the pages of *Radical Therapist*—not to mention almost all the perspectives advanced by radical psychologists. Yet in the frenetic early 1970s, these sentiments registered as both significant and meaningful especially for those struggling better to situate themselves productively in a political struggle against a social system that appeared devotedly dedicated both to endless warfare abroad and the suppression of activism and freedom at home.

It is also significant to remember how these political concepts grew directly out of an enormously persuasive and prevalent analysis of mental illness as fully societal in origin. And important as well was the degree to which mental health was understood on the left as directly related to political engagement. For instance, an African American woman in the 1960s succinctly informed an interviewer: "Black power is my mental health."[55] And as the ubiquitous Claude Steiner observed in the early

1970s, groups like the Black Panthers "are of great value in that they clearly offer an alternative to the usual self-defeating scripts which are so commonly seen among black people." Antisocial personality problems could be solved by radical politics, Steiner added, a fact "confirmed for me, at the height of the Black Panthers' militant period (1969), by a group of probation officers from Alameda County, where the Panthers' headquarters are located, who had observed a decrease of delinquent behavior in black youths who joined the Black Panther Party."[56] The story was just the same for disaffected white students. Seymour L. Halleck, director of psychiatric health services at the University of Wisconsin at Madison in the 1960s, also recommended to depressed or anxious teens and young adults that they could help themselves psychically by becoming more politically active and working on behalf of social justice.[57] And subsequently women's consciousness-raising groups would argue that what suburban housewives needed was not Valium or antidepressants but rather feminism.[58]

IV

Yet there were drugs—marijuana, peyote, psilocybin, and especially LSD—that were not considered problematically pacifying but rather compatible with, indeed enhancing of, antimilitarist and progressive politics. A significant thread of debate at the Dialectics of Liberation conference in London in 1967 concerned how best to think about the possible uses of psychedelic drugs in the wider struggle for political revolution. LSD was a psychic revolution in feeling, Allen Ginsberg averred. Acid was a beautiful thing. Not that Ginsberg denied having had scary experiences. He confessed in London that he had already had six bad acid trips; these simply came with the territory known as consciousness. No hallucinogen was ever going to be ingested completely free of risk. Individual sanity was fragile in any event. And yet for Ginsberg and countless others who argued for the wondrous possibilities of flower power, psychedelic drugs provided the sort of life-changing experiences whose benefits far outweighed their dangers. LSD could be therapeutic. In addition, acid appeared to promote both introspection and nonviolence. As Ginsberg discoursed on it, LSD made you aware "of what your own feelings are" and gave you a recognition of "the movements of your own mind, including the movements toward hysteria." LSD broke down the barriers between persons, and this enacted a new vision of the potentialities for humanity. With a new "level of awareness," a person became capable of "treating a person as person and not as role," Ginsberg argued, "not as uniform, not as cop, not as capitalist, not as communist, not as Maoist, not as Allen Ginsberg," but simply as human. As Ginsberg inquired: "What's the point of having enemies when you can have friends?" Such individual gestures represented a "drop in the void," Ginsberg admitted, but we had to recognize our oneness if "a new society based on a new consciousness" was ever successfully to come into being. And as Ginsberg urged, LSD helped persons "to dehypnotise" and "decontrol" themselves.[59]

For Ginsberg there was a direct link between psychedelic consciousness and the achievement of mental health. The two were not antithetical. Alter consciousness and everything changes. This also became Timothy Leary's mantra.[60] In his LSD guidebook, *The Politics of Ecstasy* (1968), Leary discoursed at length on this precise issue, observing how the "interior journey" provoked by psychedelic drugs could serve as cure for all kinds of socially induced neuroses and psychoses. Or as Leary put it in his own words, the ingesting of acid and psilocybin mushrooms "enable each person to realize that he is not a game-playing robot on this planet to be given a Social Security number and to be spun on the assembly line of school, college, career, insurance, funeral, goodbye."[61] Claude Steiner also accepted the possibilities of LSD, observing in 1974: "Our vision and hearing are encapsulated in a rational shell which takes out 90% of their sensing capacities. I believe that psychedelic drugs and rock music are used by many young people to shatter this shell. . . . LSD, mescaline, peyote bring back the visions which we have forgotten how to see: a rose becomes, once again, a wondrous universe of texture, color, and smell."[62] An endorsement of a psychedelic drug from radical psychologists was hardly surprising. Rather more remarkable was that a scattered band of far more mainstream psychiatrists had been openly championing the therapeutic properties of LSD for nearly twenty years.

Surveying psychiatric research on LSD since the early 1950s, a psychoanalyst wrote in 1963 how LSD treatments had proved themselves a uniquely effective means to "cut through the intellectualizations and other dysjunctive processes which people use to avoid meaningful communication with each other and thereby to get to their fantasies and emotions."[63] Patients on LSD were shown to experience "an elated state in which the processes of ego-reconstruction result in reinforcement of the integrative functions of the ego."[64] LSD treatments were also said to have the potential to cure chronic alcoholism.[65] And in an especially provocative case, a physician reported how a patient on LSD had been able for the first time to admit and address his "unconscious hostility toward minority groups."[66] Researchers could not contain their amazement at the therapeutic powers of LSD. As psychiatrist Don Jackson—an original member of the research team around Gregory Bateson—wrote in 1962 of a patient with chronic depression until treated with LSD: "In seventeen (now nineteen) years of practicing psychotherapy I have never seen as much change in an individual with a rigid obsessional character. The change has been permanent. While it has leveled off, there has been no backsliding since our first Encounter using LSD."[67]

Nor did researchers see a problem with the fact that the mind on acid resembled the schizophrenic mind. On the contrary, the resemblance caused considerable excitement. As *Scientific American* reported in 1955, researchers in Boston concluded (after six years of clinical trials with LSD) that because they could reproduce "psychosis" in otherwise healthy subjects, it might be possible to use LSD as "a remarkable new tool for the investigation of psychotic states."[68] Quite soon, though, the idea that a psychedelic trip resembled the psychotic experience was turned on its head. It was not that psychedelic drugs recreated a psychotic state but rather that psychotics were (and naturally, as it were) already on psychedelic trips, and that this constant state of natural tripping (like the acid trip) brought an unprecedented perceptiveness into the ordering of the cosmos.

Psychosis came in the 1960s to be widely reinterpreted as an especially intense kind of sanity that was incapable of being lured or co-opted by the shams and fakeries and con games of ego and power that characterized so much of what passed for "normal" in the "square" world. As one former mental patient (and LSD experimenter) would summarize the matter: "What Western societies have been calling 'psychosis' is very often, if not usually, in part an awakening, a growth or individuation process, or an attempt by the organism to function more naturally, completely, or healthily."[69] Gregory Bateson proposed similar conclusions about the "curative" elements of schizophrenia as early as 1961.[70] Thus the madman came to be seen as seer and prophet, whether in the voice of the visionary Chief Bromden who narrated Kesey's *Cuckoo's Nest* (written after the author's own hallucinatory experiences on acid while working as an orderly on a mental ward) or in the widely celebrated rants and meditations of poet, playwright, and asylum inmate Antonin Artaud.

"So a sick society invented psychiatry to defend itself against the investigations of certain visionaries whose faculties of divination disturbed it," wrote Artaud in the 1940s.[71] And he also wrote in an open letter to the medical directors of lunatic asylums: "We protest against any interference with the free development of delirium. It is as legitimate, as logical as any other sequence of human ideas or acts. The repression of anti-social reactions is as chimerical as it is unacceptable in principle. All individual acts are anti-social. Madmen, above all, are individual victims of social dictatorship."[72] No surprise then that by the early 1970s, Artaud's writings came to be interpreted by the radical psychology movement as the purest articulation of essential truths about society's suppression of individuals' inner consciousness and the political dimensions of the psychotic experience. And no surprise that Laing's madness-mythologizing *The Politics of Experience* would become in these years a cult classic.

Even the *American Journal of Psychiatry*—in between publishing Cotter and McConaghy—published an essay in 1968 that defended hippies and suggested that their LSD experimentation represented a useful means to achieve heightened *political* consciousness. LSD brought into being "a new self" opposed to all destructive human tendencies, or so psychiatrist Harry R. Brickman, director of the Los Angeles Department of Mental Health, suggested. Brickman openly mocked his less imaginative colleagues who put "flower children" on a "derogatory scale" ranging from "the condescending to the acerbic," and who chose to diagnose hippies as suffering from "withdrawal from 'reality,' avoidance of oedipal struggles, reaction formation against, projection, and denial of aggressive drives." Instead, what Brickman proposed was that the hippies' fascination with LSD indicated instincts and qualities both hopeful and utopian. Brickman suggested that an understanding of acid could explain the hippie's "deliberate self-removal from the societal nexus." What the acid trip induced, Brickman wrote, was "a death experience in which the consciousness of self is fragmented or extinguished," and from which there resulted lasting insight into the "union of life and death and self and nonself." Scarcely able to contain his enthusiasm, Brickman continued:

> This insight powerfully suggests to [the hippie] that the "ego games" he has been playing, in which he feels essentially different and apart from others and from the natural world, are but acculturative illusions. The subject then often realizes that he can never be all "good" and his "enemy" or antagonist can never be all "bad"—that both qualities reside in all persons. This insight, together with a diminished need to externalize destructive aggression . . . helps energize the subject's nonviolence toward not only his "hip" colleagues but toward the "straight" world as well.[73]

For Brickman the counterculture represented nothing short of a potential for the formation of a new society committed to nonviolence as the only proper means to resolve human conflicts. In this and other ways, LSD became imagined as an essential gateway drug for an entire generation of people in search of a better and more humane future. LSD was far more than a powerful adjunct to psychoanalytic procedures. LSD was also the key to unlocking a new politics.

V

And yet at the Dialectics of Liberation Congress in 1967—where Ginsberg spoke of the need to reconsider the human and of the beneficence of LSD—there was chaos and conflict. Black Power activist Stokely Carmichael spoke fiercely (and to great applause) of the need for armed and coordinated anti-imperialist struggle within the West; his speech veered toward the apocalyptic: "We're gonna burn the system to the ground."[74] Psychotherapist Paul Goodman spoke in defense of nonviolence, noting how "it is necessary to keep in the back of one's mind that the only real revolution is humanity and peace."[75] John Gerassi, a member of the Vietnam War Crimes Tribunal, angrily denounced the political uselessness of the counterculture, observing that hippies were tolerated simply because "they are not a threat" to "the Establishment."[76] Others by contrast (like Ginsberg) saw in the flower power of the counterculture the only genuine solution to societal ills. Anthropologist Gregory Bateson stated that the spiral of violence in Vietnam must be causing President Lyndon Johnson considerable distress. "You know, I don't believe President Johnson's really happy," Bateson commented. Yet an audience member angrily shouted back that Johnson was most likely "enjoying himself" and had not the slightest moral qualms about his militarist endeavors. Antipsychiatrist David Cooper questioned the revolutionary benefits of LSD, suggesting that hallucinogens could cause the Argentine revolutionary Che Guevara to lay down his guns in the struggle against imperialism. Ginsberg responded (only half in jest) that LSD could also lead Che to fight *harder* for world liberation. No wonder that Marxist feminist Sheila Rowbotham, who attended the congress, would later write that the gathering had been "more of a two-week-long trauma than a conference."[77]

Only philosopher Herbert Marcuse appeared willing to thread a path through the theoretical impasses and oversized egos in which the Dialectics of Liberation event had gotten mired. Like Laing and Cooper, Marcuse emphasized that psychoanalysis and psychiatry had emerged as "powerful instruments of suppression." (The following year, Mar-

cuse would go on to write that the work of psychiatrists in a "sick society" was making the individual "normal" by "normalizing his strains
and stresses," or "to put it more brutally: making him capable of being
sick, of living his sickness as health, without his noticing that he is sick
precisely when he sees himself and is seen as healthy and normal."[78])
Yet at the same time Marcuse also saw the possibility of using therapy as a tool for political education. He denounced the indiscriminate
use of "violence" in revolutionary rhetoric and sought to distinguish
between violence used to protect life and violence used to destroy it. He
spoke hopefully that "the imperialist world system" had already begun
to show signs of potential collapse, even as he acknowledged (following Gerassi) that many hippies were engaged in "mere masquerade and
clownery" and were consequently "completely harmless." But Marcuse
also observed (following Ginsberg) that there were in the counterculture
many hippies who were seeking "a new sensibility against efficient and
insane reasonableness." And these hippies deserved praise. Sounding a
lot like a radical therapist, Marcuse said: "There is the refusal to play the
rules of a rigged game, a game which one knows is rigged from the beginning, and the revolt against the compulsive cleanliness of puritan morality and the aggression bred by this puritan morality as we see it today
in Vietnam among other things." The difficulties ahead for liberation
movements in the West were immense, Marcuse concluded in London,
but he urged his listeners to take note of how critical it remained not to
succumb to the "defeatism" that was spreading through the liberation
movements already in 1967.[79]

It has become conventional to emphasize that the 1960s were not just
an era of sex, antiwar protest, drugs, and rock 'n' roll. It was also the
birth moment of the conservative backlash that would come to dominate
the next generation or more.[80] But another way to think about 1967—
one that comes into sharp relief once the decade is examined through
the lens of the insanity trip—was that far from being a moment of na-
ive optimism, the year already saw the onset of tremendous confusion,
anguish, and fear within the New Left and the counterculture about the
possibilities and hopes for progressive social change.

Social change and individual self-transformation both turned out to
be not so easy. Furthermore, it was quite unclear what the relationship
could be between individual and social change. Which was the precursor
to the other—or did they have to operate in dialectical tandem? Activists
had been worrying about this for some time. In addition, when individuals

turned to left activism, did they simply play the same power games as their right-wing adversaries? Was left politics just another ego trip? Would it be better to refuse to play the games of power altogether? Or was "dropping out" just depoliticized self-indulgence? There were no simple answers.

6

Person Envy

The invisible woman in the asylum corridor
sees others quite clearly,
including the doctor who patiently tells her
she isn't invisible—
and pities the doctor, who must be mad
to stand there in the asylum corridor
talking and gesturing to nothing at all.   Robin Morgan, *Monster* (1972)[1]

I

An influential and absolutely indispensable aspect of both
antipsychiatric thought and radical therapy during the
late 1960s and 1970s was the feminist insurgency. Feminism challenged the outrageous power of psychiatrists to
ensure obedience to mystiques of femininity in their female patients. Psychologist Naomi Weisstein may be credited with breaking the door down with her oft-reprinted
"Kinder, Küche, Kirche as Scientific Law: Psychology
Constructs the Female" (1968), in which she argued how
women were routinely characterized psychologically as
"inconsistent, emotionally unstable, lacking in a strong
conscience or super-ego, weaker, 'nurturant' rather than
productive, 'intuitive' rather than intelligent, and, if they
are at all 'normal,' suited to the home and the family."[2]

But legions of angry women, on and off the couch, were to follow—rejecting the assumptions about women's minds and exposing the vapid dogmatism, retrograde notions of gender roles, and insidious emotional manipulation (not to mention undertheorized countertransference and lechery) at work in too many doctor-patient encounters. In these and other respects, feminists assailed the disciplines of psychology and psychiatry and maintained that society *made* persons—and especially women—sick. "Cultures that practiced female infanticide were at least honest in how they felt about women," wrote sociologist Pauline Bart angrily in 1971. "Better we should have been exposed on a mountain side as infants, than to have the death of a thousand cuts which is the fate of women, particularly intelligent women, in our society."[3] Such sentiments were far from unusual at this moment.

Yet there developed also in the early 1970s a second immensely more influential and divergent strand of antipsychiatric thinking—one whose complex overlaps with feminist therapy on the one hand, and whose eventual damage to the reputation of antipsychiatry on the other, have not been adequately accounted for. Popular psychological self-help guidebooks promising greater joy and self-fulfillment were antipsychiatry for the masses. Self-help flourished in the early 1970s. Almost one in every six best-selling books fit into this category—a much higher percentage of titles than ever before. Hundreds of millions of self-help books sold during the decade.[4] These best-selling titles routinely rejected the psychiatric status quo. Theirs was an alternative approach to therapy that did not require countless dollars spent on endless hours in analysis—money and time, the books argued, that was most likely going to be wasted in any event. What new pop psych books offered, as psychiatrist Thomas A. Harris wrote on the opening page of *I'm OK—You're OK* (1969)—one of the earlier and most popular self-help manifestos of the era—was "a new answer to people who want to change rather than to adjust, to people who want transformation rather than conformation."[5] Pop psych was "radical therapy" turned populist, and without the "radical." Pop psych emphasized taking control and *individual* responsibility. "No more probing into your forgotten past," intoned the back cover of psychologist Jerry Greenwald's *Be the Person You Were Meant to Be* (1973). "Dr. Greenwald puts the tools for reconstructing your life squarely into your hands and shows you how to use them."[6] Pop psych thereby tapped into a long-standing postwar suspicion that psychiatry actually induced the very same problems it claimed to resolve. Pop psych was presented as the opposite of psychiatry—replacing a preoccupation with "guilt," "fear," "dependency," "self-rejection," or "living in the

past" with "bold but simple techniques for taking charge of your unhealthy behavior patterns," as the cover of psychologist Wayne Dyer's
Your Erroneous Zones (1976) announced.[7]

Feminist therapy and pop psych thus shared some general commonalities with radical therapy. Both sought to democratize counseling and
therapy. Both expressed profound ambivalence—if not open hostility—
at the whole notion of psychiatric "expertise." An essential message of
both was: Professionals offered no special skills, only special degrees.
Everyone was (or could become) his or her own therapist. And finally,
both addressed a deep yearning in the 1970s for personal validation; everyone hungered for "strokes" in order to grow into more fully "actual-
ized" (and thus happier) human beings.

Yet the sharp distinctions between these two 1970s outgrowths of
antipsychiatry also cannot be underestimated and remain crucial. Feminism and feminist therapy still always offered a *social* diagnosis of mental illness, even as feminists grappled (as had radical therapy) with the
tensions between how to change society and how to change the individual. Which led to what? Did a person need to change first, or was
transforming society a prerequisite for personal transformation? Where
did the damages to persons originate, and what were the mechanisms by
which those damages might be undone? Pop psych, by contrast, stripped
away the idea that there was a sick society, or that anything quite so abstract as "society" caused mental anguish. Change was represented in
terms that were individual and always possible. Change was not essentially social; everyone could and should change him- or herself by him-
or herself.

Perhaps most significantly, pop psych shifted discussion away from
women's issues per se, and sizably expanded its potential audience by
doing so. Self-help literature liked to package its message as broadly
gender neutral, often alternating anecdotes about men and women. Yet
there can be no question that the pop psych bonanza depended in no
small part on how these self-help books thematized (without explicitly
admitting they were doing so) the miserableness above all of *men's* exis-
tences—the rivalries and insecurities, dissatisfactions and agonies large
and small—that daily beset the so-called (and only supposedly) stronger
sex. Whether the attention also to male vulnerabilities should be counted
among one of feminism's unintended successes, or actually an end-run
around feminism, is a question that must remain open. But indisputably, in the effusion of competing platitudes generated in the ascent of
pop psych, the very idea of individual empowerment that was such a
significant component of the feminist project was hopelessly perverted.

When Wayne Dyer announced in 1976 that change was easy—"You are in charge of yourself! You can be whatever you choose to be. And since the choice is yours, why not choose to be happy rather than depressed, successful rather than overlooked, adventurous rather than timid?"—it was apparent that the era of the social diagnosis had pretty well run its course.[8]

II

In September 1970, at a historical moment when fewer than one in four psychologists in the United States were women, the women's caucus of the American Psychological Association demanded at the APA annual meeting that a million dollars in "reparations" be paid on behalf of the many female patients who had suffered mistreatment by their therapists. The women affirmed that "male chauvinist" therapists had systematically denigrated the personhood of female patients who expressed interest in activities besides being a mother or a housewife. They argued that therapists who systematically worked to pressure women to "fit in" needed to be actively challenged. They demanded that "liberated" therapists (male or female) reject the concept of a "well-adjusted woman" upon which psychological diagnoses of female patients were so often based. In sum, they insisted that it was past due to put a stop to the era in which male therapists were allowed to get away with pressuring their female patients into "a more passive acceptance of what society defined as their proper role in a male dominated world."[9] As for the million dollars in reparations, the women's caucus said it would be used to get women out of mental hospitals as well as to develop new therapies specifically meant to address the mental health needs of women in a society where (as caucus spokeswoman Phyllis Chesler announced) "both psychotherapy and marriage function as vehicles for keeping a woman in her place."[10]

The reparations demand went nowhere, but feminists made a persuasive case. It was not difficult in the late 1960s and early 1970s to amass anecdotal instances of male therapeutic "piggishness." Piggishness was evident in many prominent psychiatric and psychological assessments of (what were understood to be) the appropriate roles and satisfactions that came with femininity. The case studies documented in *Schizophrenic Women: Studies in Marital Crisis* (1964) had in hindsight with astonishing blatancy directly emphasized that schizophrenic women required adjustment to their responsibilities as wives and mothers.[11] Harvard psychiatrist Joseph C. Rheingold's tome *The Fear of Be-*

ing a Woman (1964), which he had dedicated "to my women patients," concluded with the argument that only when women "grow up without dread of their biological functions and without subversion by feminist doctrine" could they "attain the goal of a good life and a secure world in which to live it."[12] Psychiatrist Erik Erikson that same year also opined that a woman "harbors an 'inner space' destined to bear the offspring of chosen men," and that "the modalities of woman's commitment and involvement, for better *and* for worse, also reflect the ground-plan of her body."[13] In 1965 psychologist Bruno Bettelheim proclaimed during a symposium at MIT that "as much as women want to be good scientists or engineers, they want first and foremost to be womanly companions of men and to be mothers."[14] Over and over the ambitious and successful woman was diagnosed as unhappy, as suffering from an unhealthful masculine identification, and/or as having chosen a professional life only in order to have an "acceptable outlet for aggression and hostility."[15] The policing of women's emotional choices by male experts in the 1960s was remarkably consistent.

No one did more to dramatize the means by which the psychiatric profession came to systematically crush the hopes and dreams of independent-minded women than Phyllis Chesler. In the opening pages of her groundbreaking study, *Women and Madness* (1972), Chesler took the illustrative stories of four remarkable women—Elizabeth Packard, Ellen West, Zelda Fitzgerald, Sylvia Plath—who came to be "treated and/or imprisoned by male psychiatrists—most of whom were, quite literally, agents for their husbands." Chesler pointedly extended the insights of Erving Goffman in her chapters on "Asylums" and "The Female Career as a Psychiatric Patient," in which she emphasized the astonishing degree to which "women, by definition, are viewed as psychiatrically impaired—whether they accept or reject the female role—simply because they are women." There was valuable insight as well, Chesler argued, in the critiques offered by R. D. Laing and Thomas Szasz of psychiatric practice, even as these also devalued or misidentified the psychological binds of being female in contemporary society. As Chesler wrote, the double bind had a specific female dimension: "Women are seen as 'sick' when they act out the female role (are depressed, incompetent, frigid, and anxious) and when they reject the female role (are hostile, successful, sexually active, and especially with other women)."[16] In short, society psychically crippled its women.

There was in addition powerful anecdotal evidence of women who had been labeled sick by psychiatrists for alleged infractions of feminine decorum. Mothers who neglected their appearance or refused to have sex with their husbands (because they did not want to run the risk of having yet more children) were committed to mental hospitals. Single women who decided to wear jeans or boots and expressed a desire to find their own way in life were committed to mental hospitals by their parents. Married women who fell in love with other men were committed to mental hospitals by their husbands. "'Crazy' is when a woman doesn't want to live with her husband any more," wrote the feminist activist who documented these actual cases in 1972. "'Sane' is when she decides to wear a skirt and apply for a job at Bell Telephone."[17]

By the early 1970s cases like these were increasingly taken by feminists as proof that society was fully responsible for women's mental disorders. As Pauline Bart wrote retrospectively in 1974, it was no coincidence that the brightest women among her cohort in graduate school a decade earlier had developed stress-induced intestinal problems or that three had attempted suicide (one had succeeded) and another had been committed to a mental hospital. "Before the Women's Movement," Bart concluded, "we *were* being driven crazy, and the helping professions, for we were all in therapy, were mainly helping us into our madness."[18] More empirical sociological research also concluded that women were being institutionalized not because they were somehow more prone to insanity, but because "woman's role in modern industrial societies has a number of characteristics that may promote mental illness."[19]

In response to these insufferable conditions, women frequently expressed both frustration and outrage. But they found that therapists interpreted expressions of anger as further confirmation that more psychiatric treatment was required. With disarming candor the psychoanalyst Theodore Reik—who had been trained by Sigmund Freud and who founded the National Psychological Association for Psychoanalysis in New York—repeatedly revealed that his female patients were unwilling to accept his insights into their states of mind. "When you listen to me a long time without saying anything, I often have the impression that what I say is silly woman's stuff and without value," one patient told Reik. "It is as if you do not consider it worth your while to speak to me." Reik recollected how another female patient responded more sharply to his interpretations: "Goddam, I don't know why I am here. Fuck yourself!"[20] And a third female patient had this exchange with Reik: "When I told a patient in her forties that she had wanted to be a boy like her brother, she began to curse and abuse me, saying 'Fuck you' and 'Go to hell!' and other unladylike expressions."[21] But these challenges to his authority did not cause Reik to doubt his own judgment. At no point did Reik allow for the possibility that outbursts from female patients reflected the legitimacy of their frustrations *with him.* (It was left to radical feminist Shulamith Firestone to point out that Reik's commentaries on women read "like a Freudian jokebook."[22]) Yet by the early 1970s even the densest of analysts and other MDs could see that an extraordinary number of women were increasingly uncomfortable with their treatment.

Women in therapy were reportedly becoming so uncooperative that a proposal in 1971 sought to introduce a new diagnostic phenomenon. Called "the angry woman syndrome," it described patients who took "fiendish delight in deriding their husbands" and who exhibited a "baleful disregard for decency." These women were superficially well adjusted and successful in their lives, but they nonetheless "strike out blindly, frightened by any threat to their not being the sole center of attention." In short, their behavior revealed patterns that "at times border on psychotic with paranoid and aggressive overtones."[23] In 1972 there was a second proposal for another new category of client called "the intractable female patient." These were women who initially presented "exactly the kind of patient with whom the young resident in particular hopes to work." But looks could be deceiving. In reality these women were supreme manipulators who used their feminine wiles to turn psychotherapy "into a quagmire from which escape is ever more difficult." The psychiatric solution for the intractable female was for therapists to set "a firm discharge date reasonably early" and to insist that the husband "assume a posture of strength and resolution—especially toward his wife." This was because the intractable female patient most desired to be dominated by men, the essay concluded, and though she might repeatedly test the resolve of men to dominate her, "she really hopes that she will not win."[24]

There was, however, another (differently misogynist) means by which some psychiatrists addressed the problems of their female patients. William Masters and Virginia Johnson concluded their *Human Sexual Inadequacy* (1970) by noting with sharp dismay how "frequently" they had received patient reports "of tragic psychotherapeutic malpractice, that of the therapist seducing the essentially defenseless patient into mutual sexual experience." As they also observed: "Even if only 25 percent of these specific reports were correct, there still would be an overwhelming issue confronting these professionals serving as therapists in the field of human sexual dysfunction."[25] Female patients often articulated how they initially felt flattered by the attention. "I think that he just finally couldn't resist me any more," one female patient said of her affair with her therapist. "I was so happy that my therapist loved me," said another patient who had slept with her shrink. "Who cared about anything else?" But the thrill seldom lasted. "The depression, the feelings, the fear got worse and worse," said a woman about her affair with her psychiatrist. "The more upset I got, the more librium he gave me."[26] As for the male therapist, he may have been less conflicted; the issue of whether to have sex with clients was openly debated during a panel at the annual meeting of the hip-minded Association for Humanist Psychology in 1971.[27] Even famed antipsychiatrist David Cooper rationalized having sex with "a quite tall and quite attractive" young woman in his care who had been diagnosed with schizophrenia as somehow a political act (since he thereby rejected a conventional "doctor-patient relationship, unbalanced in power terms, that excludes any mutuality in the sense of a free interchange of experience").[28] By this time, it was not a secret that many therapists were participating in (what was euphemistically called) "overt transference."[29]

Popular accounts of sex with female patients veered between voyeuristic glibness and open acceptance. For instance, the underground cult film *Coming Apart* (1969) depicted with eerie verisimilitude a New York psychotherapist (Rip Torn) who decides (for the murkiest of reasons) to set up a hidden movie camera in his office so he can film his sessions with female patients; more than once, these involve sexual intimacy. And psychiatrist Martin Shepard's *The Love Treatment* (1971), which supposedly documented the real-life stories of patients who had affairs with their psychiatrists, amounted to soft-core titillation. In his own "confession," Shepard recounted how he had agonized over whether or not to have sex with an "attractive" lesbian patient after she told him she wished now to have sex with men—but remained "most fearful of being penetrated." Shepard reasoned that since she would likely have difficulty finding the right man for the job—"a man with the wisdom of a sage and the patience of a saint"—he thought to volunteer himself (believing he represented his patient's best shot "to experience the pleasures of heterosexuality"). That he held back did not prevent him from having lasting regrets at his cowardice. "I *knew* that it was my own conventionality," he wrote remorsefully, "that kept me from taking the properly helpful, if unorthodox, step."[30] It was left to Phyllis Chesler to summarize angrily any sexual contact between female client and male psychiatrists as "legally a form of rape and psychologically a form of incest."[31] Women asked by their male therapists if they were interested in "making it" were often equally outraged.[32]

Finally, another standard narrative among psychiatrists was that women in therapy needed more and more medications. A new chemical class of tranquilizers was a pharmaceutical gold mine at least since

Librium (chlordiazepoxide) was marketed in 1960, and the blockbuster antianxiety drug Valium (diazepam) soon followed in 1963. Into the early 1970s pharmaceutical companies were marketing medications for women with ads that were truly amazing above all for the frankness with which they indicated how the right drugs could produce in female patients a desired (and desirable) femininity.[33] Furthermore, these ads also positioned *psychiatrists* as victimized by hostile or disagreeable female patients. They particularly identified with frustrations felt by psychiatrists who were dealing with depressed or anxious female patients. In every instance the ads promised a drug guaranteed to help, even as they also blatantly reinforced for the therapist a fully normative conception of what women should be.

For example: An ad from 1968 (for the antidepressant Aventyl) included a black-and-white photograph of a middle-aged woman looking haughtily at the camera while her hand clutched her neck—a wedding ring conspicuously visible. The text read: "Do you have patients who try to hide anguish behind arrogance?" It continued:

> You see many depressed patients who conceal their real emotional lives beneath a veneer because it lets them hide from the finality of their depression. Before they come to you, few can recognize their despair. Even while seeking your help, they may continue attempting to hide from you as well as themselves.

The ad (from Eli Lilly) offered a drug to help the therapist as well as the female patient "see behind the veneer and accept the reality."[34]

Other ads focused on those female patients who presented as spiritless and intensely disinterested in their appearance or domestic responsibilities. An ad from 1968 showed two color photographs of the same young and pretty woman wearing a skirt and ballet slippers; these photos were clearly meant as portraits taken "before medication" and "after medication." In the first she sits despondently in a chair, wires attached to her ankles and wrists lying limply at her side. In the second, she stands and looks directly into the camera, a smile on her face, as the wires—now taut—keep her on her feet. The text states that the antidepressant Vivactil (from Merck Sharp & Dohme) is "particularly suitable for withdrawn and apathetic patients." Thus the drug takes responsibility for (literally) pulling the woman out of her stupor—though the imagery also unmistakably and unabashedly likens the young woman to a puppet on a string.[35]

In 1971 advertising directed at the problems of female patients

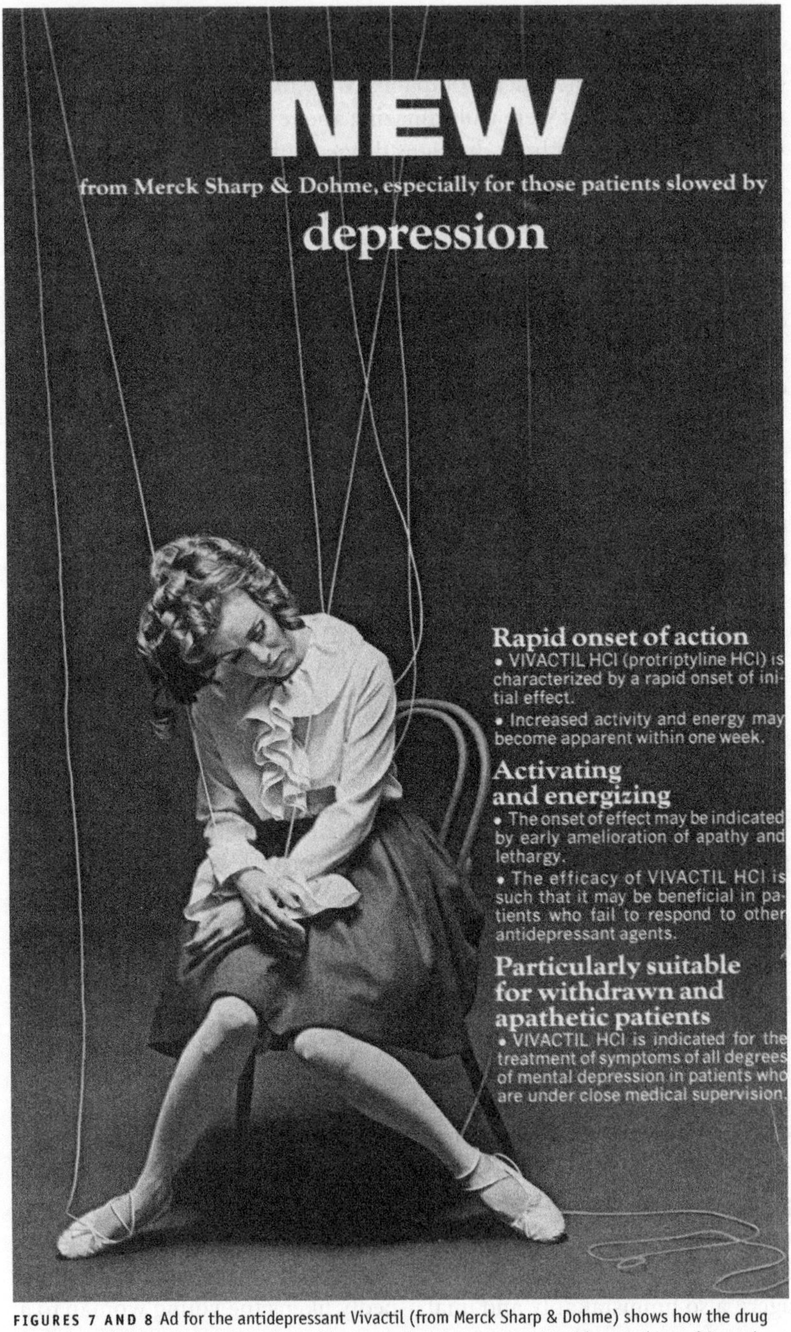

NEW

from Merck Sharp & Dohme, especially for those patients slowed by

depression

Rapid onset of action
• VIVACTIL HCl (protriptyline HCl) is characterized by a rapid onset of initial effect.
• Increased activity and energy may become apparent within one week.

Activating and energizing
• The onset of effect may be indicated by early amelioration of apathy and lethargy.
• The efficacy of VIVACTIL HCl is such that it may be beneficial in patients who fail to respond to other antidepressant agents.

Particularly suitable for withdrawn and apathetic patients
• VIVACTIL HCl is indicated for the treatment of symptoms of all degrees of mental depression in patients who are under close medical supervision.

FIGURES 7 AND 8 Ad for the antidepressant Vivactil (from Merck Sharp & Dohme) shows how the drug can pull a young woman out of her stupor like a puppet on a string. Reprinted from *Archives of General Psychiatry* 18 (June 1968).

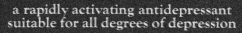

a rapidly activating antidepressant
suitable for all degrees of depression

VIVACTIL®HCI
PROTRIPTYLINE HCI

It has proved to be useful when the depression is characterized by the following symptoms: suicidal drive, excessive crying, apathy, withdrawal, psychomotor retardation, fatigue, insomnia, depressed mood, anxiety, agitation, feeling of guilt, and anorexia.

• Clinical studies thus far have shown VIVACTIL HCI to be characteristically lacking in sedative and tranquilizing properties.

NOTE: Should not be used concomitantly with MAO inhibitors. When patients receiving a monoamine oxidase inhibitor (MAOI) are to be treated with VIVACTIL HCI, an interval of several days to several weeks should elapse between use of the two drugs to permit dissipation of the effects of the MAOI. Contraindicated in patients with pyloric stenosis, glaucoma, or a tendency to urinary retention. May block the antihypertensive effect of guanethidine and similarly acting compounds.

For additional prescribing information, please see following page.

pointed more specifically to the psychological distresses experienced by young mothers and wives, and self-reflexively acknowledged the rise of women's resistance to their assigned tasks. "A lot of little things are wrong," read the caption below two photographs—the first of a young woman in a mini skirt standing glumly with her hands clasped in front of her while laundry fluttered unattended on a clothes line, and the second of an attractive woman's face superimposed over a shot of dried weeds and dirt. The caption continues: "Headaches, diarrhea, this rash on my arm. And sometimes I think I don't like being married." The ad (from Pfizer) concluded with: "Guilt, and somatic symptoms and concerns caused by anxiety respond particularly well to Sinequan (doxepin)."[36] That same year, further copy (also from Pfizer) presented a photograph of a young wife with her small child. "Once an anxious, withdrawn schizophrenic . . . Navane (thiothixene) helped bring her home," read the ad. "Helping the patient return to a normal environment and avoid rehospitalization," continued the text. Then there was a second photograph showing the same wife cuddling her child warmly while her husband sat beside her, his hand reassuringly resting on her shoulder.[37]

There is no evidence whatsoever that mainstream psychiatry registered these drug advertisements as anything but innocuous. Instead, in 1972 a survey of recent research into "the depressed woman" stated that this condition would be "the epidemic of the seventies," and that many female patients' "lack of energy" prevented them "from carrying out customary homemaking chores" or from caring properly for their children, which placed these children in "a group that is especially at risk" for emotional problems. Here, too, drugs—especially antidepressants—were said to be an excellent adjunct to psychological treatment.[38] Criticism was left to feminists. As radical psychologist Nancy Henley bitterly wrote in 1971, the fact that women were being "steered" toward "drugs that tended to pacify rather than eliminate them" merely suggested "that perhaps women are less expendable from the point of view of the dominant culture than are blacks."[39]

Moreover, from a feminist perspective psychiatrists were agents of adjustment whenever they stated that the answer to women's problems lay in terms that were private and individual, rather than social and interpersonal. "The prevalence of psychotherapy in American life is another force working to stabilize oppression by reconciling women to their condition," several radical feminists wrote in 1971. They added: "All of us—women in particular—are encouraged to believe that our individual 'hang-ups,' although they are the results of objective social conditions, are to be treated as isolated, idiosyncratic cases."[40] This rep-

resented a constant refrain from feminists. "I am tired of thinking of myself as Crazy," a woman in 1970 wrote in an open letter to her psychiatrist. "The whole psychological thing is based on the premise that there
are INDIVIDUAL problems rather than a social problem which is political."[41] On this feminists could agree.

Feminists could also agree that the entire cultural project of assigning
sharply distinct gender roles to men and women was laughable. Meredith Tax wrote in a widely circulated publication, *Woman and Her Mind*
(1970), that women were quite literally "made stupid by the roles they
are pushed into," adding (with explicit reference to R. D. Laing) that
"this remorseless stifling of a girl's intelligence and ego, this socialization
into a life of service, this continued undermining of any possibility of
independent achievement outside of the prescribed realm, all constitute
a condition one could describe as female schizophrenia."[42] Likewise, a
psychology graduate student wrote in 1970 how women "are trained"
for only a handful of "particular roles in this society," and that when
these roles "fail to satisfy," there was always still the role of "Sickie." As
she also added of the "Sickie" role: "Could it be that we have been pro-
grammed to self-destruct when our tolerance for living in this America
gets very low?"[43] Or as psychology professor Michele Hoffnung Garskof wrote in 1971, "A woman who feels dissatisfied with her suburban
home and family, a young wife who does not want children, or a woman
who is sexually aggressive is likely to be labeled 'disturbed.' The definitions of who is 'sick' and what constitutes a 'cure' have similar built-in
biases."[44] That same year the *Village Voice* sought to drive the point
home, publishing a satire that inverted the roles of men and women and
then offered wise words to a young bridegroom as he prepared anxiously for marriage:

> Oh lucky you! You are finally bridegroom to the woman of your
> dreams! But don't think for a minute that you can now relax and
> be assured automatically of marital happiness forever. You will
> have to *work at it*. While she may only have eyes for you *now*,
> remember that she is surrounded every day by attractive young
> men who are all too willing to tempt her away from you. And as
> the years go by, you will lose some of the handsome muscularity
> of your youth: you will have to make up in skill and understand-
> ing what you will lack in the bloom of youth.[45]

Humor, however, was understandably in short supply. It was really
not that funny when a woman informed her psychiatrist she was having

difficulty reaching orgasm with her husband, only to be informed that her "frigidity" was a result of penis envy (or any number of related intrapsychic causes). There continued to be widespread and persistent acceptance among psychiatrists and psychologists that sexually unfulfilled women were "frigid," and that only vaginal orgasms were the proper and "mature" response to sexual stimulation (not the clitoral orgasm which was considered the "infantile" response). When the American Psychological Association at its annual meeting in 1970 sponsored a symposium on the topic of women's "frigidity," it neglected to invite a woman to participate in the panel discussion, and the men on the panel uniformly "defined sexual adequacy of women in terms of male pleasure."[46] Such attitudes of the "Psychiatric Establishment" came increasingly to be interpreted by feminists as efforts to stifle and oppress women by keeping them separated from other women—and prevent them from identifying how their feelings of estrangement (from their bodies, from their lives) were the result of broader social forces. As the Radical Caucus of the American Psychiatric Association announced at the 1970 APA convention: "It's not penis envy or inner space or maternal urges or natural passivity or hormone-caused emotionality that determines our lives." And the caucus continued: "We don't want your crazy trips laid on us. We want LIBERATION NOW."[47]

At the same time a few more thoughtful therapists were beginning to recognize that the deepest desire of many women was not some secret longing to be men, but rather to be treated like human beings. A fine example might be the case of clinical psychologist Sheldon B. Kopp. Kopp was the author of *If You Meet the Buddha on the Road, Kill Him!* (1972), a wildly successful (and still in print) Zen-inspired self-esteem guide whose title he explained like this: "Killing the Buddha on the road means destroying the hope that anything outside of ourselves can be our master. No one is any bigger than anyone else. There are no mothers or fathers for grown-ups, only sisters and brothers."[48] Kopp wrote movingly in 1974 of a depressed female patient who was seeking for the first time to be something other than a caretaker as housewife and mother. She anxiously recounted to Kopp her bizarre fantasies of biting the heads off men—fantasies she recognized full well fit snugly in "the Freudian trip of women as castrated, penis-envying inferiors," and which might certainly have been reductively analyzed by Kopp as explicable by "the neurotic demandingness of some nutty dame who just wanted to be a man." But Kopp provided another interpretation: Not that "she wanted to become a man and consequently suffered from *pe-*

nis envy, but that she simply wanted a life of her own and what she was expressing was *person envy*." What Kopp saw, and encouraged his colleagues to begin to see as well, was that any woman who felt guilt and confusion about desiring a career outside of marriage and motherhood suffered from nothing other than "legitimate human longings to fulfill her own purpose."[49] In this way the spiritually inclined New Age psychologist Kopp was not threatened or dismissive of a young woman's emergence from subordination and self-sacrifice, but instead was able to acknowledge and validate her yearnings to be more fully human. That male therapists whose attitude toward their profession was more than a little unconventional were often the ones taking the lead in acknowledging women's humanity helped bring about moments of unusual alliance between feminism and pop psychology.

III

In response to social conditions in which women so frequently felt painfully trapped and emotionally stifled, feminist therapists developed a potpourri of techniques. For instance, many feminists turned to the holistic approach of Gestalt psychotherapy as promoted by Paul Goodman and Fritz Perls.[50] Gestalt emphasized the taking of responsibility for the choices one has made in one's life. The idea was that it was not particularly useful to muck around in a patient's childhood; what needed to be addressed was what was evident in the here and now. Gestalt feminist therapy encouraged women to understand their "personal power" and to "use more powerful and assertive language."[51] In addition there was the concept of a client-centered therapy, which had been adapted from the work of psychologist Carl Rogers, a key early progenitor of the human potential movement. Client-centered therapy posited that the therapist should not direct therapy toward a definitive end or interpretation, but rather should function more as empathic facilitator and gentle guide. It further argued that each person had the capacity to control his or her own personal growth and that such personal growth was necessarily good.[52]

And feminist therapy adapted as well concepts promoted by psychologist Abraham Maslow, who believed that "self-actualization" was the aim of all human beings. Persons sought to delight and trust in their lives and to achieve (what Maslow named) "peak-experiences." Maslow's popular *Toward a Psychology of Being* (1962) might well have been addressed directly to the future women's liberation movement: "The thing to do seems to be to find out what *you* are *really* like inside, deep

down as a member of the human species and as a particular individual."
Maslow also argued that mental illness was socially produced: "Sick
people are made by a sick culture; healthy people are made possible by a
healthy culture." He urged that "we must not fall into the trap of defining the good organism in terms of what he is 'good for' as if he were an
instrument rather than something in himself, as if he were only a means
to some extrinsic purpose."[53] Minus a preference for gender-specific language, Maslow's concepts required only the slightest tweaking before
they could be applied to the lives of women in American society, which
is what Betty Friedan's *The Feminine Mystique* (1963) succeeded in doing. In Friedan's universe the lives of men were represented as everything women wanted but were forbidden to have. And Friedan waxed
lyrical in her characterization of the magical freedoms associated with
masculinity: "Down through the ages man has known that he was set
apart from other animals by his mind's power to have an idea, a vision,
and shape the future to it. He shares a need for food and sex with other
animals, but when he loves, he loves as a man, and when he discovers
and creates and shapes a future different from his past, he is a man, a
human being." By contrast, according to Friedan (who greatly admired
the work of Maslow), the woman's plight was that she was not allowed
to self-actualize. Friedan wrote that American culture "does not permit
women to accept or gratify their basic need to grow and fulfill their potentialities as human beings, a need which is not solely defined by their
sexual role."[54] If he had cared at all about feminism, Maslow could not
have put it better himself.

Feminist therapists also turned to the transactional analysis (TA) of
psychiatrist Eric Berne, author of the hugely successful *Games People
Play: The Psychology of Human Relationships* (1964). Berne had argued—as had psychiatrist Thomas Szasz before him—that individuals
inevitably engaged with one another in the playing of roles. In Berne's
view these roles trapped people in an inability to achieve meaningful intimacy and authentic relationships. (In many respects, the notion of "role
playing" in Berne's theories also represented an extension of the "double
bind" concept proposed several years earlier by Gregory Bateson's research team; Berne's work on emotional cul-de-sacs acknowledged the
influence of both Szasz and Bateson.) For feminists theorizing their own
alienation from their marriages, their sexuality, and their lives, the focus of transactional analysis on "role playing" became a most powerful and commonsense concept. There appeared to be very little about
the oppressions experienced by women in society that could *not* be ex-

plained with the help of Berne's idea that all relationships were functions of "role playing." Like Rogers, Maslow, or Perls, Berne had said very little specifically about women in society; it had not been his purpose to reflect on the oppressive conditions confronted by women. But this did not prevent the wholesale adaptation of TA by feminist therapists.

The Radical Psychiatry Center in Berkeley, for instance, promoted women's problem-solving groups whose techniques were often derived from TA and were based on methods elaborated by Berne in *Transactional Analysis in Psychotherapy* (1961) and *Games People Play*. Among other things Berne had coined the concept of "stroking," which he had defined as one person's validation of another person's *"recognition-hunger."*[55] All persons needed strokes in social transactions, which meant that they required being heard and acknowledged; and so in women's groups at the Radical Psychiatry Center, when two women paired off they were encouraged to ask for and provide affirmation for each other. As a participant wrote in *Radical Therapist*: "The group observes closely, making sure that strokes are given openly and received in like manner."[56] As Berne had proposed, and his disciples elaborated, persons who received sufficient strokes in life were capable of greater spontaneity, awareness, and intimacy; but far too often individuals suffered from "stroke deficit." According to TA, individuals who did not receive enough strokes tended to play more games in life, and thus became more manipulative and difficult in their human interactions. And women suffered unduly from stroke deficit.

Their stroke deficit, feminist therapists further argued, led women to engage in games that only made things worse for them and for the people around them. For one thing, stroke-deprived women were especially vulnerable to transactions that amounted to "stroke barter." This meant that a woman seeking love (but not receiving enough of it) willingly allowed herself to nurture a man in exchange for the crumbs of affection she received in return. This amounted to "stroke exploitation," an exchange that transformed strokes "into a commodity with object value rather than the free, unlimited expression of human affection that they can be." Marriage too often became a form of stroke exploitation having been entered into on the basis of a stroke barter: "I won't sleep with you unless you marry me" was the classic scenario.[57] The theory was also that TA groups could help women overcome their distrust and insecurity built up from years of suffering stroke deficits by establishing solidarity with one another. The aim of the radical TA groups for women was to identify—and demolish—the self-defeating "scripts" and "games" in which women so often found themselves enmeshed. Thus among other things the Radical Psychiatry Center utilized "permission exercises" designed to help individuals "do things they want to do, but can't, because they have internalized prohibitive and inhibitive parental messages."[58] Despite their occasional differences, then, feminist therapy, radical therapy, and pop psychology also frequently blurred into one another.

Feminist self-help groups and clinics sprang up everywhere in the course of the 1970s. In the Boston area alone more than a dozen feminist therapy organizations were established. A conference on feminism and therapy attracted several hundred participants.[59] New groups like the Feminist Psychology Coalition in New York and the Feminist Therapy Collective of Philadelphia were organized "to provide individual and group therapy services promoting the growth of responsible, autonomous individuals who are able to choose and create options for living which transcend the traditional norms and boundaries of sex roles."[60] There were calls for a nationwide referral service designed to help women connect with feminist therapists wherever they might be.[61] Feminist therapists came to be seen as vital to the process of overcoming the debilitating effects of society and social expectations on women's lives. As an early feminist therapist wrote, "The feminist-oriented therapist will have a sensitive awareness of what it means subjectively to be a woman in a male-dominated society, to be bewildered by the conflicting stereotypes and hounded by a sense that she's damned if she does (assert herself) and damned if she doesn't."[62]

Women's consciousness-raising (CR) groups, established in the late 1960s, continued to flourish during the 1970s. The aim here was to rewrite the traditional rules of psychotherapy so that women would be allowed to "stay in touch with our feelings," as Kathie Sarachild, who helped to originate the concept of CR groups, wrote in 1968. Sarachild added: "In our groups, let's share our feelings and pool them. Let's let ourselves go and see where our feelings lead us. Our feelings will lead us to ideas and then to actions."[63]

All did not always run smoothly, however. Historians of American feminism have gingerly acknowledged that the power-sharing therapeutic strategies adopted by women often led to severe internal conflicts within groups and to countless hours of self-examination that yielded painful paralysis rather than practical insight or effective action.[64] The aim of "structurelessness" within women's groups, as Jo Freeman tactfully pointed out in 1972, may have been "a healthy counter" to an "over-structured society," but it was also "becoming a goddess in its own right."[65] Moreover, as feminist therapist Hogie Wyckoff wrote, women were just as capable as men of playing the "Lefter Than Thou" game in which some participants professed "to be more revolutionary or more radical" than other participants.[66] Wyckoff herself experienced this in late 1971 when "the New Radical Psychiatry Group" broke with her group, the Berkeley Radical Psychiatry Center, over charges that she and other RaP leaders had "become anti-creative as a result of the power structure."[67]

There were further problems—some intrinsic to the nature of therapy itself, some to the inevitable impotence of therapy in a fundamentally unjust society. It was not proving enough for women to separate themselves from men and dismantle or reject the heterosexist and male-dominant paradigm that so often accompanied the profession of psychotherapy. Women-only facilities or women-focused therapies had their own homosocial problems. An informative case study was a difficult situation that developed at the Elizabeth Stone House. Founded in 1974 in Jamaica Plain, Massachusetts, by a small group of former mental health patients to offer peer counseling to women with psychological problems, Elizabeth Stone House was one of the first residential mental health crisis programs in the nation designed solely for women. (The house took its name from a nineteenth-century mental health activist who had been committed to an asylum in the 1840s for changing her religion from Methodist to Baptist.) But cofounder Mary Raffini lasted only a couple of years as director despite her dream of establishing a feminist alternative to the traditional mental hospital for women. The stress was too great, and tensions between the women at the center frequently ran too high. "I know that the house cannot exist on good intentions or anarchy," Raffini mournfully concluded in announcing her resignation.[68] Along related lines, women who worked in therapeutic settings with female (as opposed to male) professionals found that this did not necessarily mean that everything suddenly got better. In her poem, "Ode to My Analyst," a woman mocked the notion that female therapists were somehow automatic improvements over male therapists ("on your way out tell my secretary to double your dosage she says dryly / thanks see you thursday I say" concluded the poem).[69] And no matter what the gender of the therapist, the burdens of femininity could linger. As one woman phrased it, the oppression she suffered was not just due to male disrespect or catcalls, but also "the mother in me": "The negative image of woman which has been instilled in me from birth."[70]

It was not only for these reasons, however, that some feminists announced that feminist therapy would never be enough to alter society in any fundamental respect. Even feminist therapy, some of the most radical commentators contended, was its own kind of "adjustment." Perhaps all feminist therapy could offer was "a catalyst not a cure," as the feminist journal *Off Our Backs* concluded in 1973.[71] Or as a lesbian psychology student at Berkeley noted in 1975, while feminist therapy was helping some lesbians "grow strong inside ourselves," feminist therapy "can never by itself be effective for mass revolutionary change."[72] And some leading feminists rejected the usefulness of therapy (feminist or otherwise) altogether. Marxist feminist Shulamith Firestone, for example, argued that since therapy had historically "proven worse than useless," it needed to be replaced "with the only thing that can do any good: political organization."[73] And some feminists were even harsher. Psychologist Dorothy Tennov dismissed psychotherapy in 1971 as "a monster in our midst" and "a kind of opiate."[74] She considered feminist therapy to be no better than the generic masculine variety, rhetorically inquiring: "*What is feminist therapy?* I find the two terms mutually contradictory." Tennov tersely stated: "Feminists do not practice *therapy* on their sisters."[75] And inspired partly by reading Thomas Szasz, radical feminist philosopher Mary Daly arrived at a comparable conclusion in *Gyn/Ecology* (1978), noting that "the very concept of 'feminist therapy' is inherently a contradiction" and that "Radical Feminist Therapy" centers functioned as "Taming Centers, where independent gynergetic being [*sic*] is treated as a source of disease."[76]

The concept of changing the roles women played in society saturated the movement's goals of psychological transformation and political liberation alike—but what was the relationship between these two goals? Female misery was widespread, but was it remediable through feminist therapy? Could psychoanalysis be properly retooled to incorporate a feminist ethos? As feminist psychiatrist Carol Wolman observed in 1975: "Feminism is intrinsically therapeutic and all good therapy whether done by and for men or women, must be feminist—in other words, it must include a feminist analysis of the clients' thoughts and behavior patterns and an effort to help the client overcome his or her own internal sexism, which is so self-crippling." But Wolman also acknowledged that feminist therapy should not be considered an end in itself. "As women working for the mental health of women, we have an important job—to heal our battered sisters and strengthen each other for the fray," Wolman wrote. "But we must remember that therapy only helps individuals, it doesn't change the system. In order to do that we must work together—collectively and politically."[77] Thus while some groups were overtly political—and especially those self-designated "consciousness-raising" groups—others confined themselves to the task of mutual assistance in personal problem solving.[78] Both kinds of groups were understood by many feminists as crucial to social transformation. Women's lives would not change if the roles they were forced to play did not change, and these roles would never change until women freed themselves from the games in which society had trapped them.

Such considerations may have seemed circular, but the yearnings that lay behind them were profound. Feminists felt deeply how frequently women had been expected to suppress the human urge "toward self-actualization, toward mastery of the environment, and toward fulfillment of one's potential" and to become "adjusted to a social environment with associated restrictive stereotypes."[79] But knowing this did not mean knowing what to do about it. And it did not alter the simple fact that women too often experienced existence much like Alice did in Wonderland, when she had asked: "Who am I then? Tell me that first, and then, if I like being that person, I'll come up: if not, I'll stay down here till I'm somebody else."[80]

IV

Men's testimonials from this era demonstrated how much men were also being pressured to play according to certain societal roles, and not all of them were naturals in those roles. Penis and person envy alike, after all, were not just the preserve of women. Men were hampered by inhibitions and locked in conflicts with one another as they too struggled with the difficulties they experienced in attempting to achieve "self-actualization."

Masculinity (like femininity) required schooling. Men had to be taught to be men, and the surest sign that they were slipping in their responsibilities and roles as men was the mental state of the women with whom they were sharing their lives. If wives were "intractable" or "angry," something must be wrong with the husbands; they were too diffident and milquetoast. In these respects a (in hindsight appallingly normative) form of social diagnosis continued to operate throughout the 1960s and into the 1970s and, in fact, was a logical extension of a double bind theory that had often posited much the same analysis of the husband of a schizophrenogenic mother.[81]

Conventional therapeutic literature directed at psychiatric professionals had seldom bothered to avoid condescension in its summaries of the foibles and failings also of the men in families with mentally disturbed

children. It highlighted that the schizophrenogenic wife and mother often shared her life with a weak and unassertive husband and father who
had failed to carry himself as a proper man. If the psychiatric treatment
for female patients insisted that they had to adjust to their femininity,
the psychiatric advice to men—whether in treatment or not—was that
they had to adjust accordingly to their rightful masculinity. Women
who were not reconciled to their roles as wives and homemakers were at
special risk of producing mental illness in their children or themselves,
it was true, but men, too, needed to buck up. As anthropologist Jules
Henry observed in *Pathways to Madness* (1971), the idea of a submis-
sive father was so pervasive in the literature on schizophrenic children
it amounted to "a psychiatric cliché," and "case records of disturbed
children are littered with notations like: 'Father is passive, inadequate,
withdrawn.'" And yet Henry only partially distanced himself from this
idea. (He did remark that "it is hard to imagine that there is anything
inherent in 'excessive' paternal passivity which makes a child emotionally ill," but at the same time, he also concluded that "a problem in a
clinically 'passive' man is that the little activity in which he does engage
is often pathogenic."[82]) But the fathers of disturbed children were certainly not the only focus for elaborations of appropriate masculinity; the
dominant culture was full of such elaborations, and many men struggled
with them.

Some more feminist-identified male therapists opted for the route of
self-criticism. They noted how they too suffered from patriarchal values and were stuck playing "stereotyped scripts," as radical psychologist Claude Steiner observed.[83] In this regard an especially moving autobiographical account came from radical psychiatrist Michael Glenn. In
1973 Glenn reflected on his own emotionally troubled existence "growing up a white man in America," a process that had "trained me to be
an oppressor." Material advancement and career success were always
of preeminent importance to Glenn, while "being a person had little to
do with anything." He had felt tremendously uncomfortable in his own
body as a boy, he admitted, and his contact with girls was driven by a desire to dominate and control them. "I could not treat women as people,"
Glenn wrote, "and thus could not be a man myself." A young marriage
during graduate school quickly "became harsh and cruel as I extracted
emotional sustenance from my wife while at the same time insisting on
my being in command." The relationship floundered after she joined the
women's movement and began to articulate her frustrations. Glenn confessed that he still "could not avoid hurting her deeply in order to get
away from my own pain." And soon thereafter the marriage came to an

end. Glenn generalized from his own problems to the problems he saw with traditional therapies:

> Therapists attempt to brainwash women just as they try to brainwash gays, the young, radicals, and any others who defy today's oppressive social laws. They deny their patients' perceptions, telling a woman she isn't really angry at her husband, but at the boredom of her life. They encourage her to develop a hobby. They tell patients they "really feel" something they don't feel. They tell a woman she "really feels" inadequate and dependent on her husband, instead of angry and resentful; or that her sense of inadequacy is *really* responsible for her anger. They urge their patients to adjust to the "reality" of their lives. . . . They use their power to gain selfish, unfeeling ends: denying women abortions in situations where psychiatric opinions are essential for gaining permission; encouraging them to stay in messy family situations, where their husbands beat them or keep them virtually chained to their house; telling women who have sexual difficulties to "loosen up," without investigating the context in which their resentment and lack of sexual responsiveness might be entirely justified; and so on.[84]

Yet at other times feminist male introspection slid fairly effortlessly into flakiness. "Men are oppressed," wrote a contributor to the Berkeley-based journal *Issues in Radical Therapy*. "We are taught that there is no need for feelings—that they only get in the way of efficient and successful action."[85] Self-absorption at times hovered close to self-pity. The culture denied men their right to be passive without feeling ashamed. "I wish I wasn't forced to make a pass at a girl," said a young man during his group therapy session in 1972. "But if I don't make a pass, she thinks I'm a fag or a mamma's boy."[86] In still other instances the therapeutic advice to feminist men swerved into the rudimentary and ridiculous. A member of the Berkeley Radical Psychiatry Center wrote that "becoming aware of one's breathing" was essential in men's ability to reclaim their feelings. "Men tend to breathe only into their chests," he noted, which in turn caused men to keep "a tight anal sphincter. This literally 'locks out' a lot of feeling and sensitivity." (Though this male feminist belatedly critiqued his own insufficient leftism, in an addendum he observed how he now felt that his article, "though by no means irrelevant, is lacking in a broader analysis of how the oppression men experience is the direct result of living and working in a capitalist society."[87])

It was left to Claude Steiner to capture most succinctly the all too self-serving dynamics among men working so earnestly to be better male feminists. Steiner noted how men across Berkeley were "going around saying, 'Oh God, I'm such a pig.'" But he further observed that "self-hatred does not help," and men who were engaging in it demonstrated a tendency to "retreat into a passive stance, a stance which is often laced with a whining little boys' game called 'All or Nothing at All,' and which is bolstered by subtle but powerful passive power plays." In other words, the conduct of these "effeminists" represented but a slight improvement over the conduct of more overtly macho men.[88] Theirs was only an old chauvinism dressed up to look like a new game.

When mainstream pop psychology self-help analyzed the lives of men, the cross-section portrait it painted was rife with insecurity, pain, and anxiety. Men were like frightened children. "I'm not really a lawyer," a thirty-five-year-old lawyer told psychiatrist Eric Berne. "I'm just a little boy."[89] And Thomas Harris in *I'm OK—You're OK* advised readers to be aware of the child within themselves, as well as to "be sensitive to the Child in others, talk to that Child, stroke that Child, protect that Child," not only within every woman, but also within every man.[90] Men would not survive in the world without women to care for them, as psychologist Joyce Brothers told her female readership. While, as Brothers noted, "for self-centeredness, there is nothing to beat the male in contemporary society," she additionally observed that "we tend to forget how dependent men really are."[91] Many men, moreover, according to psychologist Jerry Greenwald, ended up serving as doormats to other men and to their wives because they had failed to be "self-starters," or because they suffered from "nice-guy-itis." Men frequently were pushed around by greedy, themselves self-involved or fearful-of-commitment women. They had "emotional constipation," or were psychologically deformed by rigid or abusive fathers or they narcotized themselves with alcohol against the boredom induced by their spouses.[92] In general, according to Wayne Dyer, men needed desperately to learn to overcome their "self-defeating behavior."[93] Men, said clinical psychologist Herbert Fensterheim and his wife Jean Baer, too often possessed "no control of their lives" and were victims of their own "unassertiveness," lacking the wherewithal to demand job promotions, meet desirable women in bars, or initiate more playful sex with their wives.[94] Passivity was not only bad for one's mental health, it was bad for one's physical well-being, observed Dyer, who went so far as to suggest that people who did not take control of their lives and destinies gave themselves diseases (including cancer).[95]

What pop psychological self-help ultimately sold men (and women) was motivation, consolation, and reassurance—in terms that were often as bland and banal as possible. It above all offered flattery and hope—a stark contrast to the more admonishing norms of traditional psychiatry or the auto-critique of radical therapy. With compulsive repetitiveness, pop psych dismissed mainstream "talk" therapy—"its seeming foreverness, its high cost, its debatable results, and its vague esoteric terms."[96] It was de rigueur to mock the reflex contemporaries had to "go to psychoanalysts" in response to the inevitable daily "frustration and boredom and anxiety . . . the lack of fulfillment in our lives."[97]

Much emphasis in pop psych was placed on the nonverbal. "Talking is usually good for intellectual understanding of personal experience," wrote psychologist William C. Schutz, "but it is often not as effective for helping a person to *experience*—to feel."[98] In *Please Touch* (1970), an excellent participant observer memoir of the human potential movement, Jane Howard noted how much pop psych began from the premise that "we can learn a lot more than we might suppose about each other without ever exchanging a single sentence, and that many sentences that do get uttered are wasteful, dishonest and evasive."[99] Furthermore, and since bodies stored pain, the most useful therapy had principally to be physical in nature, as psychologist Arthur Janov advocated through his "Primal Scream" cure and psychologist Alexander Lowen addressed with Bioenergetics.[100]

At the same time there was in much pop psych literature a tacit acknowledgment that despair and dread and miserableness were right below the surface of many people's lives. And here the impact of antipsychiatric thought was most strongly reflected. Families were accused in pop psych materials of perpetrating a double bind on children (with whom readers were enjoined always most closely to identify). Gestalt theorist Fritz Perls observed, for instance, that "it makes all the difference to a child who has built a castle in the garden, whether the mother is interested and appreciative, or whether she shouts, 'Look how dirty you are! What a mess you have made! You really ought to be ashamed of yourself.'"[101] And Arthur Janov also noted how a young child developed emotional disorders because he "cannot understand that it is his parents who are troubled."[102]

Yet in the final analysis pop psych proved also hopelessly contradictory in its injunctions. Sometimes pop psych urged *less* spontaneity.

"People say they want to 'let go,'" wrote psychoanalysts Mildred Newman and Bernard Berkowitz. "What they really need to do is take
hold."[103] Sometimes it urged *more* spontaneity. Psychologist Jess Lair insisted her life only got better the day she set "letting go as a life goal."[104]
Sometimes childhood traumas mattered not at all (as in Gestalt); sometimes they were the key to everything (as in Primal Scream). And sometimes pop psych merely urged (in a distinctly obnoxious macho manner)
that the world was a combat zone where only the strong survived, and in
which one needed adeptly to arm oneself accordingly. "Through my own
experience, I learned that striving for a positive mental attitude will get
you nowhere unless you have the ammunition to back it up," declared
Robert J. Ringer in his classic antialtruism treatise, *Winning through Intimidation* (1974).[105] Life was not about self-improvement, it was about
self-advancement. As Ringer wrote in *Looking Out for Number One*
(1977), the goal in life was to eliminate any relationship in which "your
accounts payable to someone have far outgrown your receivables" and
thus to maintain only "value-for-value friendships."[106] Pop psych managed, in other words, to promise everything to everyone, and to confuse
many while sowing stress in the process.

Sociologist Micki McGee has concluded that economic pressures in
the 1970s fostered a culture especially conducive to the popularity of
self-help. The roadblocks to personal success during a financial down-
turn made the promises of self-realization and human potential particularly marketable.[107] And Barbara Ehrenreich and Deirdre English offered a compatible analysis in 1978 when they observed how pop psych
philosophizing often purveyed, in the guise of sensitive advice, nothing
more than the ethos of "the modern consumption-centered economy,"
one in which everyone was supposed to "capitalize on our assets and cut
our losses, maximize the return on our (emotional) investments, and in
general put all our relationships—whether with lovers, co-workers, or
family members—on the psychic equivalent of a cash 'n' carry basis."[108]

There is no question that pop psych represented a deradicalization of
the earlier antipsychiatric impulses of feminist therapy. More strikingly,
pop psych also represented a remarkably creative compromise formation
between the old-style patriarchal psychiatry and an (at least partial) effort to entertain the grievances put forward by feminism. What remains
something of a mystery, however, is how, within the wider conservative
backlash unrolling from the 1970s onward against everything the 1960s
were said to have stood for, antipsychiatry, radical therapy, and feminism
eventually came widely to be held responsible for fueling an entire generation's fixation with narcissism and self-indulgence. This view not only

obscured the fact that feminism's goal had never been self-indulgence for women but rather self-respect. It also actively and aggressively buried the fact that the rise of a wider culture of narcissism had little or nothing to do with either antipsychiatry or feminism, but rather with the efflorescence of pop psychology—an efflorescence that had far more to do with soothing the self-doubts and fears of men than it ever had to do with either political radicalism in general or feminism in particular.

7

A Fashionable Kind of Slander

What indeed is "mental health"? Who indeed is "normal"? Were slave-holders "normal"? Did Nat Turner have a "problem with authority"? . . . If a man drops a bomb on people he doesn't even see or know, he is doing his duty. And if a man is *afraid* he might want to kill someone, he, of course, needs help or guidance or treatment to prevent a fear from becoming a deed; whereas if a pilot should become horrified at the thought of what *he* might do, the bombs he might cause to fall on fellow human beings, he would need that same "treatment"—presumably so that he will get over his hesitations and "do his duty."

Robert Coles, 1970[1]

I

By the end of the 1960s, pronouncing the student activist mentally unstable had become a popular pastime among psychiatrists and psychologists and other social scientists. In 1969, University of Chicago professor (and expert on adolescence) Bruno Bettelheim began to pronounce on the psychological maladjustments he claimed to see in campus radicals. Speaking before a House Special Subcommittee on Education in March of that year, Bettelheim opined that campus radicals flocked to follow strong father figures like Ho Chi Minh and Mao because they had lacked strong or decisive fathers.[2] Bettelheim concluded that "many of these kids are very sick. They need psychiatrists."[3] A year earlier political scientist Leo Rosten (author of *The Joys of Yiddish*) made a related but different point in an open letter to a student radical. "You say your generation 'wants to be understood,'" Rosten wrote bitterly. "'Understanding'? You don't even understand that when you call me a 'motherfucker' you are projecting your unresolved incestuous wishes on me. The technical name for such projection, in advanced form, is paranoia."[4]

In 1969 a contributor to the *American Psychologist* posited that the radicals themselves could often be characterized as having the same "authoritarian personality and the lust for power" that they criticized in their elders; the radicals were just "play acting." He also speculated that young persons who congregated at protest marches were not interested in social change but rather sought only "the sense of drama, the feeling of participation, and the excitement of being caught up in a group experience."[5] Another contributor responded to this piece by contending instead that protesters were seeking "a symbolic killing of the primordial father."[6] Even campus psychiatrists delivered bad news, though their analysis took yet another turn. Dana Farnsworth, director of Harvard University Health Services, argued that student activists were "obsessed, rigid, dogmatic, lacking in sense of humor and perspective, intolerant and often overly suspicious in their modes of thinking."[7] And numerous prominent social commentators followed suit. Sidney Hook, George Kennan, Jacques Barzun, Irving Kristol, Nathan Glazer, and H. Stuart Hughes each offered his own unflattering diagnosis of young radicals' mental states, identifying all sorts of possible analytic explanations for student radicalism.[8] Not atypical (and certainly influential) was the mammoth study, *The Conflict of Generations* (1969), in which sociologist Lewis S. Feuer argued that (what he identified as) the "pathological element in the student movement" was principally derived from an unacknowledged and unresolved oedipal struggle.[9]

Nor were African American civil rights activists exempt from such dismissive diagnoses. An article in *Archives of General Psychiatry* in 1968 noted that "the stress of asserting civil rights in the United States these past ten years and the corresponding nationalistic fervor of Africo-Asian nations during the same period has stimulated specific reactive psychoses in American Negroes." Its authors proposed the new diagnostic category of "protest psychosis," which they described as "colored by a denial of Caucasian values and hostility thereto. This protest psychosis . . . is virtually a repudiation of 'white civilization.'"[10] Despite a wealth of empirical studies that found radicals to be quite well adjusted, then, a popular conception of both white and black activists as having a few screws loose began aggressively to be promoted.[11]

In 1970 psychiatrist Robert Coles offered his own rebuttal to derogatory psychological summaries of the student and civil rights activists. Coles was appalled and rhetorically inquired: How was it symptomatic of "oedipal conflict" to oppose poverty in America? Why was it "passive-aggressive," "paranoid" or "exhibitionist" (or possibly even "psychotic") to object fervently to the Vietnam War? What psychiatric validity or relevance did it have to surmise that young demonstrators must be "products of permissive child-rearing practices"? These were just a few examples, Coles wrote, of what was turning out to be a particularly "fashionable kind of slander."[12]

Labeling student radicals mentally ill was a means to avoid addressing their ideas. And it had happened before, Coles observed, reminding his readers how civil rights volunteers who traveled south during Freedom Summer in the early 1960s had been characterized as "wild, impetuous, thoughtless, self-destructive, and masochistic," not to mention "irrational, deluded by a host of absurd and dangerous fantasies, violence-prone, and in some serious way, antisocial." It was all nonsense, Coles added, citing his extensive professional experience observing these young people.[13] But it hardly mattered that the slanders had no basis in reality. Repeated often enough, they acquired a life all their own. Coles recounted how "a decidedly sensitive and well-educated Southern judge" committed an African American civil rights worker to a mental hospital on account of his antiracist activities. In the asylum the young man told Coles:

> It's quite a setup they've got. We protest our inability to vote, to go into a movie or restaurant everyone else uses, and they call us crazy, and send us away to be looked over by psychiatrists and psychologists and social workers and all the rest of them. The questions I've had put at me since I've been here! Were you a *loner* when you were a boy? Did people consider you *rebellious*? Were you *popular* or *unpopular* as a child? When you were younger did you have trouble *taking orders* from your parents or your teachers? Did your mother *discipline* you firmly, or did she more or less let you do as you please?

This was all too reminiscent, commented Coles in 1970, of how the Soviet Union dealt with dissent. The situation in the United States was not as "blatant and absurd" as it was in the USSR, but it was distressing nonetheless when activists—"rather than listened to (and thoroughly applauded

or severely criticized) for the substance of what they propose or advocate"—are instead "to be condemned for their 'personality problems.'"[14]

And yet, and despite attempts to defend 1960s radicalisms, by the
early 1970s new criticisms were being raised especially against the counterculture. Two psychoanalysts writing in 1974, for instance, deemed
the counterculture to be profoundly "maladaptive." They noted how
"the life style of the counter-culture involves a concern with violence
and cruelty, a preoccupation with the sexually perverse, an attachment
to noise, an anti-intellectual mood, and an effort to erase the boundary
between art and life." They additionally argued that the sex life of youth
in the counterculture had "a child-like pregenital quality" and "certain
regressive anal and oral features, such as disorder, dirt, obscenities and
oral rage."[15]

By the later 1970s a further new critical narrative also about radicalism had begun to take shape. Sixties activists—having failed to bring
down "the establishment"—were crumbling under catastrophic feelings
of clinical melancholia. Psychedelic drugs and the anarchic lifestyle that
accompanied their use had not led to a glorious new social order. Shattering the nuclear family had not resulted in new communal arrangements that met the emotional needs of its participants. The generation of
1968 was on the verge of a collective nervous breakdown.

In early 1976 the *New York Times* reported on its front page how
"the rebellious, idealistic generation of adolescents" who had come of
age during the social upheavals of the 1960s were now "experiencing a
generational malaise of haunting frustrations, anxiety and depression."
As they approached thirty years of age, many former activists and members of the counterculture were seeking professional counseling to cope
with problems ranging from suicidal tendencies to alcoholism. Psychiatrists hypothesized that the chaotic character of the 1960s caused these
many young people to develop unrealistic expectations about society
and themselves—only to see those expectations dissolve into disillusion-
ment. As a psychiatrist quoted in the article summarized matters: "A lot
of these kids were led to believe the world would be handed to them on
a silver platter. They got spoiled by permissive parents, and aren't prepared for a cruel world."[16]

In short: Initially critics attacked the New Left for its politics. Subsequently, they attacked both the New Left and the counterculture for
something rather more elusive and diffuse: a change in the emotional climate. Increasingly, youth activists and their cohort were derogated not
only for their misdirected rage but also for promoting a more generalized
self-indulgence—and not only in themselves but in the broader culture as

well. Radicals and hippies were accused of having destroyed the nuclear family and for spurring a society-wide phenomenon of "the triumph of the therapeutic."[17] And ultimately, in a peculiar twist, the destruction of the family and the rise of a therapeutic culture were both blamed not least on antipsychiatry.

Eventually, antipsychiatry would be reviled for its purported extremist refusal to believe in the medical reality of mental illness. In the meantime, however, the demerits of antipsychiatry were more frequently mixed with a welter of other complaints about the New Left and the counterculture—as well as feminism. In a battery of contradictory assessments, cultural commentators rushed to decry, variously: the militancy of antiwar protesters, the ludic excesses of drug-using hippies, and the selfish desires of women for emancipation. But they also decried the effusion in the 1960s and 1970s of pop psychology and the relentless demand to "find yourself" and "get in touch with your feelings" and the generalized transformation of US society into "the culture of narcissism."[18] In the ensuing cacophony, antipsychiatry, the New Left, and feminism frequently were all three lumped together as inexcusable revolts against domesticity. Amid a growing chorus of calls to restore the nuclear family, antipsychiatry would often be refigured as just another subset—albeit an especially appalling one—of the wider pop psychological and human potential movements, not least in order to make a roundabout, though certainly powerful, plea for a nostalgic return to the familial model of the 1950s.

As the 1970s turned into the 1980s influential commentators advanced a view that the 1960s rebellions had done Americans much more psychological harm than good. "One thing many of us are certain of is that parent-child relationships and family life have deteriorated badly in modern times," a psychologist wrote in the early 1980s.[19] And the damage extended far beyond families. After the debacles of the 1960s, the United States had emerged as a "Psychological Society," having taken on "the tone of a giant psychiatric clinic."[20] More specifically, a sociologist in 1982 further noted how "the counterculture's radical impulse" and its "structural and moral fragility" were factors that "contributed to its downfall." He added how the "delegitimation of utilitarian culture, and with it the stripping away of moral authority from major American social institutions: government, law, business, religion, marriage and the family" meant, moreover, that there could be "no simple return to normalcy."[21] Intent on bringing down the system, this perspective concluded, former radicals had nowhere left to go once the 1960s rebellions ended. The counterculture had unraveled the cohesiveness of American society due to its feckless pursuit of interpersonal experimentation and preoccupation with therapeutic self-discovery.

Especially influential in this regard was the best-selling work of Christopher Lasch, who identified what he saw as a central contradiction of the "so-called counterculture": that its "fascination with personal relations, which becomes increasingly intense as the hope of political solutions recedes," actually concealed "a thoroughgoing disenchantment with personal relations." The counterculture liked to applaud its own propagation of "emotional liberation." But this was wholly misleading, Lasch thought. Many young people were actually motivated only by "the ideologies of impulse gratification" and "a rejection of intimacy and a search for sex without emotion" (as well as, in Lasch's dismissive summary, a "celebration of oral sex, masturbation, and homosexuality")—all of which taken together had worked with great efficacy to undermine the emotionally and existentially sustaining force that was the traditional nuclear family.[22]

Lasch also condemned antipsychiatry in particular, especially for the ways it had been (in his account) put to use by radical therapists. Indeed, much of what was wrong in the 1970s in the United States, Lasch elaborated, could be blamed on the disproportionate impact of antipsychiatric thinking. "When The Radical Therapist argued that 'therapy is change—not adjustment,' it took the position, in effect, that politics itself is a form of therapy," Lasch wrote, adding that "radical" therapists stated how they wanted to abolish therapy—even though the opposite was closer to the truth. They wished nothing other than "to model education, law enforcement and spiritual salvation on what has variously been called non-directive therapy, reality therapy, behavior therapy, or client-centered therapy, in which 'no strict demands are made on the patient, nor is he admonished in any way.' The critics of 'mental illness,'" Lasch opined, "would abolish the hospital only to make the whole world a hospital." Antipsychiatry, according to Lasch, resulted in "the very nightmare it seeks to avert—the ultimate anti-Utopia, a society run by 'doctors.'"[23] For Lasch, the assault by radical therapists on a normative perspective was thoroughly disagreeable.

Lasch additionally lambasted antipsychiatry for the ways it had been (in his account) put to use by feminists. Lasch wrote: "Caught in the crossfire of generational revolt and the revolt of women, the domestic revival expired. Once again the family found itself under heavy criticism, this time as the symbol of a sentimental privatism universally repudiated in an equally sentimental search for 'community.' Feminists condemned domestic life more bitterly than before, drawing on the writings of Laing,

Cooper, and other theorists of the revulsion against domesticity to buttress their increasingly comprehensive indictment."[24] In a sophisticated
turn of argument, Lasch suggested that without a patriarchally organized family unit within and against which to contend, the ability of
children (in his imagination, always male) to mature appropriately became fatally compromised. In Lasch's words: "The decline of the classic bourgeois family had important psychic results: the collapse or near-
collapse of privacy and inner life, the impoverishment of imagination
and fantasy . . . and the waning of the capacity for self-discipline and
self-regulation."[25] Interestingly, here was a version of the double bind—
but revamped for an *anti*-antipsychiatric perspective—positioned to provide a rationale for the idea that healthful family life required (the return
of) a forceful and authoritative father.

   Other versions of attacks on antipsychiatry managed to blur together
the work of Laing with—of all people—Theodor Adorno and his team's
study from 1950, *The Authoritarian Personality*. In their best-selling
The War over the Family (1983), sociologists Brigitte Berger and Peter L.
Berger named Adorno and his colleagues as main progenitors of postwar cultural problems, directly linking them to the rise of a "commune
movement in America and Western Europe" in the 1960s. (About these
communes, the Bergers wrote further that they amounted to one of "the
most rigidly authoritarian and destructive movements of our time.") The
Bergers also condemned *The Authoritarian Personality* because of its
contention that "(right-wing) authoritarianism has its roots in the type
of family produced by bourgeois-capitalist society," a view (the Bergers
added) that was "but one small step" away from "the kind of analyses
advanced by R. D. Laing" and other radical psychiatrists "who look
upon the bourgeois family as the major obstacle to healthy and non-
repressed individuals."[26]

   By the 1980s, in sum, and despite an ongoing rich variation of emphases, a thoroughly revisionist history of the 1960s had begun to fall
into place. Although balanced in tone and scholarly in format, Robert
Bellah and colleagues' *Habits of the Heart* (1985), a best-selling study of
American values, also elucidated how a 1960s obsession with "finding
oneself" had wrought incalculable havoc in American society. "Therapy" was the culprit, the authors wrote, because "the very language of
therapeutic relationship seems to undercut the possibility of other than
self-interested relationships." "Therapy" served only to increase (not decrease) Americans' anxieties. The incessant push for fuller self-expression
largely crippled Americans' capacity for meaningful intimacies. The fervor associated with the 1960s not only failed to change the world, it

CHAPTER SEVEN   **174**

also effectively impoverished the ways in which people chose to relate to one another. As the authors wrote, "the therapeutic conception of life" that had dominated the 1960s and 1970s enforced such a "relentless insistence on consciousness and the endless scanning of one's own and others' feelings while making moment-by-moment calculations of the shifting cost/benefit balance" that it ultimately became "so ascetic in its demands as to be unendurable."[27] This interpretative frame was not pretty, but it would certainly be the one that stuck.[28]

How could it happen that an antipsychiatric suspiciousness of the ever-expanding tentacles of psychiatry and therapy that the New Left and the counterculture had used *against* medical practitioners and mental hospitals—also as a means to powerfully critique social and political relations and institutions more generally—could again by the later 1970s and 1980s be turned *against* the left? The antipsychiatric impulse—burgeoning in the 1950s within a right-wing populism and libertarianism—had shifted for over a decade leftward to become part and parcel of the antiauthoritarian counterculture in the 1960s. But by the 1980s, 1960s radicalism and the counterculture found themselves held responsible for the very same therapeutic society they had once denounced.

II

In the 1970s discussion among left-leaning theorists turned on which aspects of antipsychiatry might be salvaged while others should be jettisoned. Left observers with qualified sympathy for the antipsychiatric challenge attempted to defend at least some of its elements—even while distancing themselves from what they perceived as its excesses, inaccuracies, and unfortunate lapses into incoherence. For instance, while British Marxist psychologist Peter Sedgwick would later comprehensively lambast antipsychiatry (in *Psycho Politics*, which appeared in 1982), during the early 1970s, he struck a more ambivalent tone.[29] On the one hand he agreed with antipsychiatrists that it was likely "that 'schizophrenia' is a pretty useless dustbin category for a variety of psychic ills which have little logically or biologically in common with one another." But on the other hand Sedgwick endorsed the medical model of madness, insisting that mentally ill people really were ill. Sedgwick took aim at simplistic critiques of psychiatrists as the henchmen of a capitalist conspiracy to tame deviance, noting sarcastically not only how he would be "perfectly happy to see as many mentally-ill persons as possible treated, fully and effectively, in this society," but also—in a poignant and evocative aside—that "if capitalism could really 'adjust' people, through psychiatry or any other technology, who would want to quarrel with it?"[30]

Marxist intellectual and cultural historian Russell Jacoby attempted as well to weave his way through the possible advantages of antipsychiatric thought for the purposes of political theorizing. Jacoby contended that mentally sick persons really did require psychiatric attention, even as he averred how mental illnesses certainly had societal origins. "Both are true," Jacoby argued, noting analogously how "the victim of an automobile accident is not to be turned away by the politically aware doctor with the remark that he or she is not a victim of a specific car accident but a victim of an obsolete transportation system kept alive by the necessities of profit." And yet what had happened to the potentially so useful social diagnosis, he lamented, was that it had become banalized, with far too many "radical" therapies articulating a "mysticism without politics." It was no wonder then, he surmised, that "endless talk on I and thou" and an increasing preoccupation with wounded subjectivities were replacing political activism, and that so many former radicals were now caught up with "pop existentialism," having effectively confused (as had, Jacoby noted, Laing himself) "psychic first aid with liberation."[31]

Yet as the accusations against the New Left accumulated, and as partial defenses of antipsychiatry mixed with critiques, antipsychiatric ideas, both in culture and in science, continued nonetheless also to be put forward as though they remained doctrinally correct and only required further energetic defense. These ideas appeared in Nancy Milford's *Zelda* (1970), a biography that recounted Zelda Fitzgerald's descent into a socially produced madness; and they appeared in Toni Morrison's *The Bluest Eye* (also 1970), a tragic tale of how white racism engendered mental illnesses in African Americans. They appeared in actress Frances Farmer's *Will There Really Be a Morning?* (1972), her account of the horrors of her commitment to mental hospitals. Antipsychiatric concepts appeared on Broadway in Peter Shaffer's smash hit, *Equus* (1973), which featured a Laing-like psychiatrist, and they appeared on screen in Miloš Forman's *One Flew Over the Cuckoo's Nest* (1975), which gave Jack Nicholson the chance to bring Ken Kesey's Randle Patrick McMurphy back for a memorable encore. Here and elsewhere a key concept was that mental hospitals functioned more like political prisons than genuine therapeutic centers.

This was a view popularized especially effectively in Marge Piercy's *Woman on the Edge of Time* (1976), her influential speculative science fiction novel in which an asylum inmate has a visitor from 2037—a

distant time when society has become nonhierarchical, pantheistic, an-
tipatriarchal, ecologically attuned, and polymorphously perverse. There
are still insane asylums in the future, this visitor explains, but no one
would ever be committed involuntarily to them:

> Our madhouses are places where people retreat when they want
> to go down into themselves—to collapse, carry on, see visions,
> hear voices of prophecy, bang on the walls, relive infancy—get-
> ting in touch with the buried self and the inner mind. We all lose
> parts of ourselves. We all make choices that go bad. . . . How can
> another person decide that it is time for me to disintegrate, to re-
> integrate myself?[32]

Back in the evil 1970s, however, psychiatrists are sinister figures and
the main character is involuntarily committed and diagnosed paranoid
schizophrenic. Widely taught in humanities courses at universities and
colleges across the country, Piercy's novel was also heatedly discussed
within feminist circles.

At the same time a medley of research experiments were confirming
the destructive power of asylum settings and the inadequate empirical
grounding of many psychiatric practices. Psychiatry continued to be beset by doubts about its efficacy and rigor. Experiments found psychotherapy to function no better than a placebo when it came to patients'
mental health. There had been studies for years that indicated how psychotherapy was basically a mind game; for instance, psychiatrist Jerome
Frank conducted a well-known trial that concluded that patients' response to sugar wafers (presented as medication) proved *more* effective
than six months of psychotherapy.[33] Various trials also confirmed that
the success rates of treatment—whether placebo or psychotherapeutic—
depended greatly on patients' expectations; when patients believed in
a treatment, they got better no matter if they received psychotherapy
or a placebo (without any psychotherapy).[34] Even when a placebo was
not given, persons labeled "neurotic" by psychiatrists tended to improve
whether they engaged in lengthy psychotherapeutic treatments or not.[35]
By the 1970s there was additional evidence that psychotherapy had little
impact on patients confronting life crises; those who did receive immediate psychiatric treatment and those who did not tended to recover at
equal rates.[36] And an experiment conducted in 1977 at Vanderbilt University contested the entire concept of psychiatric "expertise," inviting
a group of psychiatrists and a second group of college teachers (from

fields like mathematics and history) to "treat" sets of patients twice a week for several months. Subsequent evaluations showed no difference in improvement between patients who saw actual psychiatrists and patients who spoke with professors who pretended to be shrinks.[37] Another research experiment went still further, concluding that patients' conditions not infrequently *worsened* after treatment with psychiatrists, an outcome euphemistically labeled "negative therapeutic reaction."[38]

Building on theories popularized by antipsychiatry, several social psychological experiments offered compelling evidence that "mental illness" appeared or disappeared depending on social context. Again, such research was not necessarily new; in 1951 medical anthropologist William Caudill had proposed to have himself committed to a ward of a psychiatric hospital while concealing his real identity as a trained participant observer. To get into the hospital, Caudill had told an unsuspecting psychiatrist that he was failing at writing a scholarly book, that he had been fighting so much with his wife that she had left him, and that he had begun routinely to cope with his depressions by getting drunk. These invented narratives succeeded; Caudill was admitted to a small private mental hospital for a period of two months, where he compiled an extensive ethnographic record of daily life on the psychiatric ward. Institutionalization, Caudill concluded, often made the mentally ill sicker, adding that the experiences of the patient in the mental hospital differed little in kind from the experiences of individuals in orphanages, prisons, or displaced persons camps. He wrote: "In general, the accounts of behavior or individuals in these types of settings all stress the phenomena, so many of which are noted in hospitalized mental patients, of apathy and depersonalization, regression, denial of reality, attempts to maintain threatened self-esteem, increased wish-level and fantasy, and the formation of stereotypes concerning those who control the authority and power."[39] In short, as one study from 1957 phrased it, "mental illness, it seems, is a condition which afflicts people who must go to a mental institution, but until they go almost anything they do is normal."[40] (Conversely, as a later experiment demonstrated, supposedly "insane" persons managed suddenly to improve their mental status in situations when sufficiently motivated to do so.[41])

Further psychological experimentation more directly questioned the medical classifications of "mental illness." In one such psychological experiment, the director at a mental hospital in Illinois (where, incidentally, psychiatrist Thomas Szasz had once been an intern) instructed staff to spend a long holiday weekend living on an abandoned ward in the hospital while simulating the role either of a staff member or a mental patient. What the experiment revealed was how abruptly "patients" assumed the behaviors of actual mental patients. Tensions between staff and patients quickly escalated, and a fistfight broke out between a "patient" and a staff member; at one point, a "patient" was placed in restraints for several hours by staff. Additionally, another "patient" noted how the experience of being committed induced feelings of an actual breakdown, while many "patients" subsequently reported profound feelings of depression and "dehumanization."[42] If three days on a mock mental ward could produce these reactions in "patients," what might be the emotional consequences of long-term commitment to a psychiatric facility?

The most celebrated psychological experiment of the era that sought to test the permeable boundary between sanity and madness was also the least complicated. In 1972 psychologist David Rosenhan wondered how it was that young men managed time and again to avoid military service in Vietnam by feigning mental illness. What made it so simple for so many to fool trained psychiatrists so routinely? Rosenhan recruited several friends—three psychologists, a graduate student, a pediatrician, a psychiatrist, a painter, and a housewife—to see if a similar trick could be played on several mental hospitals. Rosenhan's "pseudopatients" would arrive at the admissions unit of an asylum armed only with a single symptom: they had been hearing voices for the past three weeks, and these voices were saying the words "thud," "empty," and "hollow." Rosenhan asked his friends not to shave or shower for several days before their appointments at the hospital. He coached them on how not to swallow prescription medications. Otherwise Rosenhan requested that his "pseudopatients" adopt a minimalist approach—they would exhibit no odd behavior and would not alter significant facts about their actual personal history. (In this respect, his strategy differed substantially from the experiment performed by Caudill, since Caudill had fabricated large portions of his personal history.) The prank worked far beyond Rosenhan's expectations. All successfully gained admittance to eight different asylums, all but one with a diagnosis of schizophrenia (with the final diagnosis being manic-depressive psychosis). And the trick worked in both directions; when Rosenhan informed staff beforehand that a "pseudopatient" planned to gain admission to their hospital, suddenly dozens of persons were being diagnosed as frauds, even though Rosenhan had not actually sent anyone.

Most striking and unexpected was that the pseudopatients began to feel themselves going crazy in the asylum. Like the "patients" in the Illinois hospital (or William Caudill), pseudopatients observed how life on a mental ward damaged their self-worth. Some became anxious, wondering how they had managed so effortlessly to be admitted to a mental hospital. The diagnosis of madness based on the false claim to having auditory hallucinations proved a "self-fulfilling prophecy."[43] Feigning madness permitted "normal" persons to pass as "abnormal," but acting "sane" proved no defense against the "insane" environment of the mental hospital.[44]

By the mid-1970s Thomas Szasz had been arguing for almost twenty years that the label of "mental illness" was worse than worthless. Szasz believed that psychiatry put names to mental conditions as a cloak to mask the simple truth that the "condition" being "diagnosed" had no basis in reality. Diagnostic classifications rationalized the existence of a profession that lacked actual research to justify itself. "There is no science without classification," Szasz noted in the pages of the *American Journal of Psychiatry* in 1957, to which he added that the system of psychiatric classification "may be compared to posting a blind policeman on a new superhighway and then expecting him to enforce the speed-laws."[45] The view that psychiatry—like mental illness—was a myth gained influence as evidence accumulated that there simply was no there there, as Gertrude Stein might have said. In this fashion the antipsychiatric critique had managed to keep psychiatry on the defensive for a long time, but that time was coming to an end.

In the course of the 1960s and through the 1970s, research based on a medical model of schizophrenia had continued apace, despite (or perhaps also in reaction to) sharp criticisms from advocates of the opposing model, which situated social factors as indisputably central to the etiology of mental illness. This biomedical research posited that genetic transmission was responsible for the development of schizophrenia, and it sought to address the issue of heredity by producing data that underscored the central place of nature (rather than nurture). For instance, there were a series of blood studies conducted on chronically ill schizophrenic patients and their family members in the hope of locating patterns in the transmission of the disease, and there was also medical research that investigated the postulate that schizophrenia was an immunologic disorder. But the exploration of taraxein factors (relating to blood) was still not yielding definitive results.[46] At the same time, however, there began to be a more promising avenue of theoretical exploration: Clinical trials that excluded variables for the social diagnosis of schizophrenia became seen as an important step in bringing a medical model for mental disease out of exile.

Notably, and however paradoxically, these trials did not use biomedical methods to prove a biochemical etiology for mental illness. On the contrary, they employed *social* methods to undermine the social model. In 1966 an influential early study demonstrated how children of schizophrenic mothers who were placed in foster care within three days of their birth went on to develop schizophrenia at the same rate as children who remained with their schizophrenic mothers. This meant, or so the researchers concluded, that familial environment must be irrelevant to the transmission of the disease entity, while familial heritage was apparently quite significant.[47] A series of adoption studies followed. These largely confirmed how the biological offspring of schizophrenic mothers more often developed schizophrenia than children in control groups, even under circumstances in which these offspring had been removed from their families and therefore had no social contact during childhood with mental illness.[48] The double binds supposedly generated by schizophrenogenic parents could not have had an impact on children raised by normal foster parents. Great claims were made for this research, and for some these adoption studies represented "the straw that broke the environmentalist's back," as a review of the extant scholarship on the genetics of schizophrenia triumphantly announced in 1976.[49] Or as a leading neuroscientist put it: "If schizophrenia is a myth, it is a myth with a strong genetic component!"[50] According to this medical school of thought, anyone who believed that crazy families produced crazy children for reasons other than heredity had been decisively discredited.

The debate hardly ended there. Psychiatrists devoted to a familial and social model of schizophrenia as well as the double bind theory dismissed the adoption studies as completely invalid. For example, there was the not-insignificant issue—a concern that would continue to be argued for decades to come—that the so-called genetic studies from the late 1960s and 1970s had not found (nor had been designed to locate) the existence of an actual "schizophrenic gene."[51] Excluding one concept did not constitute proof for another theory. Furthermore, there was the problem that what the medical researchers had discovered was only what they had hoped to find. The adoption studies had inferred a schizophrenic gene from their data but had neglected or obscured factors that could have undermined this conclusion. For instance, there was the fact that the "adopted-away" children had been raised in familial settings the genetic researchers chose to label "normal," but which might well have also been schizophrenogenic. No information about childhood environment had been directly observed; all data were retrospectively collected. As family researcher Theodore Lidz succinctly noted in 1976, these genetic studies had not bothered to provide "an examination of the family milieu into which these children, both index and control, were adopted," and so "there can be no assurance that environmental factors were not relevant."[52] And while the genetic researchers had typically chosen to discount "the possibility of contaminated diagnoses" or "investigator bias," as well as the possibility that their sampling was inadequate, there remained strong complaints about these and other methodological concerns.[53] And finally, and perhaps most significantly, the studies took ample advantage of the blurry and inconsistent diagnostic criteria for what was (or was not) classed as "schizophrenia." In at least one study "manic depression" and "schizophrenia" were merged—despite the fact that these conditions were understood to be genetically unrelated.[54] The genetic theorists were thus guilty of the crime they accused their social model adversaries of committing, that is, making use of the categories of "normalcy" and "abnormalcy" in a manner that left a great deal to the quirks of imagination and speculation.[55]

The solution for medical model proponents turned out to be contained in the problem. The DSM-II had been published in 1968 because the psychiatric classification of diseases in the United States was not uniform with the International Classification of Diseases (ICD). DSM-II sought to facilitate standardization. But DSM-II had also been a placeholder. It had not eliminated the fluidity or fuzziness of diagnostic categorization. It had not revised or altered the underlying conception of a social model. And there remained signs of trouble; the Committee on Nomenclature and Statistics for the American Psychiatric Association (APA) responsible for DSM-II had clumsily acknowledged about "the mental disorder labeled in this Manual as 'schizophrenia'": "Even if it had tried, the Committee could not establish agreement about what this disorder is; it could only agree on what to call it."[56] This could not have been reassuring. Within only a handful of years, when the ICD was again scheduled for revision, the APA arranged once more for its DSM to be revised.

This time, however, the newly appointed Task Force on Nomenclature and Statistics actively took up the antipsychiatric challenge as justification for eliminating the social model. Thus, and however counterintuitively, the antipsychiatric critique that claimed the psychiatric profession had too much indiscriminate power to label people and enforce norms came to propel—not impede—the medical model proponents' reformation of psychiatric nosology and nomenclature. What psychiatry required, according to these proponents, was *more* science, even (or especially) in the absence of *new* science. The ongoing crisis in psychiatric legitimacy came to rationalize the reassertion of a medical model of mental illness.

This was nowhere made so abundantly clear as in the well-publicized scandal prompted by the Rosenhan experiment. In a manner of speaking, and although from an opposite perspective, the Rosenhan experiment received the same criticisms as had the genetic experiments where infants "adopted-away" from schizophrenic mothers developed schizophrenia. In the adoption studies environment had been said not to play a role in the development of the child's illness, which appeared to mean that genetics must be the cause of madness. Critics who advocated for the social model argued that the adoptive environment had not been examined—only assumed. In the reaction to the Rosenhan experiment, by contrast, defenders of the medical model argued that the pseudopatients may have claimed that they had acted "normally" once admitted to their asylums, but that this claim was questionable. As one critic put it, "normal" should have meant walking into the nurses' station and announcing: "Look, I am a normal person who tried to see if I could get into the hospital by behaving in a crazy way or saying crazy things. It worked and I was admitted to the hospital, but now I would like to be discharged from the hospital."[57] Furthermore, as Seymour Kety of the Harvard Medical School wrote in 1974, psychiatrists should not be admonished for diagnosing symptoms incorrectly when the symptoms presented were false. Other kinds of medical doctors would as likely be fooled by fake symptoms as psychiatrists. Kety wrote: "If I were to drink a quart of blood and, concealing what I had done, come to the emergency room of any hospital vomiting blood, the behavior of the staff would be quite predictable. If they labeled and treated me as having a bleeding peptic ulcer, I doubt that I could argue convincingly that medical science does not know how to diagnose that condition."[58] Yet the cleverest and harshest critique of Rosenhan came from psychiatrist Robert L. Spitzer of the New York State Psychiatric Institute who was chosen in 1974 to chair the task force assigned to prepare DSM-III. Even as he began his work, Spitzer announced his intentions to renovate the psychiatric nomenclature thoroughly to enable more reliable and systematic diagnoses and to produce a DSM that offered "a defense of the medical model as applied to psychiatric problems."[59]

Spitzer wrote that he considered the conclusions reached by Rosenhan to be junk. Psychiatrists had been tricked because they were not trained to anticipate fraudulent claims of mental illness. "I have no doubt that if the condition known as pseudopatient ever assumed epidemic proportions among admittants to psychiatric hospitals," Spitzer wrote sarcastically, "psychiatrists would in time become adept at identifying them, though at what risk to real patients, I do not know."[60] (However incongruently, then, Spitzer found common cause with Thomas Szasz, who also concluded that Rosenhan's study demonstrated the obvious. "To me," Szasz wrote in 1979, "it proved only that it is easy to deceive people, especially when they don't expect to be deceived."[61])

Yet Spitzer's point was ultimately less to bury Rosenhan's experiment than to make it do his work for him. Spitzer could use Rosenhan's experiment because it so effectively highlighted the *unreliability* of current diagnostic tools. What the pseudopatient experiment demonstrated was not what Rosenhan thought it did, Spitzer announced, which was how "it is clear that we cannot distinguish the sane from the insane in psychiatric hospitals."[62] On the contrary, Spitzer mockingly observed, the only thing the experiment proved was how psychiatrists had difficulty "detecting sanity in a sane person simulating insanity." But this "unremarkable finding" should not prevent further inquiry into the genuinely "serious problems with psychiatric diagnosis."[63] As Spitzer also wrote in 1974: "The reliability of psychiatric diagnosis as it has been practiced since at least the late 1950s is not good," but this was a problem that might be corrected with greater specificity in classification of diseases and their symptoms.[64]

Spitzer transformed Rosenhan's experiment into a teachable moment, taking its evidence seriously while reversing its analysis in order to push his own agenda, namely, an urgent need for more accurate and reliable psychiatric nosology—which for him also meant the revitalization of a medical model for mental illness. In short, Spitzer used antipsychiatry's exposure of the numerous weaknesses in the prior medical model of madness in order to lay the groundwork for a thoroughly reconceived biochemical paradigm. Yet this would not be the last or most unusual reversal in the history of antipsychiatry; that would involve the policy known as deinstitutionalization.

III

By the 1980s deinstitutionalization had taken firm hold. The numbers were dramatic: In 1955 there had been more than 550,000 patients in state mental hospitals; by 1985 that figure was less than 110,000 persons—a drop of 80 percent. Certainly economic factors played a strong role in the march toward deinstitutionalization. In the 1950s the revenues necessary to run state asylums were growing out of control, and many mental health practitioners enthusiastically endorsed efforts to shift those costs to programs supported by the federal government. In the 1960s and 1970s, these efforts included the expansion of entitlement programs like the Social Security Disability Insurance Program (SSDI) and the Supplementary Security Income for the Aged, the Disabled, and the Blind (SSI). As medical historian Gerald N. Grob writes: "SSI and SSDI encouraged states to discharge severely and persistently mentally ill persons from mental hospitals, since federal payments would presumably enable them to live in the community."[65] In this way, and into the 1980s, as incentives to shift costs from states to federal sources continued to grow, in-patient populations of state asylums continued to decline.[66] And institutions often unequipped to provide specialized treatments began to see increasing numbers of mentally ill patients. As one survey from 1987 reported: "More inpatient episodes occur in general hospitals without psychiatric units than any other facility."[67] The era of the dominance of the state asylum for the care of the mentally ill was effectively over.

At the same time, deinstitutionalization meant that federal dollars had to keep flowing to provide disability benefits for mentally disabled persons now seeking to make their own way in communities. Yet when Ronald Reagan became president in 1981, he cancelled those benefits as a cost-cutting measure and amid allegations of fraudulent applications from unqualified recipients. As a result hundreds of thousands of persons were abruptly purged from the eligibility rolls of SSDI and SSI. And the impact of these purges fell hard on the mentally ill. As a report in 1983 noted, "mentally disabled recipients were especially likely to have payments terminated. Although they represent only 11.2 percent of SSDI recipients, they comprise more than 28 percent of those whose benefits have been terminated."[68] The American Psychiatric Association warned in 1982 that individuals who were having their disability benefits cut included "large numbers of schizophrenics and other chronically mentally ill persons."[69] Experts observed that the consequences of this termination of benefits for the mentally ill were unambiguous, as "almost certainly many of the individuals who lost their benefits joined the ranks of the homeless."[70] In 1984, and however diplomatically, a Task Force Report of the American Psychiatric Association noted how the problems increasingly associated with the homeless mentally ill "are not the result of deinstitutionalization per se but rather the way deinstitutionalization has been implemented."[71] Or as psychiatrist E. Fuller Torrey wrote in 1997: "A final assessment of deinstitutionalization is to say that it has never really been tried. This is accurate as we now understand what services mentally ill persons need to successfully live in the community and recognize that such services, in most cases, have not been provided." What Americans witnessed in the 1980s, Torrey intoned, was not a policy of "deinstitutionalization" but rather the policy of "detreatmentization."[72]

There developed nonetheless and almost all at once other ways to tell the story of deinstitutionalization that effectively erased any perception that persons living on the streets had suffered from the callous disregard of the Reagan administration. One argument put forward was that the homeless crisis was not a genuine crisis at all. As influential Reagan advisor (and future attorney general) Edwin Meese III stated in December 1983, if there looked as though there were more persons than in past years lining up at soup kitchens for meals that Christmas season, it had nothing to do with more homelessness. Rather, Meese said, claims that there were more hungry and homeless people in 1983 than in prior years were unsubstantiated and "purely political." Meese caused quite a storm of controversy when he observed: "I think some people are going to soup kitchens voluntarily. I know we've had considerable information that people go to soup kitchens because the food is free and that that's easier than paying for it."[73] This opinion gained its adherents in the years ahead. As another defender of Reagan policies wrote retrospectively in 1992, Americans had come to accept the reality of a "national homeless crisis" during the 1980s because intense media coverage had "manufactured" the "crisis." The fact that news coverage of a homelessness "crisis" spiked during the Reagan years was itself cause for suspicion—or so went this line of argument. How else to explain the peculiar fact that "the word *homeless* or *homelessness*" had never appeared in any "library index of popular and academic periodicals" until "the year after Reagan's election"?[74]

A more pervasive (and apparently very persuasive) strategy, however, was to pin the blame for the homelessness crisis in the 1980s on the seductive appeals of antipsychiatry during the 1960s and 1970s. Medical doctor Gerald Weissmann may be credited with introducing the perspective that antipsychiatry in the 1960s led to widespread deinstitutionalization in the 1970s, which, in turn, resulted in the homelessness crisis of the 1980s. In his provocatively titled essay, "Foucault and the Bag Lady," published in 1982, Weissmann made these connections explicit, noting how "the return of the mad to the community was in accord not only with the rosy visions of fellowship and liberation that became prevalent in the sixties but also with a general distrust of arrangements made by any authority, be it juridical, governmental, or medical." Singling out Laing and Herbert Marcuse as well as Michel Foucault, Weissmann went so far as to suggest that these theorists' savage attacks on "the therapeutic reforms of bourgeois liberalism" must bear responsibility not only for the homelessness crisis, but also for severe budget cuts to psychiatric services more generally.[75]

In the blink of an eye, or so it seemed, this interpretation of antipsychiatry began to be woven into the fabric of the histories of deinstitutionalization and homelessness in America. Often this interpretation appeared only fleetingly, as in "The Deinstitutionalization Story," an essay in *Public Interest* from 1986, which declared how destructive to the mentally ill had been the idea that asylums "aggravated, if not caused, mental disability," as well as the antipsychiatric notion that "social acceptance and tolerance would reduce if not actually 'cure' mental illness."[76] Also, in "Crazy in the Streets" from *Commentary* in 1987, psychiatrist Paul S. Appelbaum cited Erving Goffman, Szasz, and Laing as he disparaged the voguish idea carried over from the 1960s that "chronic disability accompanying psychiatric illnesses, particularly schizophrenia, was not a result of the disease process itself, but an effect of archaic treatment methods in which patients were uprooted from their own communities."[77] These accounts concluded that misguided antipsychiatric theorists seeking greater autonomy for psychotics gave intellectual heft to deinstitutionalization, which in turn caused a homelessness crisis. As psychiatrist Charles Krauthammer, a graduate of Harvard Medical School and an influential columnist for the *New Republic* and the *Washington Post*, wrote angrily in 1985: "As the threshold for providing people asylum, against their will if necessary, has risen, so has the price to be paid." As Krauthammer added: "It amounts now to an army of broken souls foraging and freezing in the streets."[78] (Little wonder that one of Krauthammer's first essays for the *New Republic* in 1979 had been an often sarcastic screed against Thomas Szasz.[79])

It was only in 1990, however, that the full story of antipsychiatry's disastrous impact on the mentally ill homeless in America moved to the center from the margins. That year Rael Jean Isaac and Virginia C. Armat published *Madness in the Streets: How Psychiatry and the Law Abandoned the Mentally Ill*, which pounded the point that the romantic (yet crackpot) theories Szasz, Laing, and Goffman had espoused about mental illness led to social policies that released thousands of chronically mentally ill patients from asylums, a process that oftentimes rendered them homeless. Isaac and Armat decried not only how ideas on madness expressed by Marcuse, Foucault, Rosenhan and others had addled the brains of academics and New Left militants alike in the 1960s and 1970s, but also how so many of these same 1960s radicals also endorsed the use of psychedelic drugs to deepen their experiences. The con-

A FASHIONABLE KIND OF SLANDER

sequences of these pathetic developments were only being felt belatedly. Isaac and Armat wrote:

> The tremendously subversive implications of these ideas would only become fully apparent in the 1980s as insanity, chaos, and disorder came to occupy, physically, our public places. Public authorities were paralyzed. Their agents could not intervene to prevent appalling human degradation. To exert authority and force crazy people, however needy, into treatment was, or so the public was told, an unconscionable repression of human rights: the mad—if indeed there was such a thing as madness—had a civil right to their own reality, their alternative "lifestyle." Intervention was legitimate, said lawyers and judges, only when someone was an "imminent danger" to himself or others, and this was defined so narrowly that the individual had to be on the verge of suicide or murder.

Courtesy of antipsychiatry, and the ensuing "intellectual confusion" it had generated, Isaac and Armat argued that American society now "found itself helpless to deal with an enormous social problem destroying the quality of life of its cities." Thus, the authors portentously concluded, antipsychiatric attitudes had to be counted as "arguably the most important and destructive legacy of the 1960s."[80]

Thereafter it became a matter of some generalized consensus that antipsychiatric theories in the 1960s and 1970s might be held at least partially accountable for the homelessness crisis in the 1980s. A 1993 book delivering "the truth about homelessness" pinned the blame specifically on Szasz, because his "philosophy" had facilitated "the erosion of medical services to treat mental illness" in the course of the 1960s. The book further declared that "the perversities of the mental patients' rights movement" had only increased the anguish of mentally ill persons because it sought to deny medical treatments to the mentally ill, which in turn also had larger social consequences: "This denial of treatment causes [the mentally ill] not only to suffer but also to feel even more stigmatized and isolated. Homelessness is the result."[81] Sociologist Christopher Jencks, in *The Homeless* (1994), also traced homelessness in contemporary America back to theories promoted by Goffman, Laing, Szasz, and Foucault, because they "tried to convince the public that mental hospitals were oppressive places and that psychiatrists were agents of social control." According to Jencks the widespread absorption of antipsychiatric ideas in the 1970s meant that "many seriously disturbed patients began leaving state hospitals even when they had nowhere else to live." And the end result was that "in due course some ended up not only friendless but penniless and homeless."[82] Into the twenty-first century, even otherwise sensitive and nuanced scholarship continued (citing Isaac and Armat) to tie the fact that "the 1960's counterculture and New Left both celebrated craziness" to the troubled history of deinstitutionalization and also, however indirectly, to the homelessness crisis of the 1980s.[83]

Goffman died in 1982, Foucault in 1984, and Laing in 1989. By the 1990s it was left to Thomas Szasz to hit back at his growing legion of critics and detractors. This he did with a mix of mockery and bitterness, musing how on earth he had come to be dubbed "The Man Who Brought You Deinstitutionalization," despite the fact that he had for so long been "persona non grata in psychiatry," as well as the fact that "coercive psychiatric practices are now more popular than ever."[84] Yet for a movement whose history was as complex, contradictory, and ambivalent as antipsychiatry's has been, this latest development might simply be seen as just another twist on an already odd and twisted road.

Epilogue

"Psychiatry has recently rediscovered its roots," opens the introduction to *Society and Psychosis* (2008), an impressive collection of articles by medical anthropologists, social psychiatrists, and psychologists that seeks to document definitively a reinvigorated return within psychiatry of a social diagnosis. Of psychiatry at the end of the twentieth century, the editors of *Society and Psychosis* write: "It seemed as if its long history of interest in the impact of society on the rates and course of serious mental illness had been forgotten, overtaken by the inexorable advance of neuroscience and genetics."[1] And certainly in the decades immediately following the publication of DSM-III—and its subsequent revisions, DSM-IIIR in 1987 and DSM-IV in 1994—medical textbooks and psychiatric articles routinely announced the validity of a biological paradigm for mental disease put in place by the "neo-Kraepelinians" in 1980.[2] And there appeared to be solid evidence for doing so: A major World Health Organization (WHO) study of the incidence rates of schizophrenia based on data from ten nations, published in 1992, concluded that schizophrenia occurred with comparable frequency across diverse populations.[3] The invariance of schizophrenia reflected by the WHO data confirmed schizophrenia as the most biologically based of all mental disorders—"a devastating psychiatric disorder" whose heritability is now estimated at between 80 and 85 percent.[4]

Yet in the twenty-first century there has been a remarkable resurgence of energetic investigation into psychosocial risk factors for the development of schizophrenia. Studies demonstrate that life in an urban setting places people at far higher risk for schizophrenia than rural life.[5] Compelling evidence links life events like childhood stress and trauma to the outcomes of psychosis.[6] Research ties cannabis consumption to the onset of schizophrenia.[7] There is strong data that migration is a significant risk factor for schizophrenia.[8] And a range of studies provide durable evidence that patients diagnosed with schizophrenia in nonindustrial ("developing") countries have better outcomes than comparable schizophrenic patients in industrialized nations.[9] Looking back in 2007 on an era when a medical model routinely minimized the impact of social factors, psychiatrist John J. McGrath declared: "Schizophrenia is not the egalitarian disorder that we once thought it was."[10] Or as medical anthropologist Tanya Luhrmann has also concluded: "Social causation in schizophrenia can no longer be dismissed, because we need it—and something like a theory of social defeat—to explain one of the most important puzzles in culture and mental health today: the difference in the course and outcome of schizophrenia in developing versus developed countries."[11]

In short, psychiatry has been in the process (again) of changing its mind. It has, for instance, taken strong interest in the field of epigenetics, that is, the analysis of interplay between environment and genetic susceptibility for mental illness. Epigenetics is not inherently new—there had been calls in the 1960s and 1970s to pursue the "biopsychosocial" and to integrate social and medical paradigms.[12] Yet recent advances in molecular biology have made epigenetics that much more difficult to ignore. Now psychiatrists are far more willing to accept that genetics is not destiny, that environmental factors regulate the expression of heritable genes, and that brain development is a mediation and integration of genetic and environmental factors. As *Psychiatric News* acknowledged in 2010: "Unlike other diseases that are caused or predisposed by errors in a single gene or a few genes, the molecular basis of psychiatric disorders has turned out to be far more complex." Environmental factors can result in alterations in gene expression without alterations in DNA sequence. "In other words, a person may carry a particular gene, but if that gene is 'silenced,' the body may not make any protein from the gene and, in turn, not present the related trait."[13] As an instance of how epigenetics might work, the journal *Biological Psychiatry* has noted: "Persistent and uncontrollable stressful experiences interact with individual genetic susceptibility to alter synthesis, expression, and signaling in stress-related pathways. . . . For example, genetic variation in the serotonin transporter gene interacts with early life stress, resulting in hyperresponsivity to stressors that increase vulnerability to psychiatric disorders such as major depression."[14] All of this is part of a broader new move to revisit the "enormous influence" of "the social environment" on biological processes—with significant consequences for rethinking the relationship between the social and the biological in mental health.[15]

There has also been pioneering research on the impact of hazardous environments on epigenetic *transgenerational* inheritance. As clinical psychiatrist Mindy Thompson Fullilove commented in the *American Journal of Psychiatry* in 2009: "Massive harms, of the kind caused by neighborhood collapse, can cause heritable phenotypic alterations. Although such physiological changes are not changes to the DNA sequence itself, the epigenetic alterations can pass along the injury for one or more generations."[16] Arguably, an era of conceiving of "the social" and "the medical" as diametrically opposed and continually oscillating models for an understanding of mental illness may be over. As the *Journal of the American Academy of Child and Adolescent Psychiatry* wrote in 2005: "We are at the brink of understanding the extent to which the conceptual space between the genome and the environment contains mechanisms developed by evolution that render the designations 'genetic' and 'environmental' meaningless within that space."[17]

In the meantime, that blurry line between psychosis and sanity that proved so useful to postwar psychiatrists as they worked to expand the national agenda for mental health has found new confirmation. Medical researchers now identify risk factors long associated as symptomatic of psychotic disorders as also not uncommon in the general population. Adults who acknowledge having had hallucinations have been estimated at between 10 and 25 percent.[18] A study of children age seven and eight revealed a prevalence rate for auditory vocal hallucinations at nearly one in ten, although "most children experienced no or mild subjective burden" as a result of hearing voices.[19] Such results have led to proposals that psychosis should be placed on a continuum with normality, and to inquiries as to whether "it is possible to consider psychosis as a dimension of the human experience."[20] Such positions may also have larger implications. For instance, they may cause psychiatrists to resist "assigning a provisional diagnosis of schizophrenia and reflexively prescribing antipsychotic medications to patients complaining of 'hearing voices' in the absence of full diagnostic criteria."[21] And they may also influence the manner in which the forthcoming and hotly debated DSM-V (scheduled for publication in 2013) chooses to itemize the pathognomonic signs of schizophrenia.[22]

Identifying a blur or continuum between normality and abnormality can lead to contradictory consequences. One possibility is that individuals with only minor symptoms, who would previously have been placed in "the normal range," might now receive diagnoses that could lead "pharmaceutical companies, eager to expand their markets," to be "tempted to pounce on these new 'patients.'"[23] Yet another possibility is that individuals diagnosed with more severe conditions would interpret their difference as a gain.

There is renewed enthusiasm for "mad pride." Mad pride aims not only to put an end to the stigma surrounding psychosis, it also contends that insanity offers insight not infirmity. It champions "mental diversity" and questions whether antipsychotic medications are a necessary or desirable treatment. "We don't want to be normal," Will Hall, a diagnosed (but unmedicated) schizophrenic told *Newsweek* magazine in 2009. "For most people, it used to be, 'Mental illness is a disease—here is a pill you take for it,'" Hall adds. "Now that's breaking down."[24] Hall is a leader of the Icarus Project collective, founded in 2002, which boasts eight thousand members and its own successful Internet program ("Madness Radio: Voices and Visions from Outside Mental Health"). Dedicated to "navigating the space between brilliance and madness," the collective's "preamble" declares:

> The Icarus Project envisions a new culture and language that resonates with our actual experiences of "mental illness" rather than trying to fit our lives into a conventional framework. We see our madness as a dangerous gift to be cultivated and taken care of, rather than a disease or disorder needing to be "cured" or "overcome." Icarus is a space for people to come together and learn from each others' different views and experiences of madness. People who take psychiatric drugs and people who don't are welcome here. People who use diagnostic categories to describe themselves are welcome here, as are people who define themselves differently. The foundation of the Icarus Project is self-determination and mutual support.[25]

Nor has political critique been abandoned by the wayside. The Icarus Project queries: "Are we delusional and dysfunctional, or is it the culture we live in?"[26] And so at the end of this history we flash back to the

1970s, to the Madness Network collective and to the other organizations in the psychiatric survivors movement, even as unmodified arguments in defense of the medical model of mental illness also continue to be dusted off and rehearsed yet again.[27]

It is an ongoing tug-of-war, unsettled and unresolved, this contest between the medical and the social. The question becomes how best to bring historically fractious analyses of environmental and biological risk factors closer together. With funding flowing so overwhelmingly into medical research, social and cultural factors still often remain subordinate. Sharpened awareness that biological data alone cannot fully explicate the complex contributory sources, the likely course or the probable outcome of mental illness have not been enough (so far) to bring complete legitimacy to a revitalized social diagnosis.

Fresh controversies also emerge. Scientific inquiry into the "biological markers" of psychiatric disorders has risen dramatically. The theory goes that biomarkers can greatly assist medical researchers in estimating an individual's probability of developing illness, including mental illness. There is excitement specifically in the area of pediatric biomarker research that seeks to predict the biological vulnerability of children to psychiatric conditions—like antisocial behaviors or attention deficit hyperactivity disorder (ADHD). The positive goal of this research would be to collect physiological evidence—as opposed to less tangible or reliable data—to improve outcomes with early medical treatments (possibly even before symptoms appear). Yet ethical questions raised by this research remain. A report recently warns:

> At present, it is unclear what will happen when children are identified as being at risk of developing a psychiatric disorder or antisocial behavior in societies that are suffused by anxiety about the adverse social consequences of such conditions. . . . [W]ill ideas about the identity and the capacity of individuals begin to change? That is, how will people feel about themselves given their risk profile, and will others perceive them differently? Will "risk" and "potential" eventually dominate ideas of personal identity, health status and opportunity in rigid, coercive or stigmatizing ways? Will these ideas become institutionalized within education, law and policy? And how will such change affect the life trajectories of children identified as at risk early in life?[28]

Again, twenty-first-century concerns about the "risk profiling" of children resonate powerfully with the conspiratorial twinge expressed by antipsychiatry in the second half of the twentieth century. But past cannot be interpreted as prologue. As psychiatrist John McGrath has noted: "Renewed interest in the environment and schizophrenia should not be misread as somehow lessening the importance of genetic contributions."[29] So it would be most unfortunate if reductive interpretations of what had been at stake in the postwar era of the social diagnosis—among other things a collapsing of the social diagnosis with antipsychiatry as well as a caricaturing of antipsychiatry as involving the denial of the reality of madness—continue to complicate present efforts to reintroduce highly sophisticated and deeply thoughtful attention to environmental risk factors.

Finally, that DSM-III facilitated a new era of research into individual biochemical anomalies cannot be disputed. Yet practitioners and scholars do still debate whether DSM-III, with its vastly expanded checklists of symptoms, brought more scientific objectivity to processes of classification and treatment and a salutary end to what has been dismissed as the decades of "aimless chat" about an individual's past history and present dilemmas that psychodynamic and psychoanalytic approaches supposedly require.[30] Some suggest that the checklists often consist of highly subjective items whose seeming objectivity only masks the new imbrications of psychiatrists' work with pharmaceutical companies' investment in expanding their markets and insurance companies' insistence on justifying the cost of treatments. (And such debates are likely to intensify with the appearance of DSM-V.)

There is no question, however, that 1980 marked a turning point in the development of politically critical psychiatric theorizing. The political backlash against the 1960s and all that decade was said to have represented gathered force from that point forward. Abandoned and banished, perhaps forever, has been not only the idea that states of madness ever were—or might have been—the consequences of civilization, but also the ability to argue persuasively that what might pass for normal all too often may be insane.

Acknowledgments

Thanks to the faculty and staff at the Institute for Advanced Study in Princeton, New Jersey, where most of this book was initially drafted. Thanks especially to Danielle Allen, Nancy Cotterman, Karen Downing, Linda Garat, Eric Maskin, Donna Petito, and Joan Wallach Scott. Joan in particular steered me back from the edge at a critical juncture and Danielle provided solace and wisdom just at a moment when I was on the verge of jumping ship. Simply put, I got extraordinarily lucky.

I wish also to thank colleagues and staff at the City University of New York. Bill Kelly made everything possible, and my first dean at Baruch College, Myrna Chase, proved a terrific booster from the very beginning. The two individuals who followed Myrna in the dean's office in the Weissman School of Arts and Sciences, David Dannenbring and Jeff Peck, facilitated my research in ways both large and small. My colleagues Paula Berggren, John Brenkman, Hedy Feit, and Susan Locke have all been wonderful. Honors program director Elizabeth Bergman made a most helpful offer to assist with production expenses, and the college's director of financial services, Boo Choi, always ensured that everything was the way it should be.

I also owe far too much to the kindness and generosity of a far-flung network of academic acquaintances for their timely and instrumental encouragement and advice.

I wish to thank Rachel Adams, Marshall Berman, David Cesarani, Robert Genter, Mick Gusinde-Duffy, Kim Hopper, Jonathan Metzl, Deborah Dash Moore, Eric Sundquist, and John Tortorice. I extend a special word of thanks to Carolee Schneemann for sharing her memories of the Dialectics of Liberation Congress and for offering important clues that helped immensely as I first formulated this work. My old friend and mentor Mari Jo Buhle took time away from her own schedule to read the manuscript in its entirety and provide a brilliant and exacting critique. At the University of Chicago Press, I am grateful to my editor, Alan Thomas, and to Randy Petilos, as well as to the anonymous readers. Closer to home (at least metaphorically) my heartfelt thanks to Arno Armgort, Brendan Hart, Chris Hart, Jim Henle, John Kucich, Anne Montgomery, Kevin P. Riley, Lily Saint, Dianne Sadoff, Lucy Staub, and Michael Topp. And for Dagmar Herzog who consistently dropped everything to work on my problems, I have the profoundest respect and deepest appreciation. Without Dagmar this book would not have been less than it is; it would not have been.

Notes

INTRODUCTION

1. Jerry Farber, *The Student as Nigger: Essays and Stories* (North Hollywood, CA: Contact Books, 1969).

2. Claude Steiner, "Principles," in *Readings in Radical Psychiatry*, ed. Claude Steiner et al. (New York: Grove Press, 1975), 12–13. This essay originally appeared in *Radical Therapist* 2 (October 1971).

3. Andrew Scull, "The Fictions of Foucault's Scholarship," *Times Literary Supplement*, March 21, 2007. Also see Michel Foucault, *Madness and Civilization: A History of Insanity in the Age of Reason* (New York: Pantheon, 1965).

4. On the United Kingdom, see David Cooper, *Psychiatry and Anti-Psychiatry* (London: Tavistock, 1967). Translated into French, German, Swedish, and Spanish, Cooper's book was widely discussed and debated. On Italy, see Donata Mebane-Francescato and Susan Jones, "Radical Psychiatry in Italy: 'Love Is Not Enough,'" in *Radical Psychology*, ed. Phil Brown (New York: Harper and Row, 1973), 531–39; Nancy Scheper-Hughes and Anne M. Lovell, eds., *Psychiatry Inside Out: Selected Writings of Franco Basaglia* (New York: Columbia University Press, 1987); and Michael Donnelly, *The Politics of Mental Health in Italy* (New York: Routledge, 1992). On France, see Gilles Deleuze and Félix Guattari, *Anti-Oedipus: Capitalism and Schizophrenia* (New York: Viking, 1977). On the Netherlands, see Jan Foudraine, *Not Made of Wood: A Psychiatrist Discovers His Own Profession* (London: Quartet Books, 1974); and Gemma Blok, "'Messiah of the Schizophrenics': Jan Foudraine and Anti-Psychiatry in Holland," in *Cultures of Psychiatry and Mental*

Health Care in Postwar Britain and the Netherlands, ed. Marijke Gijswijt-Hofstra and Roy Porter (Amsterdam: Rodopi, 1998), 151–68. On West Germany, see Sozialistisches Patientenkollektiv, *Turn Illness into a Weapon: For Agitation by the Socialist Patients' Collective at the University of Heidelberg* (Heidelberg: KKRIM, 1993); and Cornelia Brink, *Grenzen der Anstalt: Psychiatrie und Gesellschaft in Deutschland 1860–1980* (Göttingen: Wallstein Verlag, 2010).

5. Fine historical overviews of the 1960s, for instance, often treat Laing as if he never existed. Laing receives not a sentence of discussion in many readers and scholarly surveys of the era. Prominent examples include Debi Unger and Irwin Unger, eds., *The Times Were a Changin': The Sixties Reader* (New York: Three Rivers Press, 1998); Alexander Bloom and Wini Breines, eds., *"Takin' It to the Streets": A Sixties Reader* (New York: Oxford University Press, 2003); Ann Charters, ed., *The Portable Sixties Reader* (New York: Penguin, 2003); and Karen Manners Smith and Tim Koster, eds., *Time It Was: American Stories from the Sixties* (Upper Saddle River, NJ: Pearson Prentice Hall, 2008). Scholarly and synthetic overviews of the decade that also neglect Laing include Charles Kaiser, *1968 in America: Music, Politics, Chaos, Counterculture, and the Shaping of a Generation* (New York: Grove Press, 1988); Todd Gitlin, *The Sixties: Years of Hope, Days of Rage* (New York: Bantam Books, 1993); David Farber and Beth Bailey, eds., *The Columbia Guide to America in the 1960s* (New York: Columbia University Press, 2001); Peter Braunstein and Michael William Doyle, eds., *Imagine Nation: The American Counterculture of the 1960s and 1970s* (New York: Routledge, 2002); Mark Hamilton Lytle, *America's Uncivil Wars: The Sixties Era from Elvis to the Fall of Richard Nixon* (New York: Oxford University Press, 2006); and Gerald J. DeGroot, *The Sixties Unplugged: A Kaleidoscopic History of a Disorderly Decade* (Cambridge, MA: Harvard University Press, 2008).

6. Important studies of developments in postwar American psychiatry and psychoanalysis include Gerald N. Grob, *From Asylum to Community: Mental Health Policy in Modern America* (Princeton, NJ: Princeton University Press, 1991); Ellen Herman, *The Romance of American Psychology: Political Culture in the Age of Experts* (Berkeley: University of California Press, 1995); Nathan G. Hale, *The Rise and Crisis of Psychoanalysis in the United States: Freud and the Americans, 1917–1985* (New York: Oxford University Press, 1995); Mari Jo Buhle, *Feminism and Its Discontents: A Century of Struggle with Psychoanalysis* (Cambridge, MA: Harvard University Press, 2000); Tanya M. Luhrmann, *Of Two Minds: The Growing Disorder in American Psychiatry* (New York: Knopf, 2000); Nancy C. Andreasen, *Brave New Brain: Conquering Mental Illness in the Era of the Genome* (New York: Oxford University Press, 2001); Robert Whitaker, *Mad in America: Bad Science, Bad Medicine, and the Enduring Mistreatment of the Mentally Ill* (New York: Perseus Books, 2002); Allan V. Horwitz, *Creating Mental Illness* (Chicago: University of Chicago Press, 2002); Jonathan Metzl, *Prozac on the Couch: Prescribing Gender in the Era of Wonder Drugs* (Durham, NC: Duke University Press, 2003); Eli Zaretsky, *Secrets of the Soul: A Social and Cultural History of Psychoanalysis* (New York: Knopf, 2004); David Healy, *Let Them Eat Prozac: The Unhealthy Relationship between the Pharmaceutical Industry and Depression* (New York: New York University Press, 2004); Christopher Lane, *Shyness: How Normal Behavior Became a Sickness* (New Ha-

ven, CT: Yale University Press, 2007); Peter Conrad, *The Medicalization of Society: On the Transformation of Human Conditions into Treatable Disorders* (Baltimore: Johns Hopkins University Press, 2007); Andrea Tone, *The Age of Anxiety: A History of America's Turbulent Affair with Tranquilizers* (New York: Basic Books, 2009); David L. Herzberg, *Happy Pills in America: From Miltown to Prozac* (Baltimore: Johns Hopkins University Press, 2009); Gary Greenberg, *Manufacturing Depression: The Secret History of a Modern Disease* (New York: Simon and Schuster, 2009); Ethan Watters, *Crazy Like Us: The Globalization of the American Psyche* (New York: Simon and Schuster, 2009); and Jonathan M. Metzl, *The Protest Psychosis: How Schizophrenia Became a Black Disease* (Boston: Beacon Press, 2009). These texts do not propose the analyses of antipsychiatry and psychiatry advanced here.

7. Edward Shorter, *A History of Psychiatry: From the Era of the Asylum to the Age of Prozac* (New York: John Wiley, 1997), 277; and Jonathan Engel, *American Therapy: The Rise of Psychotherapy in the United States* (New York: Penguin, 2008), 186.

8. J. Allan Hobson and Jonathan A. Leonard, *Out of Its Mind: Psychiatry in Crisis: A Call for Reform* (New York: Basic Books, 2002), 52–53.

9. "Human Potential: The Revolution in Feeling," *Time*, November 9, 1970.

10. Christopher Lasch, *The Culture of Narcissism: American Life in an Age of Diminishing Expectations* (New York: W. W. Norton, 1977).

CHAPTER ONE

1. Lawrence K. Frank, *Society as the Patient: Essays on Culture and Personality* (New Brunswick, NJ: Rutgers University Press, 1948), 1.

2. Louis E. Bisch, "How Neurotic Are You?" *Coronet* 31 (February 1952): 62–64. Among the questions posed were the following: "Are you quick to make EXCUSES for yourself or to DEFEND YOURSELF before others?" and "Do you DAYDREAM a great deal or do you FAIL TO TRY to make your ambitions come true?" Ibid., 63.

3. Oren Root, "Building Mental Health," *New York Times Magazine*, September 2, 1951, 110. Also see Dorothy Barclay, "Preventive Health for Young Minds," *New York Times Magazine*, February 14, 1954, 44.

4. See Frank, *Society as the Patient.*

5. Harold D. Lasswell, *Power and Personality* (New York: W. W. Norton, 1948), 150.

6. T. W. Adorno, Else Frenkel-Brunswik, Daniel J. Levinson, and R. Nevitt Sanford, *The Authoritarian Personality* (New York: Harper and Row, 1950), 817.

7. Joseph W. Eaton and Robert J. Weil, *Culture and Mental Disorders: A Comparative Study of the Hutterites and Other Populations* (Glencoe, IL: Free Press, 1955), 19.

8. Émile Durkheim, *Suicide: A Study in Sociology* (New York: Free Press, 1966). Durkheim's text was initially published by F. Alcan (Paris) (as *Le suicide: Étude de sociologie*) in 1897.

9. Robert E. L. Faris, *Social Psychology* (New York: Ronald Press, 1952), 347.

10. See, for example, the statistics for annual rates of admission to mental hospitals in Benjamin Malzberg, *Social and Biological Aspects of Mental Disease* (Utica, NY: State Hospitals Press, 1940). Also see Arthur R. Mangus, "Personality Adjustment of Rural and Urban Children," *American Sociological Review* 13 (October 1948): 566–75.

11. Robert E. L. Faris and H. Warren Dunham, *Mental Disorders in Urban Areas: An Ecological Study of Schizophrenia and Other Psychoses* (Chicago: University of Chicago Press, 1939). Also see H. Warren Dunham, "Current Status of Ecological Research in Mental Disorders," *Social Forces* 25 (March 1947): 321–26.

12. See especially the research conducted in New Haven by sociologist August B. Hollingshead and psychiatrist Frederick C. Redlich, which began to be published in 1952. This work—like the research of Faris and Dunham—found rates of schizophrenia to be highest among individuals in the lowest socioeconomic classes. August B. Hollingshead and Frederick C. Redlich, *Social Class and Mental Illness: A Community Study* (New York: Wiley, 1958).

13. See, for example, Robert E. L. Faris, "Some Observations on the Incidence of Schizophrenia in Primitive Society," *Journal of Abnormal and Social Psychology* 29 (April–June 1934): 30–31; and George Devereaux, "A Sociological Theory of Schizophrenia," *Psychoanalytic Review* 26 (June 1939): 315–42.

14. See, for instance, Charles G. Seligman, "Temperament, Conflict and Psychosis in a Stone Age Population," *British Journal of Medical Psychology* 9 (November 1929): 187–202; and James C. Carothers, "A Study of the Mental Derangement in Africans and an Attempt to Explain Its Peculiarities More Especially in Relation to the African Attitude to Life," *Psychiatry* 11 (February 1948): 47–86.

15. Nicholas J. Demerath, "Schizophrenia among Primitives: The Present Status of Sociological Research," *American Journal of Psychiatry* 98 (March 1942): 703.

16. S. Kirson Weinberg, *Society and Personality Disorders* (New York: Prentice-Hall, 1952), 233. Also see James Clark Moloney, *The Battle for Mental Health* (New York: Philosophical Library, 1952).

17. See Herbert Goldhamer and Andrew W. Marshall, *Psychosis and Civilization: Two Studies in the Frequency of Mental Disease* (Glencoe, IL: Free Press, 1949).

18. See Richard S. Lyman et al., *Social and Psychological Studies in Neuropsychiatry in China* (Peking: Henri Vetch, 1939), 363; and Abram Kardiner et al., *The Psychological Frontiers of Society* (New York: Columbia University Press, 1945), 431.

19. Francis J. Braceland, "Psychiatric Lessons from World War II," *American Journal of Psychiatry* 103 (March 1947): 593. The view was also Freud's own: "If the evolution of civilization has such a far-reaching similarity with the development of an individual, and if the same methods are employed in both, would not the diagnosis be justified that many systems of civilization—or epochs of it—possibly even the whole of humanity—have become 'neurotic' under the pressure of civilizing trends?" Sigmund Freud, *Civilization and Its Discontents* (London: Hogarth Press, 1949), 141.

20. Albert Deutsch, *The Mentally Ill in America: A History of Their Care and Treatment from Colonial Times*, 2nd ed. (New York: Columbia University Press, 1949), 484–87. Interestingly, postwar critics of Kraepelin's legacy seemed blithely unaware that Kraepelin had also been a pioneer in cross-cultural and comparative psychiatric investigation, conducting research in Southeast Asia, Cuba, Mexico, and the United States in the first decades of the twentieth century. See Wolfgang G. Jilek, "Emil Kraepelin and Comparative Sociocultural Psychiatry," *European Archives of Psychiatry and Clinical Neuroscience* 245 (July 1995): 231–38.

21. R. H. Felix and R. V. Bowers, "Mental Hygiene and Socio-Environmental Factors," *Milbank Memorial Fund Quarterly* 26 (April 1948): 125.

22. Karl Menninger, "The Diagnosis and Treatment of Schizophrenia," *Bulletin of the Menninger Clinic* 12 (May 1948): 101.

23. Bruno Bettelheim, "Mental Health and Current Mores," *American Journal of Orthopsychiatry* 22 (January 1952): 76–77.

24. William C. Menninger, *Social Change and Scientific Progress* (Cambridge, MA: Arthur Dehon Little Memorial Lecture at the Massachusetts Institute of Technology, 1951), 37.

25. William C. Menninger, "There Is Something You Can Do about Mental Health," *Pastoral Psychology* 12 (May 1951): 43.

26. Menninger, *Social Change and Scientific Progress*, 36–38. Emphasis in original.

27. Robert H. Felix, "Psychiatry in Prospect," *American Journal of Psychiatry* 103 (March 1947): 600.

28. Max L. Hutt, William C. Menninger, and Daniel E. O'Keefe, "The Neuropsychiatric Team in the United States Army," *Mental Hygiene* 31 (January 1947): 103.

29. See Gerald N. Grob, "Origins of *DSM-I*: A Study in Appearance and Reality," *American Journal of Psychiatry* 148 (April 1991): 427.

30. Deutsch, *The Mentally Ill in America*, 481.

31. William C. Menninger, "Psychiatric Experience in the War, 1941–1946," *American Journal of Psychiatry* 103 (March 1947): 578. Also see John W. Appel, "Incidence of Neuropsychiatric Disorders in the United States Army in World War II," *American Journal of Psychiatry* 102 (January 1946): 433–36.

32. Roy R. Grinker and John P. Spiegel, *Men under Stress* (Philadelphia: Blakiston, 1945), 36, 83, 450.

33. John Hersey, "A Short Talk with Erlanger," *Life*, October 29, 1945, 122. On Huston's documentary, *Let There Be Light*, see Gary Edgerton, "Revisiting the Recordings of Wars Past: Remembering the Documentary Trilogy of John Huston," *Journal of Popular Film and Television* 15 (Spring 1987): esp. 33–40.

34. William C. Menninger, "Lessons from Military Psychiatry for Civilian Psychiatry," *Mental Hygiene* 30 (October 1946): 581.

35. William C. Menninger and Munro Leaf, *You and Psychiatry* (New York: Scribner's Sons, 1948), 135.

36. William C. Menninger, "Tensions in Family Life," *Pastoral Psychology* 4 (April 1953): 18.

37. Lasswell, *Power and Personality*, 166.

NOTES TO PAGES 24-28

38. Ibid., 39, 162–63. Also see Harry Stack Sullivan, "The Meaning of Anxiety in Psychiatry and Life," *Psychiatry* 11 (February 1948): 1–13.

39. See Alexander H. Leighton, John A. Clausen, and Robert N. Wilson, eds., *Explorations in Social Psychiatry* (New York: Basic Books, 1957); Alexander H. Leighton, *An Introduction to Social Psychiatry* (Springfield, IL: Thomas Publishers, 1960); and Jurgen Ruesch, "Social Psychiatry: An Overview," *Archives of General Psychiatry* 12 (May 1965): 501–9.

40. Lasswell, *Power and Personality*, 118, 221. Also see Lasswell's earlier formulation of many of these positions, especially in Harold D. Lasswell, *Psychopathology and Politics* (Chicago: University of Chicago Press, 1930), Harold D. Lasswell, "The Garrison State," *American Journal of Sociology* 46 (January 1941): 455–68; and Harold D. Lasswell, "The Data of Psychoanalysis and the Social Sciences," *American Journal of Psychoanalysis* 7 (December 1947): 26–35.

41. The classic text is John Dollard, Leonard W. Doob, Neal E. Miller, O. H. Mowrer, and Robert R. Sears, *Frustration and Aggression* (New Haven, CT: Yale University Press, 1939). Also see the highly influential study *Caste and Class in a Southern Town* (1937), in which psychologist John Dollard noted that economically insecure southern whites displaced their aggression onto African Americans, while African Americans, unable to express their own frustration toward whites directly, often turned against one another in black-on-black criminality and cruelty. John Dollard, *Caste and Class in a Southern Town* (New Haven, CT: Yale University Press, 1937), 267.

42. Erich Fromm, *Escape from Freedom* (New York: Avon, 1969), 246. The book was first published in 1941. In 1951 Adorno would elaborate on Fromm's conception when he argued that the "sadomasochistic character" of fascists might be compared to the actions of bicyclists: "Above they bow, they kick below." T. W. Adorno, "Freudian Theory and Patterns of Fascist Propaganda," in *Psychoanalysis and the Social Sciences*, vol. 3, ed. Géza Róheim (New York: International Universities Press, 1951), 291.

43. Ernst Simmel, "Anti-Semitism and Mass Psychopathology," in *Anti-Semitism: A Social Disease*, ed. Ernst Simmel (New York: International Universities Press, 1946), 39, 43.

44. Adorno et al., *The Authoritarian Personality*, 232.

45. See Christiana D. Morgan and Henry A. Murray, "A Method for Investigating Fantasies: The Thematic Apperception Test," *Archives of Neurological Psychiatry* 34 (August 1935): 289–306.

46. Adorno et al., *The Authoritarian Personality*, 1.

47. See especially Richard Christie and Peggy Cook, "A Guide to Published Literature Relating to the Authoritarian Personality through 1956," *Journal of Psychology* 45 (April 1958): 171–99; and the chapter "The Authoritarian Personality and the Organization of Attitudes," in Roger Brown, *Social Psychology* (New York: Free Press, 1965), 477–546. Also see John T. Jost, Jack Glaser, Arie W. Kruglandski, and Frank J. Sulloway, "Political Conservatism as Motivated Social Cognition," *Psychological Bulletin* 129 (May 2003): 339–75.

48. Christie and Cook, "A Guide to Published Literature Relating to the Authoritarian Personality through 1956," 171. The authors were referring to

Abraham S. Luchins, "Personality and Prejudice: A Critique," *Journal of Social Psychology* 32 (August 1950): 79–94.

49. Gordon W. Allport and Bernard M. Kramer, "Some Roots of Prejudice," *Journal of Psychology* 22 (July 1946): 9.

50. Samuel H. Flowerman, "Portrait of the Authoritarian Man," *New York Times Magazine*, April 23, 1950, 9.

51. Nathan Glazer, "The Authoritarian Personality in Profile: Report on a Major Study of Race Hatred," *Commentary* 4 (June 1950): 576–77.

52. Edward A. Shils, "Authoritarianism: 'Right' and 'Left,'" in *Studies in the Scope and Method of "The Authoritarian Personality,"* ed. Richard Christie and Marie Jahoda (Glencoe, IL: Free Press, 1954), 39. Also see Paul Kecskemeti, "Prejudice in the Catastrophic Perspective," *Commentary* 11 (March 1951): 286–92.

53. Herbert H. Hyman and Paul B. Sheatsley, "'The Authoritarian Personality': A Methodological Critique," in *Studies in the Scope and Method of "The Authoritarian Personality,"* 60.

54. Herbert Blumer, "Recent Research on Racial Relations: United States of America," *International Social Science Bulletin* 10 (1958): 425, 437.

55. See also Arnold M. Rose, "Intergroup Relations vs. Prejudice: Pertinent Theory for the Study of Social Change," *Social Problems* 4 (October 1956): 173–76; Melvin M. Tumin, "Sociological Aspects of Desegregation," *American Journal of Orthopsychiatry* 29 (January 1959): 180–85; and Earl Raab and Seymour M. Lipset, *Prejudice and Society* (New York: Anti-Defamation League, 1959).

56. When two leading social psychologists inquired, "Can We Fight Prejudice Scientifically?" in an early issue of *Commentary* from 1946, their answer was at best ambivalent. In 1947 Marie Jahoda, who had coauthored the *Commentary* essay, clarified her own negative position when she documented how bigoted individuals typically remained unmoved by "anti-prejudice propaganda." As Jahoda wrote, the same weak personality structure that caused a person to become prejudiced in the first place was also a personality structure that ignored "as a defense mechanism" efforts to reeducate it—a mechanism that came into play "whenever an individual senses a danger to his ego structure—that is, whenever his self-confidence hangs in the balance." And in 1950 the authors of *The Authoritarian Personality* concluded darkly that "measures to oppose social discrimination have not been more effective" because prejudice proved "irrational in its essential nature." See Samuel H. Flowerman and Marie Jahoda, "Can We Fight Prejudice Scientifically?" *Commentary* 2 (December 1946): 583–87; Eunice Cooper and Marie Jahoda, "The Evasion of Propaganda: How Prejudiced People Respond to Anti-Prejudice Propaganda," *Journal of Psychology* 23 (January 1947): 15–25; and Adorno et al., *The Authoritarian Personality*, 973. Also see Herbert H. Hyman and Paul B. Sheatsley, "Some Reasons Why Information Campaigns Fail," *Public Opinion Quarterly* 11 (Fall 1947): 413–23.

57. See Mary L. Dudziak, *Cold War Civil Rights: Race and the Image of American Democracy* (Princeton, NJ: Princeton University Press, 2002).

58. Mary Ellen Goodman, *Race Awareness in Young Children* (Cambridge, MA: Addison-Wesley, 1952), 219–20. Emphasis in original.

59. Miriam Reimann, "How Children Become Prejudiced," *Commentary* 11 (January 1951): 93.

60. Marian Radke-Yarrow and Bernard Lande, "Personality Correlates of Differential Reactions to Minority Group-Belonging," *Journal of Social Psychology* 38 (November 1953): 253.

61. Ibid., 271.

62. Helen G. Trager and Marian Radke-Yarrow, *They Learn What They Live: Prejudice in Young Children* (New York: Harper, 1952), xi. Also see Marian Radke, Helen G. Trager, and Hadassah Davis, "Social Perceptions and Attitudes of Children," *Genetic Psychology Monographs* 49 (1949): 327–447; and Marian J. Radke and Helen G. Trager, "Children's Perceptions of the Social Roles of Negroes and Whites," *Journal of Psychology* 29 (January 1950): 3–33.

63. See Kurt Lewin, *Resolving Social Conflicts: Selected Papers on Group Dynamics* (New York: Harper, 1948), 208–9, 211.

64. Kurt Lewin, "The Practicality of Democracy," in *Human Nature and Enduring Peace*, ed. Gardner Murphy (Boston: Houghton Mifflin, 1945), 311. Emphasis in original.

65. This was an older concept introduced by sociologist Emory S. Bogardus in the 1920s. See Emory S. Bogardus, "Social Distance and Its Origins," *Journal of Applied Sociology* 9 (January–February 1925): 216–26; and Emory S. Bogardus, *Immigration and Race Attitudes* (Boston: D. C. Heath, 1928). The Bogardus "social distance" scale continued to be tested and revised through the 1950s. See Michael Banton, "Social Distance: A New Appreciation," *Sociological Review* 8 (December 1960): 169–83.

66. See Leo Srole, "Social Integration and Certain Corollaries: An Exploratory Study," *American Sociological Review* 21 (December 1956): 709–16; and Leo Srole, Thomas S. Langner, Stanley T. Michael, Marvin K. Opler, and Thomas A. C. Rennie, *Mental Health in the Metropolis: The Midtown Manhattan Study* (New York: McGraw-Hill, 1962). Also see Edward L. McDill and Jeanne Clare Ridley, "Status, Anomia, Political Alienation, and Political Participation," *American Journal of Sociology* 68 (September 1962): 205–13.

67. See Richard Kluger, *Simple Justice: The History of Brown v. Board of Education and Black America's Struggle for Equality* (New York: Random House, 1977), especially 318–19.

68. See especially Kenneth B. Clark and Mamie K. Clark, "The Development of Consciousness of Self and the Emergence of Racial Identification in Negro Preschool Children," *Journal of Social Psychology* 10 (November 1939): 591–99; and Kenneth B. Clark and Mamie K. Clark, "Skin Color as a Factor in Racial Identification of Negro Preschool Children," *Journal of Social Psychology* 11 (February 1940): 159–69. Also see Gwen Bergner, "Black Children, White Preference: *Brown v. Board*, the Doll Tests, and the Politics of Self-Esteem," *American Quarterly* 61 (June 2009): 299–332.

69. "Appendix to Appellant's Briefs: The Effects of Segregation and the Consequences of Desegregation," reprinted in Kenneth B. Clark, *Prejudice and Your Child*, 2nd ed. (Boston: Beacon Press, 1963), 170.

70. Kenneth B. Clark, *Prejudice and Your Child* (Boston: Beacon Press, 1955), 53.

71. Esther Milner, "Some Hypotheses concerning the Influence of Segregation on Negro Personality Development," *Psychiatry* 16 (August 1953): 294.

72. Abram Kardiner and Lionel Ovesey, *The Mark of Oppression: Explorations in the Personality of the American Negro* (New York: World Publishing, 1962), 381.

73. R. A. Schermerhorn, "Psychiatric Disorders among Negroes: A Sociological Note," *American Journal of Psychiatry* 112 (May 1956): 881.

74. Arnold M. Rose, "Psychoneurotic Breakdown among Negro Soldiers in Combat," *Phylon* 17 (1st Qtr. 1956): 69.

75. Martin M. Grossack, "Some Personality Characteristics of Southern Negro Students," *Journal of Social Psychology* 46 (August 1957): 128.

76. Bertram P. Karon, *The Negro Personality: A Rigorous Investigation of the Effects of Culture* (New York: Springer, 1958), 166.

77. Harold Rosen and Jerome D. Frank, "Negroes in Psychotherapy," *American Journal of Psychiatry* 119 (November 1962): 458.

78. Viola W. Bernard, "Some Psychodynamic Aspects of Desegregation," *American Journal of Orthopsychiatry* 26 (July 1956): 462.

79. For a thorough handling of this topic, see Daryl Michael Scott, *Contempt and Pity: Social Policy and the Image of the Damaged Black Psyche, 1880–1996* (Chapel Hill: University of North Carolina Press, 1997).

80. "Appendix to Appellant's Briefs: The Effects of Segregation and the Consequences of Desegregation," 170.

81. Ellen Herman, *The Romance of American Psychology: Political Culture in the Age of Experts* (Berkeley: University of California Press, 1995), 248.

82. "Psychiatrists Increase 57% in Six Years," *Science News Letter*, June 8, 1957, 361.

83. "The Mind: Science's Search for a Guide to Sanity," *Newsweek*, October 24, 1955, 61.

84. George W. Albee and Marguerite Dickey, "Manpower Trends in Three Mental Health Professions," *American Psychologist* 12 (February 1957): 61.

85. "The 'Poor' Psychiatrist," *Newsweek*, May 23, 1955, 76.

86. Quoted in Harold Lord Varney, "Mental Health: Fact and Fiction," *American Mercury* 84 (April 1957): 9.

87. Quoted in Mike Gorman, *Every Other Bed* (Cleveland: World Publishing, 1956), 30.

88. "The Mind: Science's Search for a Guide to Sanity," 60.

89. Gorman, *Every Other Bed*, 24.

90. See Rashi Fein, *Economics of Mental Illness* (New York: Basic Books, 1958).

91. See George Albee, *Mental Health Manpower Trends* (New York: Basic Books, 1959), 51–55.

92. Albee and Dickey, "Manpower Trends in Three Mental Health Professions," 61.

93. See *Hearings on the Constitutional Rights of the Mentally Ill before the Senate Subcommittee on Constitutional Rights of the Committee of the Judiciary*, 87th Cong., 1st sess., part 1 (Washington, DC: U.S. Government Printing Office, 1961), 1.

94. Quoted in "Everybody's Mental Health," *Time*, December 10, 1956.

95. Ernest Havermann, "The Age of Psychology in the U.S.," *Life*, January 7, 1957, 68, 72.

96. "Medicine: The Old Wise Man," *Time*, February 14, 1955, 62.

97. Roy Porter, *The Greatest Benefit to Mankind: A Medical History of Humanity* (New York: W. W. Norton, 1999), 519.

98. Reprinted in June Bingham and Frederick Carl Redlich, *The Inside Story: Psychiatry and Everyday Life* (New York: Knopf, 1953), 58.

CHAPTER TWO

1. R. D. Laing, *The Politics of Experience* (New York: Ballantine Books, 1968), 58–59. Emphasis in original.

2. R. D. Laing, *The Divided Self: A Study in Sanity and Madness* (Chicago: Quadrangle Books, 1960), 197. All further references are to this edition and will be documented parenthetically in the text.

3. R. D. Laing, *The Politics of the Family and Other Essays* (New York: Pantheon, 1971).

4. Seymour S. Kety, "Biochemical Theories of Schizophrenia," *Science* 129 (June 12, 1959): 1596.

5. See the posthumous anthology of Sullivan's essays collected in Harry S. Sullivan, *The Interpersonal Theory of Psychiatry* (New York: W. W. Norton, 1953). On Fromm-Reichmann's close relationship with and professional respect for Sullivan, see Gail A. Hornstein, *To Redeem One Person Is to Redeem the World: The Life of Frieda Fromm-Reichmann* (New York: Free Press, 2000), esp. 125–29.

6. See Harry Stack Sullivan, "The Theory of Anxiety and the Nature of Psychotherapy," *Psychiatry* 12 (February 1949): 3–12.

7. Frieda Fromm-Reichmann, "Notes on the Development of Treatment of Schizophrenics by Psychoanalytic Psychotherapy," *Psychiatry* 11 (August 1948): 265.

8. Philip Wylie, *Generation of Vipers* (New York: Farrar and Rinehart, 1942).

9. Edward A. Strecker, *Their Mothers' Sons: The Psychiatrist Examines an American Problem* (New York: J. B. Lippincott, 1946), 170–71. In this same passage, Strecker sketched the case of a "boy who was close to the borderline of schizophrenia" and who was subsequently driven "hopelessly insane" by a mother who continued to "baby" him with her grasping chatter: "Don't worry, lamb, momsie will make you all well. Come back to mommie soon, sweet, she needs you." Ibid., 169–70. A fine analysis of Strecker's book can be found in Jennifer Terry, "'Momism' and the Making of Treasonous Homosexuals," in *"Bad" Mothers: The Politics of Blame in Twentieth-Century America*, ed. Molly Ladd-Taylor and Lauri Umansky (New York: New York University Press, 1998), 176–80. Also see Rebecca Jo Plant, *Mom: The Transformation of Motherhood in Modern America* (Chicago: University of Chicago Press, 2010), 100–103.

10. Ferdinand Lundberg and Marynia F. Farnham, *Modern Woman: The Lost Sex* (New York: Harper and Bros., 1947), 228. See the useful discussions of *Modern Woman* and its broad cultural impact in Susan J. Douglas, *Where*

the Girls Are: Growing Up Female with the Mass Media (New York: Three Rivers Press, 1995), 47–48, and Mari Jo Buhle, *Feminism and Its Discontents: A Century of Struggle with Psychoanalysis* (Cambridge, MA: Harvard University Press, 1998), 174–78.

11. Hornstein, *To Redeem One Person Is to Redeem the World*, 133–34.

12. Joanne Greenberg, *I Never Promised You a Rose Garden* (New York: New American Library, 2004), 36.

13. Trude Tietze, "A Study of Mothers of Schizophrenic Patients," *Psychiatry* 12 (February 1949): 65.

14. Suzanne Reichard and Carl Tillman, "Patterns of Parent-Child Relationships in Schizophrenia," *Psychiatry* 13 (May 1950): 251–52. Emphasis in original.

15. John N. Rosen, *Direct Analysis: Selected Papers* (New York: Grune and Stratton, 1953), 97.

16. See, for instance, Donald L. Gerard and Joseph Siegel, "The Family Background of Schizophrenia," *Psychiatric Quarterly* 24 (January 1950): 47–73; Davide Limentani, "Symbiotic Identification in Schizophrenia," *Psychiatry* 19 (August 1956): 231–36; Melvin L. Kohn and John A. Clausen, "Parental Authority Behavior and Schizophrenia," *American Journal of Orthopsychiatry* 26 (April 1956): 297–313; and C. W. Wahl, "Some Antecedent Factors in the Family Histories of 568 Male Schizophrenics of the United States Navy," *American Journal of Psychiatry* 113 (September 1956): 201–10. Also see the comprehensive bibliographical references provided in Carol Eadie Hartwell, "The Schizophrenic Mother Concept in American Psychiatry," *Psychiatry* 59 (Fall 1996): 293–97.

17. Fromm-Reichmann, "Notes on the Development of Treatment of Schizophrenics by Psychoanalytic Psychotherapy," 265.

18. Importantly, the ethnographic practice of rendering intelligible the seemingly incoherent speech of the mentally ill would eventually be decoupled from parental blame. For a fine model see João Biehl, *Vita: Life in a Zone of Social Abandonment* (Berkeley: University of California Press, 2005).

19. Don D. Jackson, "The Question of Family Homeostasis," *International Journal of Family Therapy* 3 (Spring 1981): 8–9, 5. This was a talk given to the American Psychiatric Association in 1954, and the essay originally appeared in the *Psychiatric Quarterly Supplement* 31 (1957): 79–90.

20. See Lyman C. Wynne et al., "Pseudo-Mutuality in the Family Relations of Schizophrenics," *Psychiatry* 21 (May 1958): 205–20.

21. In this content, Bateson's prior work on communications theory should be noted. See Jurgen Ruesch and Gregory Bateson, *Communication: The Social Matrix of Psychiatry* (New York: W. W. Norton, 1951).

22. For a discussion of how the command to "be spontaneous" functions as a "double bind," see R. D. Laing, *The Self and Others: Further Studies in Sanity and Madness* (Chicago: Quadrangle Books, 1962), 151–52.

23. Gregory Bateson, Don D. Jackson, Jay Haley, and John Weakland, "Toward a Theory of Schizophrenia," *Behavioral Science* 1 (October 1956): 257.

24. Ibid., 254.

25. Ibid., 261.

26. For a thorough assessment of the largely favorable reception to the double bind hypothesis in publications in the fields of psychiatry and the behavioral

sciences during 1957–61, see Paul Watzlawick, "A Review of the Double Bind Theory," *Family Process* 2 (March 1963): 132–53.

27. Theodore Lidz et al., "The Intrafamilial Environment of Schizophrenic Patients: II. Marital Schism and Marital Skew," *American Journal of Psychiatry* 114 (September 1957): 241. Also see Theodore Lidz, "Schizophrenia and the Family," *Psychiatry* 21 (February 1958): 21–27; and Theodore Lidz, *The Family and Human Adaptation* (New York: International Universities Press, 1963). In fact, Lidz's pioneering work in this area dates to the late 1940s. See Ruth Wilmanns Lidz and Theodore Lidz, "The Family Environment of Schizophrenic Patients," *American Journal of Psychiatry* 106 (November 1949): 332–45.

28. Theodore Lidz and Stephen Fleck, "Schizophrenia, Human Integration, and the Role of the Family," in *The Etiology of Schizophrenia*, ed. Don D. Jackson (Oxford: Basic Books, 1960), 80.

29. Murray Bowen et al., "The Role of the Father in Families with a Schizophrenic Patient," *American Journal of Psychiatry* 115 (May 1959): 1020.

30. In a question that could have been—but was not—asked of virtually all subsequent clinical research of families with mentally ill children, Dr. William F. Orr wrote in 1956: "What comprises data in a study such as this when there is no clear thesis being tested, when most of the significant events occurred in the order of two decades prior to the study, and when the epitome of it, the illness of the child, has in itself created changes in the reaction of the parents to each other and to any interviewer in a setting involving the child's illness?" See William F. Orr, "Discussion" to Theodore Lidz et al., "The Role of the Father in the Family Environment of the Schizophrenic Patient," *American Journal of Psychiatry* 113 (August 1956): 132.

31. Wynne et al., "Pseudo-Mutuality in the Family Relations of Schizophrenics," 208. Emphasis in original.

32. See Lyman C. Wynne, "The Study of Intrafamilial Alignments and Splits in Exploratory Family Therapy," in *Exploring the Base for Family Therapy*, ed. Nathan Ackerman, Frances Beatman, and Sanford Sherman (New York: Family Service Association of America, 1961), 108–10, 114.

33. For example, in 1961 Lyman Wynne wrote: "The detailed delineation of the differences between schizophrenic and nonschizophrenic families is a major task of our continuing research program." Ibid., 114. And the struggle of how to differentiate "normal" from "schizophrenogenic" families would remain both intractable and persistent throughout the decade. See, for instance, *Interaction in Families* (1968), a study into family processes and mental illness by a team affiliated with the Harvard Medical School. Elliot G. Mishler and Nancy E. Waxler, *Interaction in Families: An Experimental Study of Family Processes and Schizophrenia* (New York: Wiley, 1968), esp. 243–47.

34. For the findings from the Eastern Pennsylvania Psychiatric Institute, see Iván Böszörményi-Nagy, "The Concept of Schizophrenia from the Perspective of Family Treatment," *Family Process* 1 (March 1962): 103–13, and Iván Böszörményi-Nagy and James L. Framo, eds., *Intensive Family Therapy* (New York: Harper and Row, 1965).

35. For Haley's own theories on the family origins of mental illness, see Jay

Haley, "An Interactional Description of Schizophrenia," *Psychiatry* 22 (November 1959): 321–32.

36. On the research from the Harvard School of Public Health, see Rhona Rapoport, "Normal Crises, Family Structure and Mental Health," *Family Process* 2 (March 1963): 68–80.

37. Nathan W. Ackerman, "Towards an Integrative Therapy of the Family," *American Journal of Psychiatry* 114 (February 1958): 729.

38. Nathan W. Ackerman, *The Psychodynamics of Family Life: Diagnosis and Treatment of Family Relationships* (New York: Basic Books, 1958), 343.

39. Nathan W. Ackerman, "Introduction," in *Family Process*, ed. Nathan W. Ackerman (New York: Basic Books, 1970), xiii.

40. Eleanor Perry quoted in Barry Hyams, "*David and Lisa*: Troubled Teen-Agers' Dilemma Shot in Main Line Mansion 'Institution,'" *New York Times*, May 6, 1962, 149. Unlike the film version, the original case study by psychiatrist Theodore Isaac Rubin paid minimal attention to schizophrenogenic parents. Instead, the text emphasized how extreme alienation (and even an existential loneliness) could lead to schizophrenia in young adults. On the other hand, and in this way similar to the film adaptation, Rubin's book did clearly see love as the potential cure for mental illness. See Theodore Isaac Rubin, *Lisa and David* (New York: Macmillan, 1961).

41. R. D. Laing, "Introduction," Morag Coate, *Beyond All Reason* (London: Constable, 1964), x. For Coate's discussion of how seeing the film *David and Lisa* cured her, see ibid., 119–22.

42. Betty Friedan, *The Feminine Mystique* (New York: Dell, 1963), 279, 286–87.

43. Greer Williams, "Schizophrenics Can Recover," *Atlantic Monthly* 209 (January 1962): 28. Also see Don D. Jackson, "Schizophrenia," *Scientific American* 207 (August 1962): 65–74; and Martin B. Loeb, "Mental Health: New Frontiers," *The Nation*, May 18, 1963, 418–21.

44. "Family Schizophrenia," *Time*, October 27, 1961. A more extensive replication of this familial conversation and a scholarly analysis subsequently appeared in Lyman C. Wynne and Margaret Thaler Singer, "Thought Disorder and Family Relations of Schizophrenics," *Archives of General Psychiatry* 9 (September 1963): 195.

45. Paul Watzlawick, "Rev. of R. D. Laing's *The Self and Others: Further Studies in Sanity and Madness*," *Family Process* 1 (September 1962): 167.

46. J. L. Cameron and R. D. Laing, "Patient and Nurse: Effects of Environmental Changes in the Care of Chronic Schizophrenics," *Lancet* 269 (December 31, 1955): 1386. For a fascinating report on discrepancies in Laing's writings about the rumpus room experiment, see David Abrahamson, "R. D. Laing and Long-Stay Patients: Discrepant Accounts of the Refractory Ward and 'Rumpus Room' at Gartnavel Royal Hospital," *History of Psychiatry* 18 (June 2007): 203–15.

47. On the family research at Tavistock where Laing worked at this time, also see John Bowlby, "Childhood Mourning and Its Implications for Psychiatry," *American Journal of Psychiatry* 118 (December 1961): 481–98.

48. Laing, *The Self and Others*, 97, 136, 152. Another early influence on Laing was American psychiatrist Harold F. Searles, who wrote in 1959: "My clinical experience has indicated that the individual becomes schizophrenic partly by reason of a long-continued effort, a largely or wholly unconscious effort, on the part of some person or persons highly important in his upbringing, to drive him crazy." Harold F. Searles, "The Effort to Drive the Other Person Crazy," *British Journal of Medical Psychology* 32 (1959): 1. Searles also worked at Chestnut Lodge in Maryland during the 1950s.

49. For instance, see this poem by Laing from 1970:

> Jill feels safe to be angry with Jack
> because Jack does nothing
> She is angry with Jack
> because he does nothing
> She is angry with Jack
> because he does not frighten her
> He does not frighten her
> because, doing nothing, he is useless.
> She feels safe with him,
> *therefore* she despises him
> She clings to him
> *because* he does not frighten her
> She despises him
> because she clings to him
> because he does not frighten her
> Jill knows she is inferior
> therefore, she is superior to anyone who thinks she
> is superior to him.

See R. D. Laing, *Knots* (New York: Pantheon Books, 1971), 19. Additionally see the "Jack and Jill" vignettes Laing added to the (heavily revised) second edition of *Self and Others*. An example is: "Jill loves Jack. Jack loves Jill. Jill knows that Jack loves Jill. Jack knows that Jill loves Jack. But Jacks says that it does not make any difference to him whether Jill loves him or not. As long as he loves her that is all that matters. How will Jill feel?" R. D. Laing, *Self and Others*, 2nd ed. (New York: Pantheon Books, 1969), 136.

50. R. D. Laing and A. Esterson, *Sanity, Madness, and the Family* (New York: Basic Books, 1964), 47–48, 18.

51. Ibid., 48. Emphasis in original.

52. R. D. Laing, "What Is Schizophrenia?" *New Left Review* 28 (November/December 1964): 65.

53. R. D. Laing, "Violence and Love," *Journal of Existentialism* 5, no. 20 (1965): 417.

54. R. D. Laing, "Massacre of the Innocents," *Peace News*, January 22, 1965, 7.

55. R. D. Laing, "Practice and Theory: The Present Situation," *Psychotherapy and Psychosomatics* 13 (1965): 64–65. Emphasis in original.

56. Laing, *The Politics of Experience,* 12–13.

57. Robert Coles, "Life's Madness," *New Republic,* May 13, 1967, 30.

58. In 1979 Lifton wrote: "Written before he was thirty, when still in active tension with the psychoanalytic and psychiatric traditions he was questioning, *The Divided Self* is rigorous, and equally sensitive to schizophrenic suffering and destructiveness and to psychiatric distance and maneuvers toward schizophrenic patients. Laing is willing to address nuance and entertain paradox in ways that are both visionary and responsible to the work of other serious students of madness." Robert Jay Lifton, *The Broken Connection: On Death and the Continuity of Life* (New York: Simon and Schuster, 1979), 415.

59. See Wynne's defense of Laing in Lyman C. Wynne, "Rev. of R. D. Laing, *The Politics of the Family,*" *Psychiatry* 32 (November 1969): 474–75.

60. Jules Henry, *Culture against Man* (New York: Random House, 1963), 323, 385.

61. Jules Henry, "Sham," *North American Review* 252 (May 1967): 7–8.

62. Henry, *Culture against Man,* 322.

63. Jules Henry, "American Schoolrooms: Learning the Nightmare," *Columbia University Forum* 6 (Spring 1963): 26.

64. Henry, "Sham," 6.

65. Jules Henry, *Pathways to Madness* (New York: Vintage, 1973), 106–7. Also see Jules Henry, "The Human Demons," *Trans-action* 3 (March/April 1966): 45–48.

66. See Laing, "Violence and Love," 418–20.

67. Remarks by Jules Henry, *Congress on the Dialectics of Liberation,* vol. 5 (London: Institute of Phenomenological Studies, 1967). Transcribed from the LP sound recording.

68. David Herzberg, *Happy Pills in America: From Miltown to Prozac* (Baltimore: Johns Hopkins University Press, 2009), 18.

69. Thomas M. Sullivan et al., "Biochemical Studies of Families of Schizophrenic Patients," *American Journal of Psychiatry* 122 (March 1966): 1043.

70. Thomas M. Sullivan et al., "Clinical and Biochemical Studies of Families of Schizophrenic Patients," *American Journal of Psychiatry* 123 (February 1967): 951.

71. See Heinz E. Lehmann, "'Discussion' of Robert G. Heath and Iris M. Krupp, 'Schizophrenia as a Specific Biologic Disease,'" *American Journal of Psychiatry* 124 (February 1968): 1024–27.

72. Roy R. Grinker, "Emerging Concepts of Mental Illness and Models of Treatment: The Medical Point of View," *American Journal of Psychiatry* 125 (January 1969): 865–67, 869.

73. George W. Albee, "Emerging Concepts of Mental Illness and Models of Treatment: The Psychological Point of View," *American Journal of Psychiatry* 125 (January 1969): 870–73. Also see George W. Albee, "Models, Myths, and Manpower," *Mental Hygiene* 52 (April 1968): 168–80. On Albee's career as an advocate for identifying social issues as the causation of mental illnesses, see "George W. Albee: Psychologist Sought Social Cures," *Washington Post,* July 13, 2006, B06.

74. Robert Coles, "The Limits of Psychiatry," *The Progressive* (May 1967): 32–34.

75. See Laing, "What Is Schizophrenia?"

76. Marshall Berman, "Must Man First Go Mad in Order to be Sane?" *New York Times Book Review*, February 22, 1970, 1.

77. Peter Mezan, "After Freud and Jung, Now Comes Laing," *Esquire*, January 1972, 92–97, 160–78; and "Philosopher of Madness," *Life*, October 8, 1971, 87. Also see James S. Gordon, "Who Is Mad? Who Is Sane? R. D. Laing: In Search of a New Psychiatry," *Atlantic* 227 (January 1971): 50–66; and "Philosopher of Madness," *Newsweek*, December 18, 1972.

78. Rael Jean Isaac and Virginia C. Armat, *Madness in the Streets: How Psychiatry and the Law Abandoned the Mentally Ill* (New York: Free Press, 1990), 29.

79. Richard Schickel, "A Pair of Very Grainy Pictures," *Life*, November 3, 1972, 16.

80. Angela Carter, "Truly, It Felt Like Year One," in *Very Heaven: Looking Back at the 1960's*, ed. Sara Maitland (London: Virago Press, 1988), 215.

81. David Cooper, *The Death of the Family* (New York: Vintage, 1971), 4.

82. John H. Gagnon, "The Death of the Family," *New York Times Book Review*, February 14, 1971, 4.

CHAPTER THREE

1. Erving Goffman, *Asylums: Essays on the Social Situation of Mental Patients and Other Inmates* (Garden City, NY: Anchor Books, 1961), 85. All further references are to this edition and will be documented parenthetically in the text.

2. See Mary Jane Ward, *The Snake Pit* (New York: Random House, 1946); Albert Q. Maisel, "Bedlam 1946," *Life*, May 6, 1946, 102–18; Albert Deutsch, *The Shame of the States* (New York: Harcourt, Brace, 1948); and Mike Gorman, "Oklahoma Attacks Its Snakepits," *Reader's Digest*, September 1948, 139–60.

3. Darin Weinberg, *Of Others Inside: Insanity, Addiction, and Belonging in America* (Philadelphia: Temple University Press, 2005), 76.

4. See Joost A. M. Meerloo, "The Crime of Menticide," *American Journal of Psychiatry* 107 (February 1951): 594–98; and Allen W. Dulles, "Brain Warfare: Russia's Secret Weapon," *U.S. News and World Report*, May 8, 1953, 54, 56, 58.

5. See Edward Hunter, *Brain-Washing in Red China: The Calculated Destruction of Men's Minds* (New York: Vanguard Press, 1951).

6. Quoted in *Communist Psychological Warfare (Brainwashing): Consultation with Edward Hunter, Author and Foreign Correspondent, Committee on Un-American Activities* (Washington, DC: Government Printing Office, 1958), 1.

7. See the summary account in Tim Weiner, "Mind Games: Remembering Brainwashing," *New York Times*, July 6, 2008.

8. Joost A. M. Meerloo, "Pavlov's Dog and Communist Brainwashers," *New York Times Magazine*, May 9, 1954, 33. Also see C. B. Palmer, "The War for the P.O.W.'s Mind," *New York Time Magazine*, September 13, 1953, 13, 36, 39, 42.

9. Lawrence E. Hinkle Jr. and Harold G. Wolfe, "Communist Interrogation and Indoctrination of 'Enemies of the States': Analysis of Methods Used by the Communist State Police (A Special Report)," *A.M.A. Archives of Neurology and Psychiatry* 76 (August 1956): 171–72.

10. Meerloo, "The Crime of Menticide," 598.

11. "Why Did Many G.I. Captives Cave In?" *U.S. News and World Report*, February 24, 1956, 56–72. See Elspeth Cameron Ritchie, "Psychiatry in the Korean War: Perils, PIES, and Prisoners of War," *Military Medicine* 167 (November 2002): 898–903.

12. For two valuable (if incompatible) analyses of this phenomenon, see Catherine Lutz, "Epistemology of the Bunker: The Brainwashed and Other New Subjects of Permanent War," in *Inventing the Psychological: Toward a Cultural History of Emotional Life in America*, ed. Joel Pfister and Nancy Schnog (New Haven, CT: Yale University Press, 1997), 245–67; and Timothy Melley, "Brainwashed!: Conspiracy Theory and Ideology in the Cold War United States," *New German Critique* 103 (Winter 2008): 145–65.

13. Dr. William E. Mayer quoted in "Why Did Many G.I. Captives Cave In?" 56.

14. Dr. William E. Mayer cited in Louis Jolyon West, "Psychiatry, 'Brainwashing,' and the American Character," *American Journal of Psychiatry* 120 (March 1964): 845.

15. "Torture Schools No Help," *Science News Letter*, August 4, 1956, 67.

16. William Sargant, *Battle for the Mind* (Garden City, NY: Doubleday, 1957), 239.

17. Richard Condon, *The Manchurian Candidate* (New York: Signet, 1959).

18. Albert D. Biderman, "The Image of 'Brainwashing,'" *Public Opinion Quarterly* 26 (Winter 1962): 547, 549, 550, 552–53; and Robert Jay Lifton, *Thought Reform and the Psychology of Totalism: A Study of "Brainwashing" in China* (New York: W. W. Norton, 1961), 4. Also see Edgar H. Schein with Inge Schneier and Curtis H. Barker, *Coercive Persuasion: A Socio-Psychological Analysis of the "Brainwashing" of American Civilian Prisoners by the Chinese Communists* (New York: W. W. Norton, 1961).

19. Edgar H. Schein, "The Chinese Indoctrination Program for Prisoners of War: A Study of Attempted 'Brainwashing,'" *Psychiatry* 19 (May 1956): 172.

20. Edgar H. Schein, "Reaction Patterns to Severe, Chronic Stress in American Army Prisoners of War of the Chinese," *Journal of Social Issues* 13 (Summer 1957): 27–28.

21. In this regard, note the brutally direct handling of these issues in *The Rack* (1956), a television play written by Rod Serling that concerns an Army captain who faces a military court-martial because he had succumbed to psychological torture and cooperated with the communists while a POW in a North Korean prison camp. See Rod Serling, *Patterns: Four Television Plays* (New York: Simon and Schuster, 1957), 91–135.

22. Schein, "The Chinese Indoctrination Program," 151–53, 172.

23. Robert J. Lifton, "Chinese Communist Thought Reform," in *Group Processes:*

Transactions of the Third Conference, October 7, 8, 9, and 10, 1956, Princeton, N.J., ed. Bertram Schaffner (New York: Josiah Macy, Jr. Foundation, 1957), 243. Emphasis in original.

24. Robert Jay Lifton, "Home By Ship: Reaction Patterns of American Prisoners of War Repatriated from North Korea," *American Journal of Psychiatry* 110 (April 1954): 739. Also see Harvey D. Strassman, Margaret B. Thaler, and Edgar H. Schein, "A Prisoner of War Syndrome: Apathy as a Reaction to Severe Stress," *American Journal of Psychiatry* 112 (June 1956): 998–1003. For a more pessimistic psychiatric assessment of the mental health of these repatriated prisoners of war, see Henry A. Segal, "Initial Psychiatric Findings of Recently Repatriated Prisoners of War," *American Journal of Psychiatry* 111 (November 1954): 358–63.

25. Lifton, "Chinese Communist Thought Reform," 235.

26. Lifton, *Thought Reform and the Psychology of Totalism*, 457.

27. Robert J. Lifton, "Thought Reform of Chinese Intellectuals: A Psychiatric Evaluation," *Journal of Social Issues* 13 (August 1957): 19.

28. Participants included anthropologist Gregory Bateson of the VA Hospital in Palo Alto, California; psychotherapist Frieda Fromm-Reichmann of the Chestnut Lodge Sanitarium; anthropologist Margaret Mead; behavioral scientist Fritz Redl, who had developed the "therapeutic milieu" concept for the treatment of disturbed children; psychoanalyst Bertram Schaffner, author of a widely cited examination of authoritarianism in the German family; and psychiatrist John P. Spiegel, whose *Men under Stress* (1945)—co-written with Dr. Roy Grinker—was the definitive study of combat fatigue. Also in attendance were psychologist George W. Boguslavsky, a propaganda analyst for General George MacArthur during World War II; and—although he hardly engaged Goffman— Joost Meerloo.

29. Cf. generally Erving Goffman, "Interpersonal Persuasion," in *Group Processes*, 117–93.

30. Goffman, in "Chinese Communist Thought Reform," 274.

31. Lifton, "Communist Chinese Thought Reform," 221–22.

32. Goffman, in "Chinese Communist Thought Reform," 233.

33. Erving Goffman, "Characteristics of Total Institutions," in *Proceedings of the Symposium on Preventive and Social Psychiatry* (Washington, DC: U.S. Government Printing Office, 1958), 60–61. Emphasis in original.

34. Erving Goffman, "The Moral Career of the Mental Patient," *Psychiatry* 22 (May 1959): 124.

35. Erving Goffman, "The Nature of Deference and Demeanor," *American Anthropologist* 58 (June 1956): 473–502.

36. Erving Goffman, *The Presentation of Self in Everyday Life* (New York: Anchor Books, 1959), 252–53.

37. Valuable assessments of *Asylums* and of Goffman's social theories can be found in the following: Harold W. Pfautz, "Rev. of *Asylums*," *American Sociological Review* 27 (August 1962): 555–56; Raymond M. Weinstein, "Goffman's *Asylums* and the Total Institution Model of Mental Hospitals," *Psychiatry* 57 (November 1994): 348–67; Gary Alan Fine and Lori J. Ducharme, "The Ethnographic Present: Images of Institutional Control in Second-School Research," in *A*

Second Chicago School? The Development of a Postwar American Sociology, ed. Gary Alan Fine (Chicago: University of Chicago Press, 1995), esp. 112–15; Greg Smith, *Goffman and Social Organization: Studies in a Sociological Legacy* (New York: Routledge, 1999); Philip Manning, "The Institutionalization and Deinstitutionalization of the Mentally Ill: Lessons from Goffman," in *Counseling and the Therapeutic State*, ed. James J. Chriss (New York: Aldine Transaction, 1999), 89–104; Nancy J. Herman-Kinney, "Deviance," in *Handbook of Symbolic Interactionism*, ed. Larry T. Reynolds and Nancy J. Herman-Kinney (Lanham, MD: Rowman and Littlefield, 2003), esp. 714–16; and Ian Hacking, "Between Michel Foucault and Erving Goffman: Between Discourse in the Abstract and Face-to-Face Interaction," *Economy and Society* 33 (August 2004): 277–302. Among the very few scholars who have recognized that *Asylums* concerned the nature of selfhood has been William Caudill. However, Caudill had an entirely different interpretation of what Goffman grappled with (perhaps because Caudill appeared simply to accept unambiguously the existence of a self). See William Caudill, "Rev. of *Asylums*," *American Journal of Sociology* 68 (November 1962): 366–69. Philip Manning also briefly acknowledges that Goffman "discovered that he needed a theory of the self when he analyzed aspects of mental illness and institutionalization," though his analysis remains fundamentally different from what is argued here. See Philip Manning, *Freud and American Society* (New York: Polity, 2005), 95. Yet social psychologists interested in Goffman's theories of the self wholly neglect the import of *Asylums*. Despite the thoroughness, for instance, of the more than fifty contributors to the *Handbook of Self and Identity*, none of their dozen or so references to Goffman mentions *Asylums*; they refer instead to *Presentation of Self*, characterized repeatedly as Goffman's classic statement on the self and the social world. See Mark R. Leary and June Price Tangney, eds., *Handbook of Self and Identity* (New York: Guilford Press, 2003).

38. Tom Burns, *Erving Goffman* (New York: Routledge, 1992), 142.

39. See Edwin Lemert, *Social Pathology* (New York: McGraw-Hill, 1951), and Edwin Lemert, "Legal Commitment and Social Control," *Sociology and Social Research* 30 (May–June 1946): 370–78.

40. Howard S. Becker, *Outsiders: Studies in the Sociology of Deviance* (New York: Free Press, 1963), 8–9 (emphasis in original). See also Howard S. Becker, "The Career of the Chicago Public Schoolteacher," *American Journal of Sociology* 57 (March 1952): 470–77; Howard S. Becker, "Becoming a Marihuana User," *American Journal of Sociology* 59 (November 1953): 235–42; and Howard S. Becker, "Marihuana Use and Social Control," *Social Problems* 3 (July 1955): 35–44. Also notable is the work of another graduate from the University of Chicago sociology program. See Albert K. Cohen, *Delinquent Boys: The Culture of the Gangs* (Glencoe, IL: Free Press, 1955).

41. Gary Alan Fine and Philip Manning, "Erving Goffman," in *The Blackwell Companion to Major Contemporary Social Theorists*, ed. George Ritzer (Malden, MA: Blackwell, 2003), 49.

42. Deutsch added: "I entered buildings swarming with naked humans herded like cattle and treated with less concern, pervaded by a fetid odor so heavy, so nauseating, that the stench seemed to have a physical existence of its own." Deutsch, *The Shame of the States*, 42.

43. Goffman, "Interpersonal Persuasion," in *Group Processes*, 137.

44. John Bartlow Martin, "Inside the Asylum," *Saturday Evening Post*, October 6, 1956, 25.

45. David Healy, *The Creation of Psychopharmacology* (Cambridge, MA: Harvard University Press, 2002), 97–98.

46. William L. Laurence, "Drug Found Help in Schizophrenia," *New York Times*, February 4, 1955, 28.

47. John Bartlow Martin, "Why Am I Here, Doctor?" *Saturday Evening Post*, November 3, 1956, 144.

48. John Bartlow Martin, "Disturbed Ward," *Saturday Evening Post*, October 13, 1956, 81.

49. Frank G. Slaughter, *Daybreak* (Garden City, NY: Doubleday, 1958), 320. Emphasis in original.

50. Natalie Davis Spingarn, "St. Elizabeths: Pace-Setter for Mental Hospitals," *Harper's* 212 (January 1956): 58, 62–63.

51. Edward Shorter, *A History of Psychiatry* (New York: Wiley and Sons, 1997), 228.

52. Harold Bourne, "Insulin Coma in Decline," *American Journal of Psychiatry* 114 (May 1958): 1016. Also see Deborah Blythe Doroshow, "Performing a Cure for Schizophrenia: Insulin Coma Therapy on the Wards," *Journal of the History of Medicine and Allied Sciences* 62 (April 2007): 213–43.

53. George Gulevich, Robert S. Daniels, and Philip M. Margolis, "The Decreasing Use of Electroconvulsive Therapy," *American Journal of Psychiatry* 118 (December 1961): 555–57.

54. See John A. Koltes, "Mental Hospitals with Open Doors," *American Journal of Psychiatry* 113 (September 1956): 250–53; L. C. Hurst, "The Unlocking of Wards in Mental Hospitals," *American Journal of Psychiatry* 114 (October 1957): 306–8.

55. Alfred H. Stanton and Morris S. Schwartz, "Medical Opinion and the Social Context in the Mental Hospital," *Psychiatry* 12 (August 1949): 248.

56. Alfred H. Stanton and Morris S Schwartz, *The Mental Hospital: A Study of Institutional Participation in Psychiatric Illness and Treatment* (New York: Basic Books, 1954), 169.

57. Robert Sommer and Robert Hall, "Alienation and Mental Illness," *American Sociological Review* 23 (August 1958): 418.

58. Frank Leonard, *City Psychiatric* (New York: Ballantine, 1965). In 1966 Leonard testified about the inhumane conditions at Bellevue to the New York City Council: "When an insufficient staff must control large groups of patients, simple and rigid ward routines result, and these in turn lead, naturally, to callousness and brutality. The worst of this brutality is that it is directed at the patients who are the most disturbed, because they are the hardest to control." Quoted in Martin Tolchin, "Bedlam for City Mental Patients," *New York Times*, August 29, 1966, 22.

59. Had Wiseman and Marshall distorted or exaggerated existence inside Bridgewater? The same year *Titicut Follies* was filmed, a Bridgewater inmate petitioned to be transferred to a state prison where he would not receive "treatment" for his mental illness. He contended that conditions at the state prison

were far less punitive than those at Bridgewater's "treatment center." See "Brief of Donald McEvan, Petitioner Pro Se," in *Psychoanalysis, Psychiatry, and Law*, ed. Jay Katz, Joseph Goldstein, and Alan M. Dershowitz (New York: Free Press, 1967), 700. The inmate's request for transfer to the state prison was denied. Then in *Nason v. Superintendent of Bridgewater State Hospital* (1968), an inmate at Bridgewater argued for his right to receive treatment—and he sought a writ of habeas corpus on the grounds that the substandard treatment programs at Bridgewater denied him due process. He did not get released, but he did win his demand for adequate treatment. See *Legal Rights of the Mentally Handicapped: Volume One*, ed. Bruce J. Ennis and Paul R. Friedman (New York: Practicing Law Institute, 1974), 276–77.

CHAPTER FOUR

1. Thomas S. Szasz, *The Manufacture of Madness: A Comparative Study of the Inquisition and the Mental Health Movement* (New York: Harper and Row, 1970), 282.

2. See especially James Clayton, "Edith Hough Found Ready for Release," *Washington Post*, October 28, 1958, C1; James Clayton, "Edith Hough's Plea Denied for St. Elizabeths Release," *Washington Post*, December 6, 1958, D1; and John P. MacKenzie, "Court Frees Edith Hough, Patient since '57 Slaying," *Washington Post*, July 15, 1961, C1.

3. Thomas S. Szasz, "Civil Liberties and Mental Illness: Some Observations on the Case of Miss Edith L. Hough," *Journal of Nervous and Mental Disease* 131 (July 1960): 62. For a partial rebuttal of Szasz's argument, see Joseph Goldstein and Jay Katz, "Dangerousness and Mental Illness: Some Observations on the Decision to Release Persons Acquitted by Reason of Insanity," *Yale Law Journal* 70 (December 1960): 225–39.

4. Thomas S. Szasz, "Malingering: 'Diagnosis' or Social Condemnation?," *A.M.A. Archives of Neurology and Psychiatry* 76 (October 1956): 438. Also see Thomas S. Szasz, "Some Observations on the Relationship between Psychiatry and the Law," *A.M.A Archives of Neurology and Psychiatry* 75 (March 1956): 297–315.

5. Thomas S. Szasz, "The Problem of Psychiatric Nosology," *American Journal of Psychiatry* 114 (November 1957): 405–11.

6. See Thomas S. Szasz, "Psychiatric Expert Testimony—Its Covert Meaning and Social Function," *Psychiatry* 20 (August 1957): 313–16.

7. Thomas S. Szasz, "Psychiatry, Ethics, and the Criminal Law," *Columbia Law Review* 58 (February 1958): 183–98, at 195.

8. See Thomas S. Szasz, "Politics and Mental Health: Some Remarks Apropos of the Case of Mr. Ezra Pound," *American Journal of Psychiatry* 115 (December 1958): 508–11.

9. See Richard Ballad, "Dr. Thomas Szasz: *Penthouse* Interview," *Penthouse* (October 1973): 68–74.

10. A strong critic of Szasz, sociologist Michael S. Goldstein would nevertheless in 1980 characterize him as "one of America's most well-known contemporary psychiatrists," and Szasz's writings as "one of the historical and

intellectual bases of the growing body of work criticizing the applicability of the 'medical model' to psychiatric phenomena." Michael S. Goldstein, "The Politics of Thomas Szasz: A Sociological View," *Social Problems* 27 (June 1980): 570.

11. Dorothea D. Braginsky and Benjamin M. Braginsky, "Psychologists: High Priests of the Middle Class," *Psychology Today* 7 (December 1973): 15.

12. Szasz, *The Manufacture of Madness*, xxv.

13. Jerome D. Frank, "Are You a Guilty Parent?," *Harper's* 214 (April 1957): 56, 58–59.

14. Philip Rieff, *Freud: The Mind of a Moralist* (New York: Viking, 1959), 304–5.

15. William Kaufman, "Psychiatry Is for Psuckers," *Coronet*, March 1954, 150, 152.

16. Cited in Judd Marmor, Viola W. Bernard, and Perry Ottenberg, "Psychodynamics of Group Opposition to Health Programs," *American Journal of Orthopsychiatry* 30 (April 1960): 333, 336, 338.

17. Quoted in E. Fuller Torrey, *Out of the Shadows: Confronting America's Mental Illness Crisis* (New York: Wiley and Sons, 1997), 173.

18. Quoted in Donald Robinson, "Conspiracy USA: The Far Right's Fight against Mental Health," *Look*, January 26, 1965, 32.

19. Harold Lord Varney, "Mental Health: Fact and Fiction," *American Mercury* 84 (April 1957): 8, 10.

20. Ibid., 11–12, 14. Varney had been a member of the International Workers of the World (and wrote about his experiences in the 1919 novel, *Revolt*) before moving steadily (and quite far) to the right later in his political career.

21. Christopher Slobogin, *Minding Justice: Laws That Deprive People with Mental Disability of Life and Liberty* (Cambridge, MA: Harvard University Press, 2006), 31.

22. *Durham v. United States*, 214 F. 2d 862 (D.C. Cir. 1954), http://wings.buffalo.edu/law/bclc/web/appdurham.htm.

23. Manfred S. Guttmacher, "The Psychiatrist as an Expert Witness," *University of Chicago Law Review* 22 (1954–55): 329. Guttmacher placed great faith in the wisdom of the forensic psychiatrist; he also argued that it scarcely mattered whether or not a defendant in a criminal case was proven legally to suffer from mental illness. As he wrote in 1952: "Fundamentally, why should it make any difference whether a person who has committed a criminal act was sane at the time and therefore guilty, or 'not guilty by reason of insanity'? In either case he has shown himself a menace to society who must be taken into custody and control. Why worry over whether that control is based on criminality or insanity?" Manfred S. Guttmacher and Henry Weihofen, *Psychiatry and the Law* (New York: W. W. Norton, 1952), 443.

24. Gregory Zilboorg, "A Step toward Enlightened Justice," *University of Chicago Law Review* 22 (Winter 1955): 331–35, at 332.

25. William O. Douglas, "The Durham Rule: A Meeting Ground for Lawyers and Psychiatrists," *Iowa Law Review* 41 (Summer 1956): 485, 492.

26. Jerome Hall, "Psychiatry and Criminal Responsibility," *Yale Law Journal* 65 (May 1956): 766.

27. Herbert Wechsler, "The Criteria of Criminal Responsibility," *University of Chicago Law Review* 22 (Winter 1955): 367–76, at 368.

28. For Wertham's campaign against mass culture, see James Gilbert, *A Cycle of Outrage: America's Reaction to the Juvenile Delinquent in the 1950s* (New York: Oxford University Press, 1986), 91–108.

29. Frederic Wertham, "Psychoauthoritarianism and the Law," *University of Chicago Law Review* 22 (Winter 1955): 336–38, at 337.

30. Edward de Grazia, "The Distinction of Being Mad," *University of Chicago Law Review* 22 (Winter 1955): 339–55, at 342–43.

31. Ibid., 351, 352. Even before the Durham case was decided, de Grazia had voiced his strong hesitations about the role placed by psychiatry in criminal proceedings. See Edward de Grazia, "Crime without Punishment: A Psychiatric Conundrum," *Columbia Law Review* 52 (June 1952): 746–64.

32. Robert Traver, *Anatomy of a Murder* (New York: St. Martin's Press, 1958), 62, 64.

33. Thomas S. Szasz, "Civil Liberties and the Mentally Ill," *Cleveland-Marshall Law Review* 9 (September 1960): 402, 404. Also see Thomas S. Szasz, "Hospital Refusal to Release Mental Patient," *Cleveland-Marshall Law Review* 9 (May 1960): 220–26.

34. Thomas S. Szasz, "Mind Tapping: Psychiatric Subversion of Constitutional Rights," *American Journal of Psychiatry* 119 (October 1962): 327; and Thomas S. Szasz, "Psychiatry's Threat to Civil Liberties," *National Review*, March 12, 1963, 193.

35. Thomas Szasz, quoted in Erving Goffman, *Asylums: Essays on the Social Situation of Mental Patients and Other Inmates* (Garden City, NY: Anchor Books, 1961), 364. The quotation is from Thomas S. Szasz, "Politics and Mental Health," 509.

36. Thomas S. Szasz, *Pain and Pleasure: A Study of Bodily Feelings* (New York: Basic Books, 1957), 203. Emphasis in original.

37. Thomas S. Szasz, *The Myth of Mental Illness: Foundations of a Theory of Personal Conduct* (New York: Harper and Row, 1961), 296. All further references are to this edition and will be documented parenthetically in the text.

38. See Szasz's quite definitive statement two years later: "In a sense, an individual is the end product of the *decisions* he has made. He who fails to make decisions, for the consequences of which he is responsible, is not a person." Thomas S. Szasz, *Law, Liberty, and Psychiatry: An Inquiry into the Social Uses of Mental Health Practices* (New York: Macmillan, 1963), 255.

39. It is notable how much of Szasz's analysis at this point in *The Myth of Mental Illness* was drawn from his reading of psychiatrist Harry Stack Sullivan. See Szasz, *The Myth of Mental Illness*, 267–71.

40. See also in this context the astute analysis in Thomas S. Szasz, "Blackness and Madness: Images of Evil and Tactics of Exclusion," in *Black America*, ed. John F. Szwed (New York: Basic Books, 1970), 67–77.

41. Szasz, "Politics and Mental Health," 508.

42. For an explicit critique of organic theories of schizophrenia, see also Szasz, *The Myth of Mental Illness,* 91–92.

43. Thomas S. Szasz, *Psychiatric Justice* (New York: Macmillan, 1965), 134. This is from psychiatric testimony given by Szasz before a judge in April 1962 in Onondaga County Court during a hearing for a man who had been involuntarily committed to a mental hospital.

44. Szasz, *Law, Liberty, and Psychiatry,* 205.

45. David Stafford-Clark, "Rev. of Thomas S. Szasz, *Law, Liberty, and Psychiatry,*" *Yale Law Journal* 74 (1964–65): 392.

46. See Manfred S. Guttmacher, "Critique of Views of Thomas Szasz on Legal Psychiatry," *Archives of General Psychiatry* 10 (March 1964): 245. And an anonymous psychoanalyst said of Szasz: "I don't know if you're familiar with the old saying that 'if a Hungarian has a friend, he doesn't need an enemy.'" Quoted in Ralph Slovenko, "The Psychiatric Patient, Liberty, and the Law," *University of Kansas Law Review* 13 (1964–65): 60.

47. Bernard L. Diamond, "Rev. of Szasz, *Law, Liberty, and Psychiatry,*" *California Law Review* 52 (1964): 899. Also note Jules H. Masserman's assertion that Szasz's writing amounts to "a battle cry which could quickly deteriorate into a John Birch bark." See Jules H. Masserman, "Is Mental Illness a Medico-Social 'Myth'?," *Archives of General Psychiatry* 9 (August 1963): 91–94.

48. Henry Weihofen, "Discussion," *American Journal of Psychiatry* 121 (December 1964): 548. Also see Alfred Auerback, "The Anti-Mental Health Movement," *American Journal of Psychiatry* 120 (August 1963): 105–11.

49. Many of the original documents about these events are reproduced in Jeffrey A. Schaler, ed., *Szasz under Fire: The Psychiatric Abolitionist Faces His Critics* (Chicago: Open Court, 2004), 393–402.

50. Arthur J. Goldberg, "Books for Lawyers: Rev. of Thomas S. Szasz, *Law, Liberty and Psychiatry,*" *American Bar Association Journal* 50 (November 1964): 1073. Goldberg was subsequently to become best known as the author of the majority opinion in *Griswold v. Connecticut,* which declared unconstitutional a law that outlawed contraceptives on the grounds that it violated a married couple's right to privacy.

51. Jay Haley, "A Review of a Book Review," *California Law Review* 53 (May 1965): 724. Haley was writing in response to Diamond, "Rev. of Szasz, *Law, Liberty, and Psychiatry.*"

52. Szasz, *Law, Liberty, and Psychiatry,* 229.

53. Thomas S. Szasz, "Mental Illness Is a Myth," *New York Times Magazine,* June 12, 1966, 91.

54. See Thomas S. Szasz, "The Ethics of Birth Control," *Humanist* 20 (November–December 1960): 332–36; Thomas S. Szasz, "Who Has a Right to an Abortion?" *Current* (December 1962): 52–53. Also see Thomas S. Szasz, "Bootlegging Humanistic Values through Psychiatry," *Antioch Review* (Fall 1962): 341–49.

55. Szasz, *Law, Liberty, and Psychiatry,* 212, 216, 218–19.

56. Ronald Leifer, "Community Psychiatry and Social Power," *Social Problems* 14 (Summer 1966): 20. For another example of how Szasz's idea that the

concept of mental illness was being used to police social deviance was elaborated at the time, see Thomas J. Scheff, *Being Mentally Ill: A Sociological Theory* (Chicago: Aldine Publishing, 1966).

57. Nicholas N. Kittrie, "Compulsory Mental Treatment and the Requirements of 'Due Process,'" *Ohio State Law Journal* 21 (1960): 28–51.

58. Nicholas Kittrie, "The Divestment of Criminal Law and the Coming of the Therapeutic State," *Suffolk University Law Review* 1 (1967): 44.

59. Nicholas N. Kittrie, *The Right to Be Different: Deviance and Enforced Therapy* (Baltimore: Johns Hopkins Press, 1971), 392.

60. Statement of Bruce J. Ennis, *Constitutional Rights of the Mentally Ill, Hearings before the U.S. Senate Subcommittee on Constitutional Rights of the Committee on the Judiciary*, 91st Cong., November 19, 1969 (Washington, DC: U.S. Government Printing Office, 1970), 275–76.

61. Bruce J. Ennis, *Prisoners of Psychiatry: Mental Patients, Psychiatrists, and the Law* (New York: Harcourt Brace Jovanovich, 1972), 7.

62. Bruce J. Ennis and Thomas R. Litwack, "Psychiatry and the Presumption of Expertise: Flipping Coins in the Courtroom," *California Law Review* 62 (May 1974): 693–752.

63. See Bruce J. Ennis and Paul R. Friedman, eds., *Legal Rights of the Mentally Handicapped* (New York: Mental Health Law Project, 1973).

64. See Fred Cohen, "The Function of the Attorney and the Commitment of the Mentally Ill," *Texas Law Review* 44 (1965–66): 425.

65. M. Cherif Bassiouni, "The Right of the Mentally Ill to Cure and Treatment: Medical Due Process," *DePaul Law Review* 15 (1965–66): 291.

66. See "Restructuring Informed Consent: Legal Theory for the Doctor-Patient Relationship," *Yale Law Journal* 79 (1969–70): 1533–36; and L. S. Tao, "Some Problems Relating to Compulsory Hospitalization of the Mentally Ill," *Journal of Urban Law* 44 (1966–67): 456–82.

67. Helen Garfield, "The Psychopathic Personality: Insanity or Nonconformity," *University of Colorado Law Review* 39 (1966–67): 388.

68. Leon H. Ginsberg, "Civil Rights of the Mentally Ill: A Review of the Issues," *Community Mental Health Journal* 4 (1968): 246.

69. Alan M. Dershowitz, "Psychiatry in the Legal Process: 'A Knife That Cuts Both Ways,'" *Judicature* 51 (May 1968): 372.

70. Alan M. Dershowitz, "The Psychiatrist's Power in Civil Commitment: A Knife That Cuts Both Ways," *Psychology Today* 2 (February 1969): 47.

71. This is not speculation; Dershowitz knew the ideas of Szasz and respected them enough to have them included in his coedited anthology on psychiatry and the law. See Jay Katz, Joseph Goldstein, and Alan M. Dershowitz, eds., *Psychoanalysis, Psychiatry, and Law* (New York: Free Press, 1967), 471–77 and 575–79.

72. Richard Arens, "The Durham Rule in Action: Judicial Psychiatry and Psychiatric Justice," *Law and Society Review* 1 (June 1967): 80. Also see Abe Krash, "The Durham Rule and Judicial Administration of the Insanity Defense in the District of Columbia," *Yale Law Journal* 70 (1960–61): 905–6.

73. The Durham rule was set aside in the case of *United States v. Brawner*, 471 F. 2d 969 (1972). For a history of the insanity defense, see Christopher

Slobogin, "The Guilty but Mentally Ill Verdict: An Idea Whose Time Should Not Have Come," *George Washington Law Review* 53 (1985): 494–527; and Paul S. Appelbaum, *Almost a Revolution: Mental Health Law and the Limits of Change* (New York: Oxford University Press, 1994), 163–209.

74. David L. Bazelon, "Psychiatrists and the Adversary Process," *Scientific American* 230 (June 1974): 21.

75. David L. Bazelon, "Institutionalization, Deinstitutionalization, and the Adversary Process," *Columbia Law Review* 75 (June 1975): 906.

76. Donald W. Loria, "Psychiatrist in Workmen's Compensation Field," *Cleveland-Marshall Law Review* 17 (1968): 19–31. As the essay argued: "It would be worth trying a system whereby help would be provided on the claimant's mere statement of disability. No expert would be needed to buttress the claim." Ibid., 31. A less sympathetic use of Szasz in this regard can be found in Cornelius J. Peck, "Compensation for Pain: A Reappraisal in Light of New Medical Evidence," *Michigan Law Review* 72 (June 1974): 1355–96.

77. See especially Carl P. Malmquist, "The Role of Parental Mental Illness in Custody Proceedings," *Family Law Quarterly* 2 (1968): 363–64; and Brigitte M. Bodenheimer, "New Approaches of Psychiatry: Implications for Divorce Reform," *Utah Law Review* (April 1970): 210.

78. Joel Jay Finer, "Psychedelics and Religious Freedom," *Hastings Law Journal* 19 (1967–68): 724. Leary was an early enthusiast of Szasz's work, writing in 1961 that "*The Myth of Mental Illness* is the most important book in the history of psychiatry." See "A Letter from Timothy Leary, Ph.D., July 17, 1961," http://www.szasz.com/leary.html. Also note that Szasz was invoked in the context of how the law should respond to the potential impact on society of mind-altering drugs. See "'Defective Delinquent' and Habitual Criminal Offender Statutes: Required Constitutional Safeguards," *Rutgers Law Review* 20 (1966): 761–62. And see a medical doctor's telling reference to Szasz in a defense of methadone treatment programs against charges of abuse and misuse: Robert G. Newman, "Special Problems of Government-Controlled Methadone Maintenance Programs," *Contemporary Drug Problems* 1 (1971): 189.

79. Robert T. Roth and Judith Lerner, "Sex-Based Discrimination in the Mental Institutionalization of Women," *California Law Review* 62 (1974): 790.

80. Benna F. Armanno, "The Lesbian Mother: Her Right to Child Custody," *Golden Gate University Law Review* 4 (1973–74): 9.

81. Szasz, *Law, Liberty, and Psychiatry*, 249.

82. Diane Crothers, "Rev. of Thomas S. Szasz, *The Manufacture of Madness*," *Women's Rights Law Reporter* 1 (Spring 1972): 67.

83. "Introduction," in *Radical Therapist*, ed. Jerome Agel (New York: Ballantine Books, 1971), x.

84. "Insane Liberation Front," in ibid., 108.

85. See Sherry Hirsch et al., eds., *Madness Network News Reader* (San Francisco: Glide Publications, 1974).

86. "The Sociological Approach," in *Radical Psychology*, ed. Phil Brown (New York: Harper and Row, 1973), 1.

87. Windcatcher, "Toward Total Revolution," *Good Times*, April 9, 1970, 8.

88. Quoted in "Shrinks Get Their Heads Together," *Liberated Guardian*, May 1, 1970, 15.

89. Pandora, "Disturbed Hospital," *Willamette Bridge*, April 17–23, 1970, 14.

90. Karl Menninger, "Psychiatrists Use Dangerous Words," *Saturday Evening Post*, April 25, 1964, 12.

91. Seymour L. Halleck, "The Psychiatrist and the Legal Process," *Psychology Today* 2 (February 1969): 26. Also see Seymour L. Halleck, "A Critique of Current Psychiatric Roles in the Legal Process," *Wisconsin Law Review* 1966 (1966): 379–401.

92. Petitioner's Brief in *Donaldson v. O'Connor*, reproduced in Bruce J. Ennis and Paul R. Friedman, eds., *Legal Rights of the Mentally Handicapped*, vol. 1 (New York: Mental Health Law Project, 1974), 262. In 1975 the US Supreme Court would decide *Donaldson v. O'Connor* in a landmark decision, determining that involuntary commitment was unconstitutional when an individual did not pose an imminent danger to himself or others.

93. Walter Goodman, "The Constitution v. the Snakepit," *New York Times Magazine*, March 17, 1974, 21.

94. Decades later Pirsig recanted his rejection of psychiatry. Fighting depression, Pirsig saw a psychiatrist in 2006. "He said it's a chemical imbalance," Pirsig told a British interviewer, "and he prescribed some pills and the depression has gone." Tim Adams, "The Interview: Robert Pirsig," *Observer*, November 19, 2006, http://www.guardian.co.uk/books/2006/nov/19/fiction.

95. L. Ron Hubbard, "Crime and Psychiatry," June 23, 1969, http://freedom.lronhubbard.org/page080.htm.

96. Citizens Commission on Human Rights, http://www.cchr.org/#/faq/mission-statement.

97. David J. Rissmiller and Joshua H. Rissmiller, "Evolution of the Antipsychiatry Movement into Mental Health Consumerism," *Psychiatric Services* 57 (June 2006): 864.

98. In an anthology on emotional life in American cultural history, note the reference to Szasz (and R. D. Laing) as among the "intellectuals on the political left [who] rejected psychiatry" in the 1960s. See Nancy Schnog, "On Inventing the Psychological," in *Inventing the Psychological: Toward a Cultural History of Emotional Life in America*, ed. Joel Pfister and Nancy Schnog (New Haven, CT: Yale University Press, 1997), 7.

99. See Szasz, "Malingering: 'Diagnosis' or Social Condemnation?," 432–43.

100. On electroshock "treatment," see Thomas S. Szasz, "From the Slaughterhouse to the Madhouse," *Psychotherapy* 8 (Spring 1971): 64–67.

CHAPTER FIVE

1. Susan Sontag, "Approaching Artaud," *New Yorker*, May 19, 1973, 74.

2. Mary Barnes, "Reflection," *Salmagundi* 16 (Spring 1971): 197. Barnes was a schizophrenic patient of R. D. Laing and Joseph Berke at Kingsley Hall and was often singled out as a success story of the "antipsychiatric" treatment of mental illness. See Mary Barnes and Joseph Berke, *Mary Barnes: Two*

Accounts of a Journey through Madness (New York: Harcourt Brace Jovanovich, 1971).

3. Sontag, "Approaching Artaud," 78–79.

4. Allen Ginsberg, "Consciousness and Practical Action," *Congress on the Dialectics of Liberation*, vol. 16 (London: The Institute of Phenomenological Studies, 1967). All further references are from this LP sound recording of Ginsberg's address.

5. On the Catonsville Nine, see Marian Mollin, *Radical Pacifism in Modern America: Egalitarianism and Protest* (Philadelphia: University of Pennsylvania Press, 2006), 169–81.

6. Thomas Merton, *Raids on the Unspeakable* (New York: New Directions, 1966), 48–49.

7. Norman Mailer, *The Armies of the Night: History as a Novel, the Novel as History* (New York: Plume, 1994), 120.

8. See Joanna Burke, *An Intimate History of Killing: Face-to-Face Killing in Twentieth-Century Warfare* (New York: Basic Books, 2000), esp. 159–203.

9. These questions no doubt informed the avid reception to the social psychological experiments on obedience to authority conducted by Stanley Milgram. See especially the retrospective reflections on My Lai in Stanley Milgram, *Obedience to Authority* (New York: Harper and Row, 1974), 183.

10. Herbert Marcuse, "Reflections on Calley," *New York Times*, May 13, 1971, 45.

11. See Richard A. Falk, Gabriel Kolko, and Robert Jay Lifton, eds., *Crimes of War: A Legal, Political-Documentary, and Psychological Inquiry into the Responsibility of Leaders, Citizens, and Soldiers for Criminal Acts in Wars* (New York: Random House, 1971).

12. Arlo Guthrie, *Alice's Restaurant*, Reprise Records, 1967. Discussions of the deleterious psychological impact of warfare also appeared in the underground press. For an excellent example, see Isidore Ziferstein, "Psychological Habituation to War: A Sociopsychological Case Study," *Long Beach Free Press*, June 24, 1970, 5, 13, 14, and July 8, 1970, 4, 14–15. This essay originally appeared in *American Journal of Orthopsychiatry* 37 (April 1967): 457–68.

13. Wade Hudson, "Strike Another Match," in *The Madness Network News Reader*, ed. Sherry Hirsch et al. (San Francisco: Glide Publications, 1974), 50.

14. Joseph Berke quoted in Robert Boyers and Robert Orrill, eds., *R. D. Laing and Anti-Psychiatry* (New York: Harper and Row, 1971), 275.

15. Bert Kaplan, "Introduction," in *The Inner World of Mental Illness: A Series of First-Person Accounts of What It Was Like*, ed. Bert Kaplan (New York: Harper and Row, 1964), xi.

16. Mary Ellen Hombs and Mitch Synder, *Homelessness in America: A Forced March to Nowhere* (Washington, DC: Center for Creative Non-Violence, 1982), 43. The quotation is attributed to Anthony E. Colletti of the Mental Patients Liberation Project in New York.

17. Howard Levy, "Prison Psychiatrist: New Custodian," *Liberated Guardian*, June 3, 1970, 15. On the Levy case, see A. N. Kurtha, "The Court-Martial of Captain Levy," *International and Comparative Law Quarterly* 17

NOTES TO PAGES 122-125

(January 1968): 206–9; and Staughton Lynd, "Soldiers of Conscience," *The Nation*, October 19, 2006.

18. Richard Kunnes, "Psychiatry: Instrument of the Ruling Class," *Radical Therapist* 1 (April–May 1970): 4.

19. Saul Wasserman, "Does Psychiatry Pacify or Liberate?" *The Free You*, May 26, 1970, 7.

20. See especially August B. Hollingshead and Fredrick C. Redlich, *Social Class and Mental Illness: A Community Study* (New York: Wiley, 1958), and Leo Srole et al., *Mental Health in the Metropolis: The Midtown Manhattan Study* (New York: McGraw-Hill, 1962). Subsequent research continued to confirm these findings.

21. Dennis Jaffe, "Number Nine: Creating a Counter-Institution," in *The Radical Therapist*, ed. Jerome Agel (New York: Ballantine Books, 1971), 220. Also see Dennis T. Jaffe and Ted Clark, *Number Nine: Autobiography of an Alternate Counseling Service* (New York: Harper and Row, 1975).

22. James M. Statman, "Community Mental Health as a Pacification Program," in *Toward Social Change: A Handbook for Those Who Will*, ed. Robert Buckhout (New York: Harper and Row, 1971), 372–73. Skepticism toward community psychiatry was not limited to those on the radical left. Also see H. Warren Dunham, "Community Psychiatry," *Archives of General Psychiatry* 12 (March 1965): 303–13; and Lawrence Kubie, "Pitfalls of Community Psychiatry," *Archives of General Psychiatry* 18 (March 1968): 257–66. Also note the comments of Judge David Bazelon in 1970: "When poverty, or racism, or crime is labeled a mental health problem, then society can defer to the experts for its solution, and everyone else is free to go on with business as usual." David Bazelon, "Follow the Yellow Brick Road," *American Journal of Orthopsychiatry* 40 (April 1970): 562–67.

23. See B. F. Skinner, *Science and Human Behavior* (New York: Macmillan, 1953), esp. chaps. 5 and 11.

24. See O. Ivar Lovaas, John P. Berberich, Bernard F. Perloff, and Benson Schaeffer, "Acquisition of Imitative Speech by Schizophrenic Children," *Science* 151 (February 11, 1966): 705–7. Also see O. Ivar Lovaas, Benson Schaeffer, and James Q. Simmons, "Building Social Behavior in Autistic Children by Use of Electric Shock," *Journal of Experimental Research in Personality* 1 (October 1965): 99–109. Also see Gordon D. Jensen and Mariette G. Womack, "Operant Conditioning Techniques Applied in the Treatment of an Autistic Child," *American Journal of Orthopsychiatry* 37 (January 1967): 30–34.

25. Lloyd H. Cotter, "Operant Conditioning in a Vietnamese Mental Hospital," *American Journal of Psychiatry* 124 (July 1967): 63–64.

26. See Robin Winkler, "Operant Conditioning in a South Vietnamese Mental Hospital," *Rough Times* 2 (July 1972): 7. *Rough Times* was the new name for *Radical Therapist* after the RT Collective wished to clarify its disavowal of all therapeutic practices.

27. E. Fuller Torrey, *The Death of Psychiatry* (Radnor, PA: Chilton Book, 1974), 72.

28. Frank Ervin, Vernon Mark, and William Sweet, "Role of Brain Disease

in Riots and Urban Violence," *Journal of the American Medical Association* 201 (September 11, 1967): 895. Their letter was reprinted in Frank H. Marsh and Janet Katz, eds., *Biology, Crime, and Ethics: A Study of Biological Explanations for Criminal Behavior* (Cincinnati: Anderson Publishing, 1985): 123–24.

29. Vernon H. Mark and Frank R. Ervin, *Violence and the Brain* (New York: Harper and Row, 1970), 156. Also see Richard Moran, "Biomedical Research and the Politics of Crime Control: A Historical Perspective," *Crime, Law, and Social Change* 2 (September 1978): 335–57.

30. Quoted in "Violence on the Brain: Lobotomies Are Back," *Rough Times* 2 (April 1972): 6.

31. See John Trumpbour, "Blinding Them with Science: Scientific Ideologies in the Ruling of the Modern World," in *How Harvard Rules*, ed. John Trumpbour (Boston: South End Press, 1989), 226–27.

32. Lee Coleman and Stephen Wong, "The Unholy Alliance: Social Control as Therapy," in *Madness Network News Reader*, 129.

33. Sherry Hirsch, "Violence in the Streets," in ibid., 137. This essay originally appeared in *Madness Network News* (December 1973).

34. Nathaniel McConaghy, "Aversive Therapy of Homosexuality: Measures of Efficacy," *American Journal of Psychiatry* 127 (March 1971): 142.

35. David Perlman, "The Psychiatrists and the Protestors," in *Toward Social Change*, 63.

36. Quoted in Ronald Bayer, *Homosexuality and American Psychiatry: The Politics of Diagnosis* (Princeton, NJ: Princeton University Press, 1987), 103.

37. Bernard Weiner, "A Clockwork Cure," *The Nation*, April 3, 1972, 433–36.

38. B. J. Mason, "New Threat to Blacks: Brain Surgery to Control Behavior," *Ebony*, February 1973, 68.

39. Alberto C. Mares, "A Hard Way to Go on All Fronts: Social Control in Prisons," *Rough Times* 4 (December 1974): 7, and Alberto Mares, "A Program to Cripple Federal Prisoners," *New York Review of Books*, March 7, 1974. Also see Alan Eladio Gómez, "Resisting Living Death at Marion Federal Penitentiary, 1972," *Radical History Review* 96 (Fall 2006): 58–86.

40. See "Mind Destroying Facilities," *Rough Times* 3 (November 1972): 19; and Cercie Miller, "Update on Behavior Mod. in Prisons," *Rough Times* 4 (1975): 14.

41. Phil Brown, "Preface," in *Radical Psychology*, ed. Phil Brown (New York: Harper and Row, 1973), xv–xvi. Emphasis in original.

42. Claude Steiner, "Manifesto," in *Readings in Radical Psychiatry*, ed. Claude Steiner et al. (New York: Grove Press, 1975), 6. As Steiner added: "The first Radical Psychiatry Manifesto was written in the summer of 1969 on the occasion of the annual American Psychiatric Association Conference in San Francisco, which was widely disrupted by members of the Women's Liberation, Gay Liberation, and Radical Therapy movements." Ibid.

43. Ronald Leifer, *In the Name of Mental Health: The Social Functions of Psychiatry* (New York: Science House, 1969), 226.

44. Edward Ben Elson, "Eddie's Manifesto," *Take Over* 2 (November 1, 1972): 8.

45. Phil Brown, "Preface," in *Radical Psychology*, xvi.

46. Peter Roger Breggin, "The Killing of Mental Patients," *Freedom* (June/July 1973): 5. *Freedom* was a publication of the Church of Scientology.

47. The Radical Therapist Collective, "Introduction," in *The Radical Therapist*, ed. Agel, ix, xi.

48. Michael Glenn, "Manifesto," *Radical Therapist* 1 (April–May 1970): 2.

49. Claude Steiner, "Guiding Principles of a Community 'RaP' Center," in *Toward Social Change*, 370.

50. Hogie Wyckoff, "Permission," in *Readings in Radical Psychiatry*, 112.

51. Michael Glenn and Richard Kunnes, *Repression or Revolution? Therapy in the United States Today* (New York: Harper and Row, 1973), 34.

52. Claude Steiner, "Principles," in *Readings in Radical Psychiatry*, 12. This essay originally appeared in *Radical Therapist* 1 (December 1970–January 1971).

53. Claude Steiner, "Radical Psychiatry: Principles," in *The Radical Therapist*, ed. Agel, 6.

54. Roy Money, "The Personal and the Political," *Radical Therapist* 2 (September 1971): 15.

55. Emma Jones Lapsansky, "'Black Power Is My Mental Health': Accomplishments of the Civil Rights Movement," in *Black America*, ed. John F. Szwed (New York: Basic Books, 1970), 13.

56. Claude Steiner, *Scripts People Live: Transactional Analysis of Life Scripts* (New York: Grove Press, 1974), 91.

57. See Seymour L. Halleck, *The Politics of Therapy* (New York: Harper and Row, 1971). Also see Seymour L. Halleck, "Psychiatric Treatment of the Alienated College Student," *American Journal of Psychiatry* 124 (November 1967): 642–50.

58. David L. Herzberg, "'The Pill You Love Can Turn on You': Feminism, Tranquilizers, and the Valium Panic of the 1970s," *American Quarterly* 58 (March 2006): 79–103.

59. Ginsberg, "Consciousness and Practical Action" (LP sound recording).

60. Timothy Leary, "How to Change Behavior," in *LSD: The Consciousness-Expanding Drug*, ed. David Solomon (New York: G. P. Putnam's Sons, 1964), 97–113.

61. Timothy Leary, *The Politics of Ecstasy* (New York: College Notes and Texts, 1968), 159.

62. Steiner, *Scripts People Live*, 143–44.

63. Charles Clay Dahlberg, "LSD as an Aid to Psychoanalytic Treatment," in *Science and Psychoanalysis, Vol. VI*, ed. Jules H. Masserman (New York: Grune and Stratton, 1963), 255.

64. Harold A. Abramson, "Lysergic Acid Diethylamide (LSD-25): III. As An Adjunct to Psychotherapy with Elimination of Fear of Homosexuality," *Journal of Psychology* 39 (1955): 154.

65. See Erica Dyck, *Psychedelic Psychiatry: LSD from Clinic to Campus* (Baltimore: Johns Hopkins University Press, 2008), esp. 64–78.

66. Harold A. Abramson, "Lysergic Acid Diethylamide (LSD-25): XXII. Effect on Transference," *Journal of Psychology* 42 (1956): 98. Abramson remains

perhaps most notorious for his secret involvement with the CIA's MK-ULTRA program that tested hallucinogens for their possible application as psychological weapons for mind control. See Martin A. Lee and Bruce Shlain, *Acid Dreams: The Complete Social History of LSD: The CIA, the Sixties, and Beyond* (New York: Grove Press, 1992).

67. Donald D. Jackson, "LSD and the New Beginning," in *LSD: The Consciousness-Expanding Drug*, ed. David Solomon (New York: Putnam, 1964), 197. Jackson's essay originally appeared in the symposium "LSD, Transcendence and the New Beginning," ed. Charles Savage, *Journal of Nervous and Mental Disease* 135 (November 1962): 435-39. Also see the results reported in David J. Lewis and R. Bruce Sloane, "Therapy with Lysergic Acid Diethylamide," *Journal of Clinical and Experimental Psychopathology and Quarterly Review of Psychiatry and Neurology* 19 (March 1958): 19-31; and Betty Grover Eisner and Sidney Cohen, "Psychotherapy with Lysergic Acid Diethylamide," *Journal of Nervous and Mental Disease* 127 (December 1958): 528-39. Notably, far from being an outdated perspective, the view that hallucinogens can, "in a matter of hours," "induce profound psychological realignments that can take decades to achieve on a therapist's couch," was in the year 2010 making a comeback. See Roland R. Griffiths and Charles S. Grob, "Hallucinogens as Medicine," *Scientific American* 303 (December 2010): 77.

68. "Experimental Psychoses," *Scientific American* 192 (June 1955): 34.

69. Joe Kennedy Adams, *Secrets of the Trade: Notes on Madness, Creativity, and Ideology* (New York: Viking Press, 1971), 100.

70. Gregory Bateson, *Perceval's Narrative: A Patient's Account of His Psychosis, 1830-1832* (Stanford, CA: Stanford University Press, 1961), xi.

71. Antonin Artaud, "Van Gogh: The Man Suicided by Society," in *Artaud Anthology*, ed. Jack Hirschman (San Francisco: City Lights, 1965), 135.

72. Antonin Artaud, "Letter to the Medical Directors of Lunatic Asylums," in *Going Crazy: The Radical Therapy of R. D. Laing and Others*, ed. Hendrik M. Ruitenbeek (New York: Bantam, 1972), 10.

73. Harry R. Brickman, "The Psychedelic 'Hip Scene': Return of the Death Instinct," *American Journal of Psychiatry* 125 (December 1968): 766-68, 770-72.

74. Quoted in Roger Barnard, "Round House Dialectics," *New Society*, August 3, 1967, 145.

75. Paul Goodman, "Objective Values," in *To Free a Generation: The Dialectics of Liberation*, ed. David Cooper (New York: Collier Books, 1968), 112.

76. John Gerassi, "Imperialism and Revolution in America," in *To Free a Generation*, 90. On Gerassi's firsthand investigations on behalf of the International War Crimes Tribunal, see John Gerassi, *North Vietnam* (London: Allen and Unwin, 1968).

77. Sheila Rowbotham, *Woman's Consciousness, Man's World* (Harmondsworth: Penguin Books, 1974), 22.

78. To which Marcuse added this question: "Is not the individual who functions normally, adequately, and healthily as a citizen of a sick society—is not such an individual himself sick?" Herbert Marcuse, *Negations: Essays in Critical Theory* (Boston: Beacon Press, 1968), 250-51.

79. Herbert Marcuse, "Liberation from the Affluent Society," *Congress on the Dialectics of Liberation*, vol. 9. All references are transcribed from this LP sound recording of Marcuse's address. This essay appears (in slightly different form) in Herbert Marcuse, *The New Left and the 1960s* (New York: Routledge, 2005), 76–86.

80. For example, see Gregory L. Schneider, *Cadres for Conservatism: Young Americans for Freedom and the Rise of the Contemporary Right* (New York: New York University Press, 1999); Lisa McGirr, *Suburban Warriors: The Origins of the New American Right* (Princeton, NJ: Princeton University Press, 2001); David Farber and Jeff Roche, eds., *The Conservative Sixties* (New York: Peter Lang, 2003); Sean Wilentz, "The Legacy of 1967," *Rolling Stone*, July 12–26, 2007, 27–32; and Kim Phillips-Fein, *Invisible Hands: The Making of the Conservative Movement from the New Deal to Reagan* (New York: W. W. Norton, 2009).

CHAPTER SIX

1. Robin Morgan, "The Invisible Woman," in *Monster* (New York: Random House, 1972), 46.

2. Naomi Weisstein, "Kinder, Küche, Kirche as Scientific Law: Psychology Constructs the Female" (1968), reprinted in Joanne Cooke, Charlotte Bunch-Weeks, and Robin Morgan, eds., *The New Women: A Motive Anthology on Women's Liberation* (Indianapolis: Bobbs-Merrill, 1970), 143.

3. Pauline Bart, "Sexism and Social Science: From the Gilded Cage to the Iron Cage, or, the Perils of Pauline," *Journal of Marriage and the Family* 33 (November 1971): 743.

4. Eva S. Moskowitz, *In Therapy We Trust: America's Obsession with Self-Fulfillment* (Baltimore: Johns Hopkins University Press, 2001), 224.

5. Thomas A. Harris, *I'm OK—You're OK: A Practical Guide to Transactional Analysis* (New York: Harper and Row, 1967), xiii–xiv.

6. Back cover of Jerry Greenwald, *Be the Person You Were Meant to Be* (New York: Dell, 1973).

7. Front cover of Wayne W. Dyer, *Your Erroneous Zones* (New York: Funk and Wagnalls, 1976).

8. Inside front flap of Dyer, *Your Erroneous Zones.*

9. Shari Etzkowitz, "Sexism and Psychotherapy," *Radical Therapist* 2 (April–May 1971): 2. For the statistic on women in psychology, see Joy K. Rice and David G. Rice, "Implications of the Women's Liberation Movement for Psychotherapy," *American Journal of Psychiatry* 130 (February 1973): 195.

10. Quoted in Robert Reinhold, "Women Criticize Psychology Unit," *New York Times,* September 6, 1970, 28.

11. See Harold Sampson, Sheldon L. Messinger, and Robert D. Towne, *Schizophrenic Women: Studies in Marital Crisis* (New York: Prentice-Hall, 1964).

12. Joseph C. Rheingold, *The Fear of Being a Woman: A Theory of Maternal Destructiveness* (New York: Grune and Stratton, 1964), 714.

13. Erik H. Erikson, "Inner and Outer Space: Reflections on Womanhood," *Daedalus* 93 (Spring 1964): 586, 600. These ideas about gender difference were not new to Erikson in the 1960s. Also see E. H. Erikson, "Sex Differences in the Play Configurations of Preadolescents," *American Journal of Orthopsychiatry* 21 (October 1951): 667–92.

14. Bruno Bettelheim, "The Commitment Required of a Woman Entering a Scientific Profession in Present-Day American Society," in *Women and the Scientific Professions: The M.I.T. Symposium on American Women in Science and Engineering*, ed. Jacquelyn A. Mattfeld and Carol G. Van Aken (Cambridge, MA: MIT Press, 1965), 15.

15. William J. Browne, "A Psychiatric Study of the Life and Work of Dorothea Dix," *American Journal of Psychiatry* 126 (September 1969): 340.

16. Phyllis Chesler, *Women and Madness* (Garden City, NY: Doubleday, 1972), 12, 115, 118.

17. Susan Dworkin Levering, "She Must Be Some Kind of Nut," *Rough Times* 3 (September 1972): 3. Psychologist Albert Ellis told the story of a "young and potentially attractive female" who had been referred by her boyfriend because she refused to maintain her appearance for him, as well as how Ellis persuaded her that this neglect represented an "emotional disturbance." Albert Ellis, *A Guide to Rational Living* (Englewood Cliffs, NJ: Prentice-Hall, 1961), 73–77.

18. Pauline B. Bart, "Rev. of *Women and Madness*," *Society* 11 (January–February 1974): 98.

19. Walter R. Gove and Jeannette F. Tudor, "Adult Sex Roles and Mental Illness," *American Journal of Sociology* 78 (January 1973): 831.

20. Theodore Reik, *Voices from the Inaudible: The Patients Speak* (New York: Farrar, Straus, 1964), 50, 54.

21. Theodore Reik, *The Many Faces of Sex* (New York: Farrar, Straus and Giroux, 1966), 92. The anecdote continued: "When it was time for her to leave, she stood for a longer while than usual before the mirror in my anteroom, putting her hair in order. I smilingly remarked: 'I am glad to see a remnant of femininity.'" Ibid.

22. Shulamith Firestone, *The Dialectic of Sex: The Case for Feminist Revolution* (New York: Bantam, 1971), 66.

23. Nathan K. Rickles, "The Angry Woman Syndrome," *Archives of General Psychiatry* 24 (January 1971): 91, 94.

24. John H. Houck, "The Intractable Female Patient," *American Journal of Psychiatry* 129 (July 1972): 27, 30–31.

25. William H. Masters and Virginia E. Johnson, *Human Sexual Inadequacy* (Boston: Little, Brown, 1970), 388, 391.

26. Quoted in Chesler, *Women and Madness*, 145–46, 157.

27. Cited in Michael Glenn and Richard Kunnes, *Repression or Revolution? Therapy in the United States Today* (New York: Harper and Row, 1973), 82.

28. David Cooper, *The Grammar of Living: An Examination of Political Acts* (London: Allen Lane, 1974), 98, 101.

29. See James L. McCartney, "Overt Transference," *Journal of Sex Research* 2 (November 1966): 227–37. McCartney noted that he had "allowed overt ex-

pression" with his female psychiatric patients for twenty years, and that about 10 percent of these patients "found it necessary" to engage in "mutual undressing, genital manipulation or coitus." He also noted that overt transference was "not operative when the analyst and analysand are of the same sex" because "homosexuality is immature, and to allow such expression would only lead to retardation of the emotional development, and the continuance of the neurosis." Ibid., 236. Also see Judd Marmor, "The Seductive Psychotherapist," *Psychiatry Digest* 31 (October 1970): 10–16.

30. Martin Shepard, *The Love Treatment: Sexual Intimacy between Patients and Psychotherapists* (New York: Peter H. Wyden, 1971), 18–20. Also see Melva Weber, "Should You Sleep with Your Therapist? The Raging Controversy in American Psychiatry," *Vogue*, January 15, 1972, 78–79.

31. Chesler, *Women and Madness*, 136.

32. See Nancy C., "Psychotherapy as a Rip-Off," *Radical Therapist* 2 (December 1971). Reprinted in Phil Brown, ed., *Radical Psychology* (New York: Harper and Row, 1973), 490–96.

33. As Andrea Tone has observed, men were also represented as "no less in need of tranquilizers," although pharmaceutical ads directed at men "pitched anxiety and its accompanying discontents as the natural but injurious cost men paid for their success." Andrea Tone, *The Age of Anxiety: A History of America's Turbulent Affair with Tranquilizers* (New York: Basic Books, 2009), 158–59. Also see the discussion of "gender messages" in 1960s and 1970s advertisements for tranquilizers and antidepressants in David Herzberg, *Happy Pills in America: From Miltown to Prozac* (Baltimore: Johns Hopkins University Press, 2009), 73–82; and Jonathan M. Metzl, *Prozac on the Couch* (Durham, NC: Duke University Press, 2003), 127–51.

34. This ad appeared in *Archives of General Psychiatry* 18 (June 1968): 30–31.

35. This ad appeared in *Archives of General Psychiatry* 18 (June 1968): 14–16.

36. This ad appeared in *Archives of General Psychiatry* 24 (January 1971): 7A.

37. This ad appeared in *Archives of General Psychiatry* 24 (April 1971): 7–11.

38. Myna M. Weissman, "The Depressed Woman: Recent Research," *Social Work* 17 (July 1972): 19, 21–22, 25.

39. Quoted in Chesler, *Women and Madness*, 216.

40. Ellen Cantarow, Elizabeth Diggs, Katherine Ellis, Janet Marx, Lillian Robinson, and Muriel Schien, "I am Furious (Female)," in *Roles Women Play: Readings Toward Women's Liberation*, ed. Michele Hoffnung Garskof (Belmont, CA: Wadsworth Publishing, 1971), 186.

41. Nadine Miller, "Letter to Her Psychiatrist," in *The Radical Therapist*, ed. Jerome Agel (New York: Ballantine Books, 1971), 140, 142.

42. Meredith Tax, *Woman and Her Mind: The Story of Daily Life* (Boston: New England Free Press, 1970), 9–10.

43. Marilyn Salzman Webb, "Woman as Secretary, Sexpot, Spender, Sow, Civic Actor, Sickie," in *The New Women*, 97, 112–13.

44. Garskof, ed., *Roles Women Play*, 60.

45. Jennifer S. Macleod, "How to Hold a Wife: A Bridegroom's Guide," *Village Voice*, February 11, 1971, 5.

46. Dorothy Tennov, *Psychotherapy: The Hazardous Cure* (New York: Abelard-Schuman, 1975), 207. Not that these attitudes about women and sex were limited to psychiatrists and psychologists. Also see Diana Scully and Pauline Bart, "A Funny Thing Happened on the Way to the Orifice: Women in Gynecology Textbooks," *American Journal of Sociology* 78 (January 1973): 1045-50.

47. Quoted in Ellen Herman, *The Romance of American Psychology: Political Culture in the Age of Experts* (Berkeley: University of California Press, 1995), 289.

48. Sheldon B. Kopp, *If You Meet Buddha on the Road, Kill Him!* (Palo Alto, CA: Science and Behavior Books, 1972), 188.

49. Sheldon B. Kopp, "Person Envy," *Journal of Contemporary Psychotherapy* 6 (Summer 1974): 156.

50. Their key text was Frederick S. Perls, Paul Goodman, and Ralph Franklin Hefferline, *Gestalt Therapy: Excitement and Growth in the Human Personality* (New York: Delta Book, 1951).

51. Carolyn Zerbe Enns, *Feminist Theories and Feminist Psychotherapies: Origins, Themes, and Variations* (Binghamton, NY: Haworth Press, 1997), 138. Also see the Gestalt-inspired feminism described in Elizabeth Friar Williams, *Notes of a Feminist Therapist* (New York: Dell, 1976).

52. See Carl Rogers, *On Becoming a Person* (Boston: Houghton Mifflin, 1961).

53. Abraham H. Maslow, *Toward a Psychology of Being* (New York: D. Van Nostrand, 1962), 168, 4-5.

54. Betty Friedan, *The Feminine Mystique* (New York: Dell, 1963), 60, 69.

55. Eric Berne, *Games People Play: The Psychology of Human Relationships* (New York: Grove Press, 1964), 15. Emphasis in original.

56. Hogie Wyckoff, "Radical Psychiatry in Women's Groups," *Radical Therapist* 1 (October-November 1970): 16.

57. Hogie Wyckoff, "Women's Scripts and the Stroke Economy," *Radical Therapist* 2 (October 1971): 16.

58. Hogie Wyckoff, "Permission," in *Readings in Radical Psychiatry*, ed. Claude Steiner et al. (New York: Grove Press, 1975), 106.

59. Françoise Castel, Robert Castel, and Anne Lovell, *The Psychiatric Society* (New York: Columbia University Press, 1982), 238.

60. "Feminist Therapy," *Rough Times* 3 (November 1972): 5.

61. Leonore Tiefer, "A Brief History of the Association for Women in Psychology, 1969-1991," *Psychology of Women Quarterly* 15 (December 1991): 643. Although as Tiefer also noted, "criteria for inclusion on the roster" of feminist therapists proved "elusive." Ibid.

62. Betty J. Kronsky, "Feminism and Psychotherapy," *Journal of Contemporary Psychotherapy* 3 (Spring 1971): 98. Also see Karen Lindsey, "On the Need to Develop a Feminist Therapy," *Rough Times* 4, no. 3 (1974): 2.

63. Kathie Sarachild, "A Program for Feminist 'Consciousness Raising,'" in *Notes from the Second Year: Women's Liberation—Major Writing of the Radical Feminists*, ed. Shulamith Firestone and Anne Koedt (New York: Radical Feminism, 1970), 78.

64. See Herman, *The Romance of American Psychology*, 297-303. Also see

Alice Echols, *Daring to Be Bad: Radical Feminism in America, 1967–1975* (Minneapolis: University of Minnesota Press, 1989).

65. Jo Freeman, "The Tyranny of Structurelessness," *Berkeley Journal of Sociology* 17 (1972–73): 151–64. Freeman's essay also appeared in *Ms.*, July 1973, 76–78, 86–89.

66. Quoted in Claude Steiner, "Radical Psychiatry and Movement Groups Plus a Postscript," in *Readings in Radical Psychiatry*, 172–73.

67. "A Résumé of the Criticisms of Radical Psychiatry Made by the New Radical Psychiatry Group (November 1971)," in *Readings in Radical Psychiatry*, 188.

68. Mary Raffini, "Waking from a Dream: Reflections on the Elizabeth Stone House," *Rough Times* 5 (February–March 1976): 5. Despite early upheavals, the Elizabeth Stone House continues to operate. See http://www.elizabethstone house.org/.

69. Shelley Blue, "Ode to My Therapist," *Rough Times* (September 1974): 6.

70. Laurel, "Faces of My Mother," *Rough Times* 3 (September 1972): 5.

71. Tacie Dejanikus and Fran Pollner, "Feminist Counseling: A Catalyst Not a 'Cure,'" *Off Our Backs* 3 (September 30, 1973): 2.

72. Karin Wandrei, "Lesbians in Therapy," *Rough Times* 4 (November 1975): 3–4.

73. Firestone, *The Dialectic of Sex*, 71.

74. Quoted in Herman, *The Romance of American Psychology*, 389.

75. Dorothy Tennov, "Feminism, Psychotherapy and Professionalism," *Journal of Contemporary Psychotherapy* 5 (Summer 1973): 110.

76. Mary Daly, *Gyn/Ecology: The Metaethics of Radical Feminism* (Boston: Beacon Press, 1979), 281–82.

77. Carol Wolman, "Therapy and Capitalism," *Issues in Radical Therapy* 3 (Winter 1975): 4–5.

78. Dejanikus and Pollner, "Feminist Counseling," 2–4.

79. Inge K. Broverman, Donald M. Broverman, Frank E. Clarkson, Paul S. Rosenkrantz, and Susan R. Vogel, "Sex-Role Stereotypes and Clinical Judgments of Mental Health," *Journal of Consulting and Clinical Psychology* 34 (February 1970): 6.

80. Quoted in Dot Vance, "Offing Piggery in Women's Groups," *Radical Therapist* 1 (February–March 1971): 2.

81. See, for example, Theodore Lidz et al., "The Intrafamilial Environment of Schizophrenic Patients: II. Marital Schism and Marital Skew," *American Journal of Psychiatry* 114 (September 1957): 241–48; and Theodore Lidz et al., "The Father: Interfamilial Environment of the Schizophrenic Patient," *Psychiatry* 20 (November 1957): 329–42.

82. Jules Henry, *Pathways to Madness* (New York: Vintage, 1973), 294–96.

83. Claude Steiner, *Scripts People Live: Transactional Analysis of Life Scripts* (New York: Grove Press, 1974), 197.

84. Glenn and Kunnes, *Repression or Revolution?*, 75, 78–79, 83–84. This collaborative book clarifies that the use of "I" in the text always refers to Glenn. Ibid., 35.

85. Rick DeGolia, "Thoughts on Men's Oppression," in *Love, Therapy, and Politics*, ed. Hogie Wyckoff (New York: Grove Press, 1976), 180–81.

86. Quoted in Richard C. Robertiello, "After the Sexual Revolution and the Women's Liberation Movement," *Journal of Contemporary Psychotherapy* 5 (Winter 1972): 32.

87. DeGolia, "Thoughts on Men's Oppression," 189, 279.

88. Claude Steiner, "Open Letter to a Brother: Some Reflections on Men's Liberation," in *Love, Therapy, and Politics*, 170–71.

89. Cited in Harris, *I'm OK—You're OK*, 16–17.

90. Ibid., 95–96.

91. Joyce Brothers, *The Brothers System for Liberated Love and Marriage* (New York: Peter H. Wyden, 1972), 214–15.

92. Greenwald, *Be the Person You Were Meant to Be*, 31, 87, 45, 47, 94, 139, 259.

93. Dyer, *Your Erroneous Zones*, 1.

94. Herbert Fensterheim and Jean Baer, *Don't Say Yes When You Want to Say No* (New York: Dell, 1975), 17.

95. Dyer, *Your Erroneous Zones*, 19–20.

96. Harris, *I'm OK—You're OK*, xiii.

97. Mildred Newman and Bernard Berkowitz, *How to Be Your Own Best Friend* (New York: Random House, 1971), 3–4.

98. William C. Schutz, *Joy: Expanding Human Awareness* (New York: Grove Press, 1967), 11.

99. Jane Howard, *Please Touch: A Guided Tour of the Human Potential Movement* (New York: McGraw-Hill, 1970), 167.

100. See Arthur Janov, *The Primal Scream* (New York: Dell, 1970) and Alexander Lowen, *Bioenergetics* (New York: Coward, McCann, and Geoghegan, 1975).

101. F. S. Perls, *Ego, Hunger, and Aggression: The Beginning of Gestalt Therapy* (New York: Vintage Books, 1969), 177.

102. Arthur Janov, *The Anatomy of Mental Illness: The Scientific Basis of Primal Therapy* (New York: Putnam's Sons, 1971), 79–80. For an excellent sample of Janov's methods in practice, listen to John Lennon's screams on "Mother," the opening track of *John Lennon/Plastic Ono Band* (1970), Lennon's first solo album after the breakup of the Beatles. Both Lennon and his wife, Yoko Ono, had been in treatment with Janov in the months before they recorded this album.

103. See Newman and Berkowitz, *How to Be Your Own Best Friend*, esp. 49–50.

104. Jess Lair, *"I Ain't Much, Baby—But I'm All I've Got"* (Garden City, NY: Doubleday, 1972), 85.

105. Robert J. Ringer, *Winning through Intimidation* (New York: Ballantine Books, 1974), 20.

106. Robert J. Ringer, *Looking Out for Number One* (New York: Funk and Wagnalls, 1977), 242.

107. Micki McGee, *Self-Help, Inc.: Makeover Culture in American Life* (New York: Oxford University Press, 2005).

108. Barbara Ehrenreich and Deirdre English, *For Her Own Good: 150 Years of the Experts' Advice to Women* (Garden City, NY: Anchor Press, 1978), 276.

CHAPTER SEVEN

1. Robert Coles, "A Fashionable Kind of Slander," *Atlantic* 226 (November 1970): 54. Emphasis in original.

2. See "Student Protests Linked to Guilt Ideas," *New York Times*, March 21, 1969, 19. Also see Bruno Bettelheim, "Obsolete Youth: Towards a Psychograph of Adolescent Rebellion," *Encounter* 33 (September 1969): 29–42.

3. Bettelheim quoted in Donald Janson, "Chicago U. Ready for Sit-In Siege," *New York Times*, February 1, 1969, 32. Also see Bruno Bettelheim, "On Campus Rebellion," *Chicago Tribune*, May 4, 1969, 80–81.

4. Leo Rosten, "To an Angry Young Man," *Look*, November 12, 1968, 28. The original text inserted dashes in the portion of the word where there was obscenity.

5. Eli Rubinstein, "Paradoxes of Student Protests," *American Psychologist* 24 (February 1969): 136, 138.

6. Andrew N. Glatter, "On Rubinstein's 'Paradoxes,'" *American Psychologist* 24 (September 1969): 876.

7. Dana Farnsworth quoted in Arthur G. Nikelly, "Ethical Issues in Research on Student Protest," *American Psychologist* 26 (May 1971): 475–76. Also see Seymour L. Halleck, "You Can Go to Hell with Style," *Psychology Today* 3 (November 1969): 16, 70–73; Halleck, "The Psychiatrist and Youth: Joint Efforts Toward Innovative Solutions," *American Journal of Psychiatry* 126 (June 1970): 1768–70; and Halleck, *The Politics of Therapy* (New York: Harper and Row, 1972).

8. Sidney Hook, "Symbolic Truth," *Psychiatry and Social Science Review* 2 (July 1968): 22–23; George Kennan, "Rebels without a Program," *New York Times Magazine*, January 21, 1968, 22–23, 60–61, 69–70; Jacques Barzun, *The American University* (New York: Harper, 1968); Irving Kristol, "A Different Way to Restructure the University," *New York Times Magazine*, December 8, 1968, 50, 162–72; Nathan Glazer, "Student Politics and the University," *Atlantic* 224 (July 1969): 43–53; and H. Stuart Hughes, "Emotional Disturbance and American Social Change, 1944–1969," *American Journal of Psychiatry* 126 (July 1969): 21–28. See also Sidney Hook, *Academic Freedom and Academic Anarchy* (New York: Cowles, 1970), 81.

9. Lewis S. Feuer, *The Conflict of Generations: The Character and Significance of Student Movements* (New York: Basic Books, 1969), 526.

10. Walter Bromberg and Franck Simon, "The 'Protest' Psychosis: A Special Type of Reactive Psychosis," *Archives of General Psychiatry* 19 (August 1968): 155. For the wider context, see also Jonathan M. Metzl, *The Protest Psychosis: How Schizophrenia Became a Black Disease* (Boston: Beacon Press, 2009), 100–101.

11. See the hundreds of empirical research summaries—most finding student radicals to be *well* adjusted—digested in Kenneth Keniston, *Radicals and Militants: An Annotated Bibliography of Empirical Research on Campus Unrest*

(Lexington, MA: D. C. Heath, 1973). Also see Kenneth Keniston, "The Sources of Student Dissent," *Journal of Social Issues* 23 (July 1967): 108–37; Kenneth Keniston, *Young Radicals: Notes on Committed Youth* (New York: Harcourt Brace and World, 1968); Robert Michels, "Pseudoanalyzing the Student Rebels," *Psychiatry and Social Science Review* 3 (May 1969): 2–5; and Robert Liebert, *Radical and Militant Youth: A Psychoanalytic Inquiry* (New York: Praeger, 1971).

12. Coles, "A Fashionable Kind of Slander," 55.

13. See Robert Coles, "Serpents and Doves: Non-Violent Youth in the South," in *Youth: Change and Challenge*, ed. Erik H. Erikson (New York: Basic Books, 1963), 188–216; Robert Coles, "Social Struggle and Weariness," *Psychiatry* 27 (November 1964): 305–15; Robert Coles, "We Will Overcome," *New Republic* 151 (July 11, 1964): 13–14; and Robert Coles and Joseph Brenner, "American Youth in a Social Struggle: The Mississippi Summer Project," *American Journal of Orthopsychiatry* 35 (October 1965): 909–26. Additional psychiatric assessments that testified to the mental well-being of southern civil rights workers include Fredric Solomon and Jacob R. Fishman, "The Psychosocial Meaning of Nonviolence in Student Civil Rights Activities," *Psychiatry* 27 (May 1964): 91–99; and Wagner H. Bridger, "Adolescent Idealism in the Civil Rights Movement," in *Adolescence, Dreams, and Training*, ed. Jules H. Masserman (New York: Grune and Stratton, 1966), 61–67.

14. Coles, "A Fashionable Kind of Slander," 55. Emphasis in original.

15. Morton Levitt and Ben Rubenstein, "The Counter-Culture: Adaptive or Maladaptive?" *International Review of Psycho-Analysis* 1 (1974): 330–31, 333, 335.

16. Robert Lindsey, "Many Rebels of the 1960's Depressed as They Near 30," *New York Times*, February 29, 1976, 1, 40.

17. See Phillip Rieff, *The Triumph of the Therapeutic: Uses of Faith after Freud* (New York: Harper and Row, 1966).

18. See Christopher Lasch, *The Culture of Narcissism: American Life in an Age of Diminishing Expectations* (New York: W. W. Norton, 1978).

19. Bernie Zilbergeld, *The Shrinking of America: Myths of Psychological Change* (Boston: Little, Brown, 1983), 253.

20. Martin L. Gross, *The Psychological Society* (New York: Random House, 1978), 6.

21. Steven M. Tipton, *Getting Saved from the Sixties: Moral Meaning in Conversion and Cultural Change* (Berkeley: University of California Press, 1982), 29.

22. Christopher Lasch, *Haven in a Heartless World: The Family Besieged* (New York: Basic Books, 1977), 182–83.

23. Christopher Lasch, "Sacrificing Freud," *New York Times Magazine*, February 22, 1976, 72.

24. Lasch, *Haven in a Heartless World*, 135.

25. Christopher Lasch, "The Waning of Private Life," *Salmagundi* 36 (Winter 1977): 8.

26. Brigitte Berger and Peter L. Berger, *The War over the Family: Capturing the Middle Ground* (Garden City, NY: Anchor Press, 1983), 173.

27. Robert N. Bellah, Richard Madsen, William M. Sullivan, Ann Swidler,

and Steven M. Tipton, *Habits of the Heart: Individualism and Commitment in American Life* (New York: Harper and Row, 1985), 139.

28. See, in this context, Wendy Kaminer, *I'm Dysfunctional, You're Dysfunctional: The Recovery Movement and Other Self-Help Fashions* (New York: Vintage, 1993); and T. J. Jackson Lears, *No Place for Grace: Antimodernism and the Transformation of American Culture, 1880–1920* (Chicago: University of Chicago Press, 1994), 55–56, 306.

29. Peter Sedgwick, *Psycho Politics: Laing, Foucault, Goffman, Szasz, and the Future of Mass Psychiatry* (New York: Harper and Row, 1982).

30. Peter Sedgwick, "Mental Illness *Is* Illness," *Salmagundi* 20 (Summer–Fall 1972): 219, 224.

31. Russell Jacoby, *Social Amnesia: A Critique of Contemporary Psychology* (New Brunswick, NJ: Transaction Publishers, 1997), 141, 149–50.

32. Marge Piercy, *Woman on the Edge of Time* (New York: Knopf, 1976), 60.

33. Jerome Frank, *Persuasion and Healing: A Comparative Study of Psychotherapy*, rev. ed. (Baltimore: Johns Hopkins University Press, 1973), 141–43.

34. See, for instance, Arthur K. Shapiro, "Placebo Effects in Medicine, Psychotherapy, and Psychoanalysis," in *Handbook of Psychotherapy and Behavior Change: An Empirical Analysis*, ed. Allen E. Bergin and Sol L. Garfield (New York: Wiley and Sons, 1971), 439–73.

35. See Hans J. Eysenck, "The Effects of Psychotherapy," *International Journal of Psychiatry* 1 (January 1965): 97–144.

36. Louis A. Gottschalk, Ruth A. Fox, and Daniel E. Bates, "A Study of Prediction and Outcome in a Mental Health Crisis Clinic," *American Journal of Psychiatry* 130 (October 1973): 1107–11.

37. Discussed in Gross, *The Psychological Society*, 53.

38. See Suzanne W. Hadley and Hans H. Strupp, "Contemporary Views of Negative Effects in Psychotherapy," *Archives of General Psychiatry* 33 (November 1976): 1291–302.

39. William Caudill, Frederick C. Redlich, Helen R. Gilmore, and Eugene B. Brody, "Social Structure and Interaction Processes on a Psychiatric Ward," *American Journal of Orthopsychiatry* 22 (April 1952): 332. Only several years later did Caudill publicly acknowledge that he had been the observer participant who was committed to the mental hospital. See William Caudill, *The Psychiatric Hospital as a Small Society* (Cambridge, MA: Harvard University Press, 1958).

40. Elaine Cumming and John Cumming, *Closed Ranks: An Experiment in Mental Health Education* (Cambridge, MA: Harvard University Press, 1957), 102.

41. Benjamin M. Braginsky and Dorothea D. Braginsky, "Schizophrenic Patients in the Psychiatric Interview: An Experimental Study of Their Effectiveness at Manipulation," *Journal of Consulting Psychology* 31 (December 1967): 543–47. On the desire of mental patients to remain in mental hospitals, also see Benjamin M. Braginsky, Dorothea D. Braginsky, and Kenneth Ring, *Methods of Madness: The Mental Hospital as a Last Resort* (New York: Holt, Rinehart and Winston, 1969).

42. Norma Jean Orlando, "The Mock Ward: A Study in Simulation," in *Behavior Disorders: Perspectives and Trends*, 3rd ed., ed. Ohmer Milton and

Robert G. Wahler (Philadelphia: Lippincott, 1973), 162–70. Also see the comparable prison experiment conducted by Philip G. Zimbardo. See Craig Haney, W. Curtis Banks, and Philip G. Zimbardo, "Interpersonal Dynamics in a Simulated Prison," *International Journal of Criminology and Penology* 1 (1973): 69–97.

43. David L. Rosenhan, "On Being Sane in Insane Places," *Science* 179 (January 19, 1973): 254. Also see Lauren Slater, *Opening Skinner's Box: Great Psychological Experiments of the Twentieth Century* (New York: W. W. Norton, 2004), 64–67.

44. For a journalistic account of feigning madness and the experience of being committed, also see Anne Barry, *Bellevue Is a State of Mind* (New York: Harcourt Brace Jovanovich, 1971).

45. Thomas S. Szasz, "The Problem of Psychiatric Nosology," *American Journal of Psychiatry* 114 (November 1957): 411.

46. See Thomas M. Sullivan, Charles E. Frohman, Peter G. S. Beckett, and Jacques S. Gottlieb, "Clinical and Biochemical Studies of Families of Schizophrenic Patients," *American Journal of Psychiatry* 123 (February 1967): 947–52; and Robert G. Heath and Iris M. Krupp, "Schizophrenia as a Specific Biologic Disease," *American Journal of Psychiatry* 124 (February 1968): 1019–27.

47. Leonard L. Heston, "Psychiatric Disorders in Foster Home Reared Children of Schizophrenic Mothers," *British Journal of Psychiatry* 112 (August 1966): 818–25.

48. For instance, see Seymour S. Kety, David Rosenthal, Paul H. Wender, and Fini Schulsinger, "Mental Illness in the Biological and Adoptive Families of Adopted Schizophrenics," *American Journal of Psychiatry* 128 (September 1971): 302–6; David Rosenthal et al., "The Adopted-Away Offspring of Schizophrenics," *American Journal of Psychiatry* 128 (September 1971): 307–11; and Paul H. Wender et al., "Cross-Fostering: A Research Strategy for Clarifying the Role of Genetic and Experiential Factors in the Etiology of Schizophrenia," *Archives of General Psychiatry* 30 (January 1974): 121–28.

49. Irving I. Gottesman and James Shields, "A Critical Review of Recent Adoption, Twin, and Family Studies of Schizophrenia: Behavioral Genetics Perspectives," *Schizophrenia Bulletin* 2 (1976): 364.

50. Seymour S. Kety, "From Rationalization to Reason," *American Journal of Psychiatry* 131 (September 1974): 961.

51. See Jay Joseph, "Schizophrenia and Heredity: Why the Emperor Has No Genes," in *Models of Madness: Psychological, Social, and Biological Approaches to Schizophrenia*, ed. John Read, Loren R. Mosher, and Richard P. Bentall (New York: Brunner-Routledge, 2004), 67–83.

52. Theodore Lidz, "Commentary on a Critical Review of Recent Adoption, Twin, and Family Studies of Schizophrenia," *Schizophrenia Bulletin* 2 (1976): 406. Also see Theodore Lidz et al., "Critique of the Danish-American Studies of the Adopted-Away Offspring of Schizophrenic Parents," *American Journal of Psychiatry* 138 (August 1981): 1063–68.

53. Seymour Kessler, "Progress and Regress in the Research on the Genetics of Schizophrenia," *Schizophrenia Bulletin* 2 (1976): 435.

54. The study was Rosenthal et al., "The Adopted-Away Offspring of Schizophrenics."

55. A later generation of adoption studies would provide refined methodologies. See, for instance, Pekka Tienari et al., "Genetic Boundaries of the Schizophrenia Spectrum: Evidence from the Finnish Adoptive Family Study," *American Journal of Psychiatry* 160 (September 2003): 1587–94; and Karl-Erik Wahlberg et al., "Interaction of Genetic Risk and Adoptive Parent Communication Deviance: Longitudinal Prediction of Adoptee Psychiatric Disorders," *Psychological Medicine* 34 (November 2004): 1531–41.

56. *Diagnostic and Statistical Manual of Mental Disorders*, 2nd ed. (Washington, DC: American Psychiatric Association, 1968), ix.

57. Fred M. Hunter, letter to the editor, *Science* 180 (April 27, 1973): 361.

58. Kety, "From Rationalization to Reason," 959.

59. Quoted in Mitchell Wilson, "DSM-III and the Transformation of American Psychiatry: A History," *American Journal of Psychiatry* 150 (March 1993): 405.

60. Robert L. Spitzer, "On Pseudoscience in Science, Logic in Remission, and Psychiatric Diagnosis: A Critique of Rosenhan's 'On Being Sane in Insane Places,'" *Journal of Abnormal Psychology* 84 (October 1975): 448.

61. Thomas S. Szasz, "The Lying Truths of Psychiatry," *Journal of Libertarian Studies* 3 (Summer 1979): 133.

62. Rosenhan, "On Being Sane in Insane Places," 257.

63. Spitzer, "On Pseudoscience in Science," 443, 451.

64. Robert L. Spitzer and Joseph L. Fleiss, "A Re-Analysis of the Reliability of Psychiatric Diagnosis," *British Journal of Psychiatry* 125 (October 1974): 345.

65. Gerald N. Grob, *The Mad among Us: A History of the Care of America's Mentally Ill* (New York: Free Press, 1994), 290.

66. See William Gronfein, "Incentives and Intentions in Mental Health Policy: A Comparison of the Medicaid and Community Mental Health Programs," *Journal of Health and Social Behavior* 26 (September 1985): 192–206.

67. Charles A. Kiesler and Amy E. Sibulkin, *Mental Hospitalization: Myths and Facts about a National Crisis* (Newbury Park, CA: Sage Publications, 1987), 66.

68. Paul S. Appelbaum, "The Disability System in Disarray," *Hospital and Community Psychiatry* 34 (September 1983): 783.

69. Quoted in Robert Pear, "Fairness of Reagan's Cutoffs of Disability Aid Questioned," *New York Times*, May 9, 1982.

70. Ann Braden Johnson, *Out of Bedlam: The Truth about Deinstitutionalization* (New York: Basic Books, 1990), 154. Also see Dan Salerno, Kim Hopper, and Ellen Baxter, *Hardship in the Heartland: Homelessness in Eight U.S. Cities* (New York: Institute for Social Welfare Research Community Service Society of New York, 1984), 11–16. And in 1987 the *New York Times* reported on estimates that 75 percent of the homeless in New York City had been treated in psychiatric hospitals. Cited in Daniel Goleman, "Mentally Ill Poorly Supervised, Experts Say," *New York Times*, September 11, 1987, A1.

71. H. Richard Lamb, "Deinstitutionalization and the Homeless Mentally Ill," in *The Homeless Mentally Ill: A Task Force Report of the American Psychiatric Association*, ed. H. Richard Lamb (Washington, DC: American Psychiatric Association, 1984), 55.

72. E. Fuller Torrey, *Out of the Shadows: Confronting America's Mental Illness Crisis* (New York: Wiley and Sons, 1997), 87–88.

73. Quoted in Robert D. McFadden, "Comments by Meese on Hunger Produce a Storm of Controversy," *New York Times*, December 10, 1983.

74. Richard W. White Jr., *Rude Awakenings: What the Homeless Crisis Tells Us* (San Francisco: ICS Press, 1992), 241, 221.

75. Gerald Weissmann, "Foucault and the Bag Lady," *Hospital Practice* 17 (August 1982): 33, 34.

76. W. Robert Curtis, "The Deinstitutionalization Story," *Public Interest* 85 (Fall 1986): 37.

77. Paul S. Appelbaum, "Crazy in the Streets," *Commentary* 83 (May 1987): 36. Also see Paul S. Appelbaum, *Almost a Revolution: Mental Health Law and the Limits of Change* (New York: Oxford University Press, 1994), esp. 4–7.

78. Charles Krauthammer, *Cutting Edges: Making Sense of the Eighties* (New York: Random House, 1985), 71.

79. See Charles Krauthammer, "The Myth of Thomas Szasz, Libertarianism Gone Mad," *New Republic* 181 (December 22, 1979): 13–17. Krauthammer wrote: "Like the atheist who cannot stop talking about God, Thomas Szasz cannot stop talking about psychiatry." Ibid., 13.

80. Rael Jean Isaac and Virginia C. Armat, *Madness in the Streets: How Psychiatry and the Law Abandoned the Mentally Ill* (New York: Free Press, 1990), 57–58. Also see Rael Jean Isaac, "The Grate Society," *Commentary* 89 (January 1990): 67–70.

81. Alice S. Baum and Donald W. Burnes, *A Nation in Denial: The Truth about Homelessness* (Boulder, CO: Westview Press, 1993), 171.

82. Christopher Jencks, *The Homeless* (Cambridge, MA: Harvard University Press, 1994), 29 31.

83. Kyle L. Grazier, Carol T. Mowbray, and Mark C. Holter, "Rationing Psychosocial Treatments in the United States," *International Journal of Law and Psychiatry* 28 (2005): 547.

84. Thomas S. Szasz, *Cruel Compassion: Psychiatric Control of America's Unwanted* (Syracuse, NY: Syracuse University Press, 1998), 190. Also see John Monahan, "From the Man Who Brought You Deinstitutionalization," *Contemporary Psychology* 33 (June 1988): 492.

EPILOGUE

1. Craig Morgan, Kwame McKenzie, and Paul Fearon, "Introduction," in *Society and Psychosis*, ed. Craig Morgan, Kwame McKenzie, and Paul Fearon (New York: Cambridge University Press, 2008), 1.

2. See Jonathan M. Metzl, *The Protest Psychosis: How Schizophrenia Became a Black Disease* (Boston: Beacon Press, 2009), x.

3. See Assen Jablensky et al., "Schizophrenia: Manifestations, Incidence, and Course in Different Cultures; A World Health Organization Ten-Country Study," *Psychological Medicine: Monograph Supplement* 20 (1992): 1–97.

4. Shi Jianxin et al., "Common Variants on Chromosome 6p22.1 Are Associ-

ated with Schizophrenia," *Nature* 460 (August 6, 2009): 753. For a vivid literary rendering of this point, see John Wray, *Lowboy* (New York: Farrar, Straus and Giroux, 2009).

5. Carsten B. Pedersen and Preben B. Mortensen, "Evidence of a Dose-Response Relationship between Urbanicity during Upbringing and Schizophrenia Risk," *Archives of General Psychiatry* 58 (November 2001): 1039–46. Also see Jim van Os, "Does the Urban Environment Cause Psychosis?" *British Journal of Psychiatry* 184 (April 2004): 287–88; and John J. McGrath, "Variations in the Incidence of Schizophrenia: Data versus Dogma," *Schizophrenia Bulletin* 32 (January 2006): 195–97.

6. Lisa J. Phillips et al., "Stress and Psychosis: Towards the Development of New Models of Investigation," *Clinical Psychology Review* 27 (April 2007): 307–17.

7. Cécile Henquet et al., "Gene-Environment Interplay between Cannabis and Psychosis," *Schizophrenia Bulletin* 34 (2008): 1111–21.

8. Elizabeth Cantor-Graae and Jean-Paul Selten, "Schizophrenia and Migration: A Meta-Analysis and Review," *American Journal of Psychiatry* 162 (January 2005): 12–24. Also see Win Veling et al., "Ethnic Density of Neighborhoods and Incidence of Psychotic Disorders among Immigrants," *American Journal of Psychiatry* 165 (January 2008): 66–73.

9. See the findings collected in Kim Hopper et al., eds., *Recovery from Schizophrenia: An International Perspective* (New York: Oxford University Press, 2007).

10. John J. McGrath, "The Surprisingly Rich Contours of Schizophrenia Epidemiology," *Archives of General Psychiatry* 64 (January 2007): 14. For a critique of the WHO report's preliminary conclusions about transnational uniformity, see Arthur Kleinman, *Rethinking Psychiatry: From Cultural Category to Personal Experience* (New York: Free Press, 1991).

11. T. M. Luhrmann, "Social Defeat and the Culture of Chronicity: Or, Why Schizophrenia Does So Well Over There and So Badly Here," *Culture, Medicine, and Psychiatry* 31 (June 2007): 144.

12. See Roy R. Grinker, "Emerging Concepts of Mental Illness and Models of Treatment: The Medical Point of View," *American Journal of Psychiatry* 125 (January 1969): 865–69; and George L. Engel, "The Need for a New Medical Model: A Challenge for Biomedicine," *Science* 196 (April 8, 1977): 129–36. Also see George L. Engel, "The Clinical Application of the Biopsychosocial Model," *American Journal of Psychiatry* 137 (May 1980): 535–44.

13. Jun Yan, "Epigenetics Links Nature and Nurture," *Psychiatric News* 45 (March 2010): 12.

14. Rajita Sinha, "Stress and Addiction: A Dynamic Interplay of Genes, Environment, and Drug Intake," *Biological Psychiatry* 66 (July 2009): 100.

15. "Social Neuroscience: Gene x Environment x Brain x Body": Conference program for the Association for Research in Nervous and Mental Disease held at Rockefeller University in New York City on December 1, 2010.

16. Mindy Thompson Fullilove, "Toxic Sequelae of Childhood Sexual Abuse," *American Journal of Psychiatry* 166 (October 2009): 1091.

NOTES TO PAGES 191-194242

17. Douglas A. Kramer, "Gene-Environment Interplay in the Context of Genetics, Epigenetics, and Gene Expression," *Journal of the American Academy of Child and Adolescent Psychiatry* 44 (January 2005): 26.

18. Louise C. Johns and Jim van Os, "The Continuity of Psychotic Experiences in the General Population," *Clinical Psychology Review* 21 (November 2001): 1125–41.

19. Agna A. Bartels-Velthuis et al., "Prevalence and Correlates of Auditory Vocal Hallucinations in Middle Childhood," *British Journal of Psychiatry* 196 (January 2010): 44.

20. Emmanuel Stip and Genevieve Letourneau, "Psychotic Symptoms as a Continuum between Normality and Pathology," *Canadian Journal of Psychiatry* 54 (March 2009): 149.

21. Joseph M. Pierre, "Nonantipsychotic Therapy for Monosymptomatic Auditory Hallucinations," *Biological Psychiatry* 68 (October 2010): e33–e34.

22. Richard J. Linscott and Jim van Os, "Systematic Reviews of Categorical versus Continuum Models in Psychosis," *Annual Review of Clinical Psychology* 6 (March 2010): 391–419.

23. "Psychiatric Diagnosis: That Way, Madness Lies," *Economist*, February 6, 2010, 88.

24. Quoted in Alissa Quart, "Listening to Madness," *Newsweek*, May 11/May 18, 2009, 54.

25. "Gathering Preramble," in *Navigating the Space between Brilliance and Madness* (New York: Icarus Project, summer 2006), 81.

26. "Making Sense of Being Called Crazy in a Crazy World," in ibid., 16.

27. See Alison Jost, "Mad Pride and the Medical Model," *Hastings Center Report* 39 (July/August 2009): 4. Also see Linda J. Morrison, *Talking Back to Psychiatry: The Psychiatric Consumer/Survivor/Ex-Patient Movement* (New York: Routledge, 2005).

28. Illina Singh and Nikolas Rose, "Biomarkers in Psychiatry," *Nature* 460 (July 9, 2009): 204.

29. McGrath, "The Surprisingly Rich Contours of Schizophrenia Epidemiology," 16.

30. Edward Shorter, *A History of Psychiatry: From the Era of the Asylum to the Age of Prozac* (New York: John Wiley, 1997), vii.

Index

homosexuality, 27, 111, 114, 126, 129, 146, 158, 161, 172. *See also* gay and lesbian liberation
Hook, Sidney, 168
Hornstein, Gail A., 44
Hough, Edith Louise, 89–91
House Committee on Un-American Activities, 70
Howard, Jane, 163
Hubbard, L. Ron, 113
Hughes, Everett, 80
Hughes, H. Stuart, 168
"human potential" movement, 8, 153, 164, 171
Human Sexual Inadequacy (Masters and Johnson), 145
Hunter, Edward, 70–71
Huston, John, 22

I Never Promised You a Rose Garden (Greenberg [Green, pseud.]), 44
Icarus Project, 192
If You Meet the Buddha on the Road, Kill Him! (Kopp), 152
I'm OK—You're OK (Harris), 140, 162
Insane Liberation Front, 111, 124
insanity defense, 89, 91, 93, 97–98, 100–101, 104, 114
insulin coma treatment, 85
International Classification of Diseases (ICD), 181
involuntary commitment, 91, 107, 109, 114, 120, 124, 129, 144, 187
Isaac, Rael Jean, 186–88
Issues in Radical Therapy, 161

Jackson, Don D., 47–48, 51, 54, 134
Jacoby, Russell, 175
Janov, Arthur, 163
Jencks, Christopher, 187–88
Johnson, Lyndon B., 136
Johnson, Virginia, 145
Joint Commission on Mental Illness and Health, 36
Josiah Macy, Jr. Foundation, 76

Journal of the American Academy of Child and Adolescent Psychiatry, 191
Journal of the American Medical Association, 125
Joys of Yiddish, The (Rosten), 167
Jung, Carl, 37, 64

Kafka, Franz, 54
Kaplan, Bert, 121
Kardiner, Abram, 33
Kennan, George, 168
Kennedy, John F., 123
Kesey, Ken, 68–69, 86, 100, 125, 134, 175
Kety, Seymour, 182
Kierkegaard, Søren, 54
King of Hearts (de Broca), 119
Kittrie, Nicholas N., 107–8
Kopp, Sheldon B., 152–53
Korean War, 72
Kraepelin, Emil, 17, 189
Kramer, Bernard M., 28
Krauthammer, Charles, 186
Kristol, Irving, 168
Kubrick, Stanley, 126
Kunnes, Richard, 122, 130

Laing, R. D., 3–4, 6, 7, 23, 39–41, 45, 52, 54–61, 63–65, 68, 69, 113, 118, 119, 136, 143, 151, 172–73, 175, 185–88
Lair, Jess, 164
Lasch, Christopher, 172–73
Lasswell, Harold D., 14, 24–27
Leary, Timothy, 63, 111, 133
left-wing politics, 7, 29, 63, 70, 118, 120, 127, 131–32, 138, 157, 161, 165, 167–70, 174; backlash against, 164, 167–70. *See also* New Left
Legal Rights of the Mentally Handicapped, 109
Leifer, Ronald, 107, 129
Lemert, Edwin, 80
Leonard, Frank, 87